Dangerous

THE SHELLEY TAYLOR-SMITH STORY

When Wet

SHELLEY TAYLOR-SMITH
with
IAN COCKERILL

M⊙tivational PRESS®
LEADERS IN GLOBAL PUBLISHING

Published by Motivational Press, Inc.
7777 N Wickham Rd, # 12-247
Melbourne, FL 32940
www.MotivationalPress.com

Manufactured in the United States of America.

ISBN: 978-1-62865-115-7

• TESTIMONIES •

"Shelley Taylor-Smith is one of the greatest athletes the world has ever seen and probably one of Australia's most unsung heroes. Read this biography and you'll understand why." **Alan Jones AO, Leading Australian Radio Personality**

"No matter where you are in your life or sporting career this book will give you the kick in the butt to never give up on yourself."
Janet Evans, 4-time Olympic Gold Medallist, Legendary American World Record Holder 400m, 800m & 1500m Freestyle, Businesswoman & Mother of two.

"An inspiring read for anyone, whether a fellow long distance swimmer or an armchair fan with a passion for inspiration. This book will provide you a great understanding of the length's anyone can push themself to when they have a goal in mind, and exemplifies the importance of having a tough and disciplined mindset. A great read".
Patrick Hollingworth, dual Rottnest solo swimmer and Mount Everest climber, Perth, Australia

You do not have to be a swimmer to understand the power of Shelley Taylor-Smith. Her insight and passion are obvious, but the fact is, Shelley wanted to make the world better, both on an individual basis and on a global basis. In the water, as on land, she encountered obstacles – and pushed right past them. It was occasionally difficult and frustrating, but her determination and persistence set in motion a more inclusive, better world for those who follow. Her legacy – in which she beat her male competitors so consistently – led to the international governing body to create equal prize money for both men and women in the sport. Shelley's greatest achievement will live on throughout the waterways of the world.
Steven Munatones, Editor-in-Chief, Daily News of Open Water Swimming, Founder, www.OpenWaterSource.com

An extraordinary story of attitude and determination and how you can overcome obstacles at every stage in life. This book is impossible to put down, as it not only describes what it takes to be a World Champion, but because it shows that every single one of us has the ability to be champion in our own right. A must read for anyone wanting to take on their personal goals, and succeed!
Shaun Jessop, Perth, Australia Company Director, and born-again, thirty-something, ocean swimmer, Rottnest Channel Solo 2011

I read "Dangerous When Wet" training for the Rottnest Duo swim and found the book to be not only inspirational from the perspective for my upcoming endurance event, but also for everyday life. Reading about Shelley's determination, ability and hardships not only spurred me on to compete, but also inspired me to reach goals I previously believed were unachievable.

Laurie Levy SC, Barrister, Rottnest Channel swimmer, Perth, Australia

As a long distance freestyle swimmer Shelley's story has inspired me as I prepare for my own English Channel swim for September 2011. Her thought-provoking goal setting helped me set my sights on where I want to go and how to execute them in a structured manner. This has been invaluable for me in both life and business - thanks Champ!

Paul Newsome, Head Coach, Rottnest Channel Solo swimmer, www.swimsmooth.com

Get ready to be enlightened by Shelley Taylor-Smith. As a fellow female swimmer I was encouraged and inspired to follow my dreams and goals. You will learn that it is possible to push yourself beyond what you thought possible whether physically or mentally - in the pool or life. Combining motivation and humour; Shelley's life is an example that regardless of your lack of natural talent, if you're prepared to work hard & stay focused, nothing can stop you. An incredibly influential woman who shows gender does not matter in the sport of open water swimming. I would recommend this book not only to women, but anyone who needs to understand that mind over matter, truly is the key to success.

Lexie Kelly, Cayman Islands, USA. Flowers Sea Swim Coordinator, US Masters Swimmer, Open Water Source etc.

We love your book! It's been a great inspiration and insight into the open water swimming history and community.

Penny and Chris Palfrey, Townsville, Australia
www.palfreymarathonswims.com

A great book for anyone interested in being the best they can be at their passion. Shelley describes her champion mindset and how it propelled her to become arguably one of the greatest marathon swimmers in history. Shelley's book has inspired me to continue my quest to become the best open water swimmer I can be and has given me additional tools to handle adversity in long, challenging marathon swims.

Jen Schumacher, California, USA

The book is both an inspirational and memorable read for me as I have been fortunate enough to have shared many aspects of the "STS" passionate life experience and purpose! Thank you Shell Bell!!

Leith Weston, Perth, Australia. STS Supporter & Dear Friend of 30+ years, Rotto Channel Duo Partner 2001, Former Lady Razorback, Arkansas Swimmer & Teammate.

I really enjoyed the read as it inspired me to have the courage to try a new challenge in my life and succeed. It was so motivational and truly a page turner. It taught me about focus, goal setting, overcoming obstacles, and perseverance . I can't wait for the next book!

Victoria Rian, Indianapolis, USA. Teacher, 10K National Champion 40-44 age group 2010, Catalina Channel Crossing 2010 & Long Island Sound 25K 2009.

Shelley coached me in 2010 and 2011 for Rottnest Channel swim and read Shelley's book in 2009. I found her story to be a great source of inspiration and a reminder to myself to toughen up on my far more humble swimming goals. If you are trying to do something that requires dedication and perseverance, stories such as Shelley's are well worth the read."

John Edwards – Perth, Australia. Rottnest solo '07, '09, '11 and duo '10, Legal Manager, Iluka Resources.

Shelley's biography, seminars and performance coaching programs have given me the added tools to succeed in completing 20km open water swims, Ironman events and focus in everyday life. Thanks Shelley, now I'm also dangerous when wet!

Trevor van Aurich, Rottnest Channel Solo swimmer, triathlete, Director, JCA, Perth, Australia www.jcalogic.com

Shelley's story teaches you that long distance swimming is about mental toughness. Losing my niece from ovarian cancer whilst being coached by Shelley for the 2010 Rotto Channel swim was the tipping point and where everything I'd learned from Shelley fell in to place and guaranteed the one thing I could control, my mind! I've now achieved two solos and raised nearly $9000, which I couldn't have done without Shelley's game plan.

David Fairclough, Fish Biologist, Husband and Dad, Rottnest Channel Swim Solo 2010 & 2011. Perth, Australia

Your book & cd changed my life. I took on an opportunity of a life time and competed in the Rotto Channel Swim in a team. A large part is due to you helping me believe in myself and my abilities. My husband was right; you are a legend.

Julie Covich, Perth, Australia

Your book was fantastic and I am grateful for your story that has led me to believe I can overcome problems even when I'm at a very low point in life. Your book gave me inspiration to start again and move on

Shelby Aramini, Bunbury, Australia

Reading this book gave me a new outlook on life. Not only has it changed the way I look at the negatives and hurdles in my life but I remember the struggles that Shelley pushed through. You go Shelley, you have inspired me!

Karena Nicholls, Lawyer, Wollongong, Australia

I believe the Shelley Taylor-Smith story is one of the most inspirational I have read; filled with courage and one which provides hope for all Aussies.

Danny Smith, Victoria, Australia

I took your book home last night and we had a power failure. You should've seen my kids how they were trying to read the book and look at the photos in candlelight! We could not put it down.

Odette H., CBA, Manager, NSW, Australia

I love reading your book. I can't believe you knocked almost six minutes off the men's record in the '91 Atlantic City marathon swim - which stood since '79 - WOW! Love the two phrases: "If you don't quit you'll make it" & "Stuff it and flush it." I am now implementing them in my life.

Steve Bell, UK

I was captivated by your book and unable to put it down. Having been a swimmer myself (not at your level however) and a fan of Dawn Fraser my emotions coupled yours throughout the storey and I mentally lived through the build up and the swims with you.

Jenni Hill, Victoria, Australia

After reading your book and listening to the cd; I'd have to say, it's the best dollars I have spent in a very long time. What inspiring stuff! Shelley, you are AMAZING! Your story has just blown me away, with the all inspiring energy you've supplied. I found myself so absorbed in your story that I laughed. I cried. I ached. You are a true blue Australian!"

Mary Prowse, Surf Beach, NSW

The opportunity to read 'Dangerous when Wet' was fantastic preparation for my 10th Duo Rottnest Channel crossing. You helped me mentally achieve my goals when the times got tough during the race. Your greatest line in the book, for me, which I used in my head the whole way through the race, was "If you don't quit, you will Make It". Your book inspired me to complete a solo crossing. I look forward to being inspired as you coach me to achieve this goal.

Shane MacDermott, Perth, Australia, Managing Director, Westbury Investments

The obstacles Shelley faced and how she applied her positive thinking and energy in this very tough but lonely sport is bloody amazing. I read the book at a time in my life when struggling with a marriage breakdown, financial problems and depression that affected my normal positive outlook on life and my two beautiful young children. My wake up came after a serious car accident and thinking I was a failure and could not succeed. Shelley, thank you for teaching me that I can't do it on my own. Your book reminded me during my recovery where I came from, what I enjoyed and more importantly how to get back to it. Many a night after the accident I would dream of swimming again, gradually I started to BELIEVE it and more amazing I ACHIEVED this and much, much more. Thanks Shells

Jodi O'Connor. Rockingham, Australia. Mother of Joseph & Amy, Assistant Head Coach - Rockingham Swimming Club. 3 Solo Rottnest Channel Crossings.

• DEDICATION •

In Memory of my Mum, Irene Taylor (dec) and my Dad, Mervyn Taylor (dec) who nurtured the creation of a strong and assertive woman with the courage, confidence, self belief, passion and Aussie willpower to stand up for what is right and just.

To all the dreamers, goal setters, go getters... who dare to dream, dare to believe and dare to achieve your birthright.... becoming the Champions you were born to be! I applaud you. The world is a better place because of you. The world needs you to shake the person next to you and wake them from their snooze... to get up, get over it and get on with it.

Remember: if you don't quit... you will make it!

• TABLE OF CONTENTS •

• ACKNOWLEDGMENTS •

In writing these acknowledgments I am reminded of the over-whelming support and encouragement—which I now refer to as 'my balcony people'—that has sustained me through my swimming career and my life.

In particular to Dad, my hero, whose mere presence and character were an inspiration. His wisdom and optimism taught me commitment, perseverance and passion. Your spirit lives within me and drives me continually.

To my mum and Nanna, thanks for devoting your time and energy to my swimming when I was such a keen youngster. To my brother Michael and sister-in-law Lesley and nephew Myles, my aunties, uncles and cousins, I thank you all for your love and support.

To my wonderful and loving sister Liz and brother-in-law Andrew, I thank you for your unconditional love and keeping me level-headed and helping to keep my feet on the ground.

To my other hero, Mal Brown—thanks for teaching me, by example, that winners are those who give 100 per cent regardless of placing.

Now to my coaches: May Pitcher, thanks for teaching me to swim, and Ray Pitcher, who coached me to my first swag of state medals. Kevin Duff, thanks for believing in me and my dreams and never holding back my enthusiasm and drive to succeed.

To Bernie Mulroy, a coach of enormous wisdom and patience—I thank you for embracing marathon swimming with enthusiasm. I would never have achieved what I have without your constant guidance and support. Coach Colin Raven, assistant of Ray Pitcher, Kevin Duff and Bernie Mulroy, I say a huge thanks for guiding me through my tormented teenage years and supporting me through 25 years of swimming. I will always remember you for your honesty and integrity.

To coaches Laurie Lawrence and Graham McDonald, thanks for picking up the pieces and helping me keep on track after a year of chronic illness and CFS. Graham, we did it after commitment and persistence, I would never have got there without your belief in me.

To the Legend Coach, Graeme 'The Grub' Carroll—our union as coach and swimmer in the H_2O, and brother and sister out of the H_2O, has been enriching and rewarding. Your unique, easy-going, refreshing character together with your honesty, trust and integrity brought out the best in me. WOW! what a team.

To Coach Dave Ferris in New York, I thank you for making me a 'swinger', alleviating all my shoulder problems and enabling continued success.

To Nancy, Tammy and Grub as trainers/handlers in my swims— you deserve the accolades as much as me. I could never have made it without your loyalty and belief in me.

To all my competitors—male and female—thanks so much for helping me to be the best I can be and pushing me to my potential.

To my fellow teammates of Aquaclub, Warringah Aquatic, Long Island Aquatic and Arkansas Razorbacks and Palm Beach–Currumbin over the last 25 years—I thank you for your camaraderie in a team sport like no other.

In particular I would like to say thanks to the Schnarr family in New York who welcomed me into their home and hearts with such love and warmth. Together we conquered Manhattan Island numerous times.

To all my wonderful and amazing loyal friends—my 'balcony people'. The never-ending unconditional support, phone calls, letters and faxes—there is so much to be thankful for. I love you all. To mention a few: my No. 1 fan, Alan Jones AO, Laurie and Barbara Smith; 'KB' Kevin Berry; Dawn Fraser; Des Renford; Laurie Lawrence; Alana, Clem and June Paull; the Laphams; the Whiteheads; the Mohr family; the Smiths; the Westons; Tracey and Dave Buchert; Muzz; Paul Kofod; Kim Dyke; Jerome Guerette; Karen Hartley; Richard Kersh; Will Howe; Jim Schoolcraft; the Flatleys; Nancy and Mike Warnock; Judy Howard; Bob McDonald; Roger and Val Parson; Mal Brown and family; the Brooks family; Tim and Greg; the Moyles; Richard Marsh; Keith and Van; Eric Mather; Wayne Staunton; the Andersons; Lindsay May; 'Brucie' Graham Bruce; Dr Robert Hampshire; Michael de Vere; and Trish and Ben Lake. I've got so many people to thank for making things easier for me. Domestic Appliances, John Whitehead & Associates, for all your professional and sound financial advice; Luis restaurant; Sheraton

On The Park and Sheraton Towers Southgate, my homes away from home; Marathon Physical Therapy (New York), Dynamic Energy Centre, Narrabeen Sport Medicine Centre, Fisher Road Chiropractic, Kingsley Physio and Tugun Physio, who spent countless hours trying to keep my body and its parts in working order; Australia Day Council (NSW), M&M Print, Oakridge Communication Group and Leigh Maloney P.R., for helping raise my profile and my sport; Queenscliff Squash Centre, Kooka's Hair of Balmain, Maxim Pure Energy Fuel, Sunspirit Aromatherapy, Metro Brick, Caltex Oil Australia, Carrerra; NSW Academy of Sport, for recognising my sport; TYR Sport Inc, for their enduring swimwear range; Qantas, Ansett, British Airways, Air New Zealand, Cathay Pacific, and Aerolineas Argentinas—without your help I would never have been able to defend my world titles; Ando and Bumpo at Laing & Simmons Commercial, who created a job to fit with my swimming schedule; Shane, Chris and Trent at Trent Nathan, who dressed me fashionably out of the water; GIO Australia, who have remained loyal and supportive; Ross Gardiner & Friends, Ford Motor Company of Australia, Craft Canoes, Grand United Friendly Society, Darling Harbour 'Harbourside' and Muirs Holden, for believing in me, believing in my dream, and being loyal to an Australian.

And of course I am deeply grateful to Ian Cockerill, who was the first to hear my life story and believed that it should be told.

Thanks for telling it.

●

FRIENDS ARE THE PEOPLE WHO LET YOU

BE YOURSELF AND NEVER LET YOU FORGET IT .

●

• FOREWORD •

Internationally revered, Shelley Taylor-Smith, seven-time World Marathon Swimming Champion, is a household name.

In South America hundreds of thousands line the riverbanks to chant 'Shelley Shelley!!' as she ploughs by, oblivious to their adulation—she is in another zone. After she races, children swarm, she smiles, signs, laughs, waves—she is of this world again.

This same scene has been repeated countless times around the world. Shelley Taylor-Smith is an international marathon swimming star. She is feared and respected by teammates and opponents alike. Many male marathoners detest racing her because of the number of times she has lowered their colours in open races—the male ego finds it difficult to bow to a female opponent.

However, for years this single-minded athlete was barely recognised in her native Australia. She was just another pretty blonde face in the crowd and only her closest friends knew her as the smiling assassin.

Now, through the sheer weight of her achievements, Shelley Taylor-Smith has opened the Australian public's eyes to the world of marathon swimming—her world championship win in Perth, her Sydney Harbour triumph over all comers, and her amazing Sydney to Wollongong epic journey. Her persistence, longevity and single-mindedness have reaped personal rewards and recognition.

But Shelley is more than a marathon swimmer or a public figure. She is an educationalist and as such has been able to influence thousands of young Australians. She has taught them the value of dreaming, setting goals but, more importantly, acting on those goals—for without action the dream is merely a fantasy.

Shelley, by her actions, has and will continue to influence our youth.

Encore! Bravo! Bravissimo!

Good on you, mate.

LAURIE LAWRENCE OA

• INTRODUCTION •

To dream anything that you want to dream . . . *that* is the beauty of the human mind.

To do anything that you want to do . . . *that* is the strength of human will.

To trust yourself to test your limits . . . *that* is the courage to succeed.

These three sentences sum up the Shelley Taylor-Smith I know and admire.

An incredible 90 per cent of her sport is suggested to be mental. In other words it is how you manage the images produced inside your head. The most awesome piece of technology on the planet—the neck-top computer. Nevertheless it works like all computers: rubbish *in*, rubbish *out*.

Somehow Shelley Taylor-Smith, the high priestess of pain, is able to filter, like a fish, the messages which bombard her mind. How else could she cope with her constant companion?

As a student of sport I am fascinated by what makes different men and women tick. That's where this book will hook you. Shelley's refusal to be ruled by the negative self-doubt of others charts the remarkable journey of a very special Australian . . . through at times dark, angry seas to some cherished destinations.

As a bright-eyed little girl with a wonky back, she dreamed of swimming glory, only to be told by 'others' without her passion to quit because she'd never make it. Those privileged to witness her attitude to non-dreamers (people who delight in trying to reduce those prepared to risk all and explore the limits of their capabilities) can understand her response . . . Enjoy proving them wrong.

How would you feel if on the verge of adolescence you had to wear a metal brace extending from your neck to your waist. Shelley put up with that brace for 2000 days. The only time it came off was to swim and sleep . . . and even today one leg is 7mm shorter than the other.

Parents can be a handful even for the most talented off-spring . . . here she shares a wondering insight into her mother and father.

Shane Gould's three gold medals at the 1972 Munich Olympics were an inspiration to a nation. Unashamedly Shane's performances lit the fire in Shelley's belly—it has never stopped burning brightly.

'If you don't quit you'll make it!'

After two decades of exploring the edges of her mind and body's potential she overcame the bitter disappointment of missing selection for the 1976 Montreal Olympics.

Then in 1991, in front of a massive home town crowd at the World Swimming Championships in Perth, she won gold in the Marathon swim—her equivalent of Olympic gold. Australia embraced a new world champion. Her second mentor, the legendary 'big bad' Malcolm Brown, hero of the East Perth Football Club and laterly the Richmond FC in the AFL, was overcome with pride.

Unfortunately, the sport of marathon swimming is still not recognised at the Olympics but Shelley and her friends will continue to lobby FINA, the world swimming body, to have it included in the 2000 Olympics in Sydney.

The marathon marvel has been consistently beating men and women over distances in excess of 25 kilometres and loving it! A fierce competitor, she is comfortable in describing herself in the water as an 'aggressive bitch'. To be No. 1 in the world it is not enough to just dip the big toe in—only the strong survive.

Her story of survival in some of the most Godforsaken waters in the world, alongside clueless drivers in dodgy boats, is compelling to share—the after-effects of such torture often reduced hotel rooms to miniature hospital wards.

Shelley Taylor-Smith is a dream to interview. She's left me spellbound every time—a great raconteur, so many situations yet so little time. Fortunately, in this tome there's no shortage of time or the amount of water crossed.

Her darkest year was a period between late 1993 and '94, that revealed how, through her obsession with single-minded goals, she had to navigate painfully through a marriage breakdown. On top of that torment she was confronted by a cancer scare. Fortunately, she's back in full training and smiling often.

The lady is both a hero and in many ways a trendsetter. She is unlike a lot of our elite swimmers: she has no mega commercial sponsorships. Stroke after stroke, kilometre after kilometre, Shelley Taylor-Smith unconsciously is inspiring men and women everywhere with her single-minded horizontal victories.

Believe her when she says 'Dangerous When Wet'. She means it.

So take up the challenge. Get wet, enjoy the swim and the read—even share her pain. You won't be disappointed . . . in fact you'll discover how the positive effects of willpower, dedication and belief can help us all achieve our dreams.

MAX WALKER

THE • TOLL • OF • THE • BOWELS

LOSING CONTROL OF YOUR bowels ranks among life's more unpleasant experiences at the best of times. To lose control in the middle of a race watched by tens of thousands of people plumbs another depth altogether.

My public evacuation took place in a distant river in early 1993. A week earlier I'd sewn up my first World Series title. Now I wished *I* was sewn up.

My discomfort could be traced back to the 7 February final of marathon swimming's inaugural World Series. The swim was staged out of Santa Fe, one hour's flight north of Buenos Aires, in front of 100,000 delirious spectators and one Argentinian president safely ensconced on a luxury cruiser. El presidente had picked a sensible vantage point. I'd been here twice before and the last place you wanted to be was *in* the water.

The course flowed 57 kilometres down the grey-brown Rio Coronda (Coronda River), with shanties squatting ominously along its length. I say ominous because it didn't take much to figure out what sort of additives found their way into the waterway from these ramshackle dwellings. And if the shanties didn't get you, you could be reasonably sure the sewage plant would.

It was with that knowledge that I responded to the starter's gun with 29 other swimmers on that clammy Sunday morning. My trainer, Graeme 'Grub' Carroll, soon came alongside me in our boat and in short time we had established a break over the other women as I beat my way into the 20-kilometre per hour headwind. The only sour (and I mean *sour*) note in the early stages came during our passage past the El Vado sewage plant, when I swallowed a bit more water than recommended in the tourist guides.

The water wasn't the only thing sticking in my craw. Our boatman obviously didn't have a clue what he was doing. He kept running low on petrol and veering off without warning to top up his supply, leaving me to my own devices. Grub had problems of his own. The combination of wind and currents was creating a huge wash which threatened to swamp the boat. Bucket in hand, Grub was kept busy bailing all day.

Despite all this, by the halfway mark I was making good progress. I had a two-kilometre lead over my nearest female competitor and lay in fifth place overall. Then came the second miscalculation. Somehow–don't ask me how–the boat driver contrived to miss a turn and took us 400 metres in the wrong direction before he realised his mistake. Now, 400 metres might not seem that much. But when you have to swim back against a current running at eight kilometres per hour, well, *it is*. Muttering darkly, I frantically fought my way back across the river and upstream, pulling myself through mud and weeds along the bank.

When I finally made it back to where we'd left the course, I found myself in eleventh place overall and my lead over the nearest woman cut to 100 metres. There was nothing for it but to start over again. I had just begun to regain my rhythm when the third misfortune struck. My boatman had gone in search of petrol once again, depriving me of my eyes in the river. Without him, I didn't see the tree trunk jutting from the shore in time. When I thumped into it dozens of leeches promptly attached themselves hungrily to my back and arms (I still bear the scars). As if that weren't enough, my El Vado cocktail began to take effect with two hours still to go. With the nausea sweeping over me and my stomach beginning to flip, I gritted my teeth and eventually held on to win the women's race by three minutes.

Some swim. As it turned out, I wasn't the only one who'd had a rough day. Most of the women had been allotted clueless drivers and dodgy boats. One girl's boat had sunk, another's had broken down, and the organisers had neglected to inform two girls that they'd missed a cut-off time. Both had battled on to complete the swim. To rub salt into the wounds, the men received three times the prizemoney and trophies twice the size.

I'd have made my displeasure known, if only I'd had the energy. Scarcely had I been able to acknowledge my world title when the diarrhoea and vomiting struck. I was due to swim in a race at nearby Parana the following Sunday and I couldn't even move from my hotel for the next 24 hours. As much as I would have liked to quietly slip back to Australia, I knew that I'd have to try to front up. It was the first swim of the next season and, apart from being the race's debut on the World Series calendar, considerable expectation had built up around my appearance. In Argentina, this most macho of societies, they all wanted to see the señora who could beat men.

The ailing señora dragged herself out of bed and made the trip to Parana with Grub. On checking into a hotel I quickly set about turning my room into a miniature hospital ward. I was put on a drip, and doctors, nurses and translators formed a steady trickle of visitors. Apart from an Argentinian swimmer who helped with translation, none of my fellow competitors saw me for three days while the diarrhoea and vomiting continued to wreak havoc on my system. Confined to bed and a diet of bread sticks and rice, I lost four kilograms before the doctor came up with the right drip solution. After a further twelve hours my blood pressure finally returned to normal.

It was now Friday. I had not ventured out since Sunday and it was widely assumed I wouldn't show on race day. But when the doctor declared me fit I decided I'd make the effort. That night I surprised everyone when I turned up to the ceremony where swimmers are presented to the town. I must have looked like death. The following day I stayed in my room except for a light training swim. That night I couldn't sleep after all the rest I'd had, so I listened to motivational tapes instead. One line stayed with me: 'If you don't quit, you'll make it.' I adopted it for the swim.

I climbed out of bed at 4 a.m. We had a two-hour bus trip to the starting point at Hernandarias and from there it was 88 kilometres back along the Rio Parana to Parana. I've got to say my expectations were pretty low. I even wished my competitors well before the start. Yet, once the race was underway, I actually found myself leading the whole field in the early stages. That couldn't last, though, and soon swimmers started to pass me. It was pretty deflating. This was definitely going to be a long day.

As we reached the three-hour mark, Hungarian Rita Kovacs passed me to take over second spot among the women. Rita had never headed me before and we still had seven hours to go! As if that wasn't hard enough to swallow, my body chose that moment to resume the torment of the past week. It was probably the sugar in the chocolate drink that kicked it off. Whatever the reason, suddenly my diarrhoea returned. And then the vomiting. As fast as Grub was feeding me, it was coming out one or the other end. You couldn't help wonder what the swimmers behind me were making of this, but in this water they were probably blissfully unaware. After all, I wasn't really doing anything out of the ordinary. You only had to look at the shanties along the banks to remind yourself of that.

Not that it made the experience any more pleasant. It's about as humiliating as it gets in this sport. I was lucky I had an understanding trainer in Grub and was sufficiently distant from the bank most of the time for spectators to be left guessing. Embarrassment aside, my main concern was to keep my fluids level up on a stinking hot day. I was stopping every ten minutes to take another drink, but it was like pouring liquid down a drain.

This went on for hour after hour. At some point I started to lose my marbles. Everything around me became distorted and enlarged. The tankers which plied this river were big enough as it was, but in my fragile state they began to look terrifyingly huge and menacing. The chop looked like tidal waves. Poor Grub's attempts to humour me seemed like treacherous unconcern for my welfare. I began to abuse him for his apparent flippancy in the midst of my misery. It was horrendous for him. Goodness knows what the hovering Red Cross boat made of all this.

In the rare moments I was lucid I clung to one thought. If you don't quit, you'll make it. And it looked like I just might when, after an eternity of pain and humiliation, Grub shouted out that we were rounding the last buoy. It had been a surreal seven hours since Rita had passed me. She had remained just out of reach the whole time and, just when I longed for someone to swim with, nobody else could catch up with me. It felt like a solo swim. With three kilometres to go Grub barked at me once more.

'Rita's just eight hundred metres ahead! She's *dying*! Come on, you can catch her!'

From somewhere deep inside I dredged up a final, gut-busting effort. I started to haul her in, closing to 500 metres, 300 metres, 100 metres, 50 metres. But that was as close as I would get. Rita touched the wall at the finish and I followed her into third place. We turned to each other and I collapsed in her arms. The next thing I knew I was being lifted out of the water and hooked up to have my blood pressure and heart rate measured. I flopped forward like a rag doll.

Bed. That's where I wanted to be now. Instead, the organisers were trying to steer me towards the stage to be paraded before the huge crowd. There must have been upwards of 50,000 people there. They would have to wait, though. I whispered that I had nothing left in the tank (or anywhere else for that matter) and was immediately ushered to a waiting ambulance.

That's when things started to get *really* crazy. It had clearly been a slow week for the ambulance driver, because he sped off as though I was knocking at death's door. There was a steep climb from the river to the town and it felt like I was lifting off a launch pad. Suddenly the back doors flew open and all the bags and equipment started tumbling out. The attendants had to grab my stretcher to prevent me doing likewise. A vision leapt into my head of hurtling down the hill and back into the river like some excerpt from a Jerry Lewis movie. After banging on the driver's cabin the situation was retrieved, but not before Grub had a fit of hysterics. It seemed like a fitting finale to an extraordinary day.

Welcome to the glamorous world of marathon swimming.

It's a world which has led me to many a success, some major disappointments and a few home truths. I'll be sharing those with you. But, as with any autobiography, it's not so much the details which are of value. It's the insights and lessons a life can offer.

Two underlying themes have bubbled to the surface in the course of writing this book. The first is about the positive effects of willpower, dedication and belief. They are doughy kinds of words, but no less important for that. My life is essentially the story of a woman of limited talents who refused to be ruled by self-doubts or the doubts of others. A woman who set goals and who, with enormous input from those around her, achieved them. It never ceases to amaze me how much support people are prepared to lend to someone with a clear vision and direction in life.

I'm probably dancing around saying it, but it's about following your dreams. Not just following them, *pursuing* them and hunting them down. Dreams are hard won and that's why they're so valuable. In return, dreams help give us a sense of purpose. Broken down into achievable goals, they give us a reason to get out of bed each day. They help us to live life to the full. They challenge us to guard our individuality, because the non-dreamers delight in trying to reduce us to their level. Dreamers must be prepared to be different, to take risks, to explore the limits of their capabilities. I don't see it as an alternative. I see it as the *only* option for anyone who wants to lead a meaningful life.

The other theme underpinning this book may seem contradictory. It is a cautionary tale about the dangers of becoming obsessed with the goals which serve as stepping stones to our dreams. There is no question they are necessary. But when they dominate you to the extent that you ignore all other aspects of your life, you have a problem. *I* had a problem. Somewhere along the way to my dreams I forgot to tend to my relationships and my health. I forgot to stop and smell the flowers. It's a well-documented flipside to achievement and yet it's so easy to lose your way.

I went some way to regaining my perspective in the space of one dark year. Between late 1993 and late 1994 I had to contend with a marriage breakdown and a cancer scare. With my foundations crumbling, I had to rethink my priorities. I'm a changed person for it. Not that I'd necessarily do things differently if I had another chance. I firmly believe that I had to follow the path I did to arrive at the present point.

Besides, there are many things I'd never change. The emotions that welled up inside me as I stood on the dais to receive my World Championships gold medal in 1991, for example.

Now there was a dream come true. Not only had I won for my country, but I had done so in front of a hometown audience in Perth. In the absence of a berth for marathon swimming at the Olympics, this was my Olympic gold medal, the culmination of a quest which had begun nearly twenty years earlier.

A • TAYLOR • MAID

SHELLEY RAELENE TAYLOR spluttered into life at the St John of God Hospital, Subiaco, on 3 August 1961.

The first-born daughter of Merv and Irene, I already had a brother, Michael, eight years older, and in eighteen months I was to gain a sister, Lizabeth. Home was a humble three-bedroom brick veneer in the working-class Perth suburb of Morley.

Like most kids, my earliest memories are a warm and fuzzy series of disconnected images. I do recall that from the outset I was a perfectionist. I'd spend my days furiously cleaning my cubby house while my poor sister was denied entry for fear of undoing my good work.

The memories begin to assume sharper focus from the time I was about ten (being ridiculed by other kids for wearing long apricot socks to school tends to leave an indelible impression on one). We had moved from Morley to another northside address in nearby Yokine. Apart from a brief period, it was to be my home for the next fifteen years. Lizzie and I shared a bedroom which had been furnished with real attention to equality. Our beds were identical, as were the chairs and dressers. Come to think of it, we were even dressed identically for a time. People often mistook us for twins. I've never asked Mum why, but I imagine it was to lessen the chance of us fighting over things.

If we were fighting, it was more than likely our grandmother who would have to intervene. Florence Kennedy, my mother's mother, virtually raised us while our parents did shift work. If Nana was busy, my Aunt Kaye and her future husband David would take over babysitting duties while Mum worked long hours behind the Rendezvous Bar at the Rivervale Hotel. I guess she was a bit of a personality there. Leastways, the bar was known as Irene's Rendezvous.

My father Merv, meanwhile, had left the navy to join the police force when I was still a small child. He led a fairly nomadic life while we stayed in Perth. Over the years he spent time posted to the country towns of Bunbury and Narrogin, both about three hours' drive from Perth. In his spare time he worked at the vegetable markets to bring in some extra money. He made a lot of friends in the Italian community as a result and hardly a month seemed to go past without us tootling along to an Italian wedding, christening or funeral. We would also eat out at least once a week at an Italian family's home or an Italian restaurant in the area now known as Northbridge.

With all Mum and Dad's comings and goings, it was a pretty fluid family environment. We rarely had both parents at the nightly meal. When they were both home, which was mainly on weekends, they would get stuck into the garden. With Michael that much older than Lizzie and I, it often seemed like just the two of us. Which isn't to say we weren't loved. In fact, we were spoiled rotten by both our parents. And once I started swimming competitively at the age of nine, together with Nana ('keep kicking your legs, Shell!') they were my greatest fans and supporters.

I had Lizzie to thank for leading me into swimming. I was about six when we both learnt to swim during Education Department lessons in the ocean pool at North Beach. Some of that Indian Ocean water must have got into my blood, because when our parents decided Lizzie should continue swimming to help her asthma, I was happy to play the big sister and accompany her to the pool.

Our reactions were entirely predictable. Lizzie had to go, therefore she hated it. I didn't have to go, therefore I was as keen as mustard. As a further twist, Lizzie was a natural in the water. All her strokes were beautiful. I, on the other hand, exhibited all the grace of wounded buffalo. But, awkward as I was, I wasn't going to let anyone discourage me. The pool quickly became the centre of my universe. I'd go to bed with my bathers on in preparation for morning training. On the way to the pool, I'd have my cap and goggles on in the car (now that must have been a sight!). I was first through the turnstiles, first changed and first behind the blocks ready to go. If the coach was late, I'd be in the water doing the warm-up anyway.

By the time I was nine I'd shown enough enthusiasm, if not natural aptitude, to be deemed ready for competition. We'd been training morning and night in the backyard pool of swim coach Ray Pitcher, and his wife, May, had seen enough in both of us to convince her we were ready to step up a level. We were enrolled in Ray's swim school at Inglewood and Lizzie started to win races almost immediately. At the same time we joined the Tuart Hill Swimming Club and I continued to plug along determinedly, eventually picking up my first club record in breaststroke. Over the next eight years the Tuart Hill Swimming Club was to become my extended family. Every Saturday afternoon between October and April upwards of a dozen families would ritually gather at Tuart Hill High to compete in the pool and play games of continuous cricket. Dad would act as starter and Mum as timekeeeper. In the evenings the group would regretfully disperse and we would join the Hattons and the Buntings and the Cotterills for a barbeque. I can still hear the laughter and smell the sausages of those joyful Saturdays.

My parents began to take a more active interest in the sport as it became clear we had some talent. What nobody could have guessed was that, from the age of eleven, I would begin to catch up and then outstrip my sister in terms of performances. It certainly had nothing to do with God–given talent. It was simply that my fervour knew no bounds, while Lizzie had never been truly comfortable with the swimming scene. I just loved the hard work. If I missed a training session, there was something wrong with me. It was never a case of being slack. And as if my natural zeal wasn't enough, I had been electrified by Shane Gould's performance in winning three gold medals at the 1972 Munich Olympics. Now I knew what I was swimming for. I wanted to represent Australia at the Olympics. It didn't seem beyond the realms of possibility when, still aged eleven, I finally cracked it for my first state championships gold medal in the 12-years 200-metre backstroke. There was no stopping me now.

Not that fate didn't try. Within a year I was diagnosed with scoliosis, an abnormal curvature of the spine, and was also advised to quit swimming because of severe tendonitis in my shoulder. It was suggested I would never be the champion I longed to be, so it was better to give it away now. It was the last thing I wanted to hear. And, as it happened, I was in no mind to listen to such pessimistic forecasts. I'd already proved most doubters wrong by getting this far and I wasn't about to throw in the towel now. Not this little 12 year old!

The scoliosis was not so easily shrugged off. It turned out that my spine had been wonky since birth and the problem had probably been exacerbated by carrying heavy school cases for the past seven years. The net effect was a slight limp. In his wisdom, the doctor decided that the best thing for me was to be fitted with a custom-designed metal brace extending from my neck to my waist. Obviously *he* wasn't going to be wearing it. I would have to wear the brace every day until the problem was corrected or, at the very least, stabilised. Little did anyone suspect that I would wear that horrible contraption for nearly 2000 days, finally casting it off when I was seventeen. When I did, I was still 7mm shorter in one leg and to this day I occasionally lose my balance and fall over for no observable reason.

I can thank my scoliosis for two things, at least. First, it offered a compelling reason to keep swimming. As anyone with back problems knows, swimming is just about the best means of exercising and building up the muscles needed to support the spine. Second, if you'll excuse the pun, it provided the backbone to my tolerance of pain, a crucial factor in my success in marathon swimming. Not that the scoliosis itself was painful. No, it was that damned brace!

Picture, if you will, a device that wouldn't look out of place in a medieval torture chamber. The steel brace extended down my right side to my hip and was held in place by a harness which wrapped around my other side. The brace would rub my sternum raw and wear through the hips of all my skirts because of the constant rubbing. In the mornings I would have to wear it to the pool, take it off to swim, put it back on afterwards and then leave it on until I repeated the procedure for training in the evening. Apart from the pool and (most often) my bed, I would be trussed up in it seven days a week. Needless to say, the design did not find its way into mainstream corrective medicine.

Vexing as it was, the brace proved to be no hindrance to my swimming. The same year my scoliosis was diagnosed I joined Kevin Duff's Aquaclub training squad at Beatty Park and began to pursue the sport even more wholeheartedly. My life was reduced to a pattern of eating, sleeping, swimming and schoolwork. I would get my homework done by 8.30 p.m. and go straight to bed. My most treasured book, *Swimming The Shane Gould Way*, was never far from my reach. My obsession soon bled into the rest of the family (Dad was stationed back in Perth) and the household began to revolve almost entirely around my schedule and the sport. Neither of my parents had a background in swimming, but they both became involved as my budding career unfolded. In short time I was beating girls five years my senior at distance freestyle events and my father had become a starter for the West Australian Swimming Association.

It's time for a confession. Somewhere along the way I became a spoilt brat. I don't have to look too far for the reasons why. After all, my sister and I were given everything we ever wanted. If I wanted a steak, I'd have a steak. If I wanted a carrot juice, Dad would make it. Michael had left to join the army by now, so all the attention was lavished on Lizzie and me. It even extended to having a healthy and a junk alternative in the fridge.

In the training pool, I could be a perfect little vixen. I would dob my mates in at training if they didn't do all their laps. If they cut corners or went to the toilet in the middle of laps, I'd tell the coach. I can safely say I was hated by some of the other kids at the pool as a 12 year old. I was just shocking, and I don't know why I was like that. Perhaps I was *too* focused.

I resented anybody not putting in the same effort I was. I was always the first one in the water. I'd do my warm-up like it was the main set and tumble turn on people if they were on the black square. I just knew what I had to do to be the best, and God help anybody who got in my way. When I look back, I can see there were other casualties of my single-mindedness. We had cats and dogs at home, but I just didn't have any time for them. How were they going to help me achieve my goal?

They're not easy words to write, even if it was only a brief phase in my life. In mitigation, I wasn't the same person away from the pool. I was far more relaxed at school. In fact, I loved school. I was forever talking and giggling with classmates. In the absence of a 'normal' childhood, it was my social outlet. Remember, I was swimming morning and night. I never got to sleep over at friends' places. Apart from school, I really only had the chance to socialise on weekends. Even then, once I started competitive swimming I was spending more and more of my weekends at the pool. My 13th birthday was a slumber party with my swimming mates.

As far as schoolwork went, I was a model student at both Yokine Primary School and Tuart Hill High. Just as with swimming, I was dedicated and disciplined. I wasn't overly intelligent, but I worked my butt off. I was the type who always paid attention in class, always did their homework and always wore their uniform. Why does that sound apologetic? It shouldn't. I truly enjoyed study. Mum would often have to chase me away from the kitchen table after I'd spread my books all over it.

As much as I thrived at school, swimming was the undisputed focus of my life. After my unspectacular start in the sport, I was now winning all my races. My ribbons and trophies for 100 and 200-metre backstroke and 400, 800 and 1500-metre freestyle were beginning to clutter the loungeroom. Then, in 1974, my Olympic dream edged closer when I was selected to represent Western Australia at the national age championships. It was to signal the start of an unbroken run of five years in the state team. The 1976 Montreal Olympics were two years off and, according to Kevin Duff, I was on target to challenge for a spot in the Australian team. The 200-metre backstroke was earmarked as my best chance of making it.

It was all the encouragement my family needed. My father became increasingly involved in the sport, taking on the role of manager of a number of state teams, and Mum even had stints as a manageress. In 1975 all four of us went to Adelaide with the state team for the age group championships. As I reflect on it now, without wishing to appear ungrateful, I wonder whether there was an unhealthy emphasis on my achievements. Make no mistake, it wasn't enough that I was competing. I was expected to win. It became so I doubted that I would ever be able to do enough to satisfy my parents, especially my mother.

It may have been the spin put on the situation by a sensitive child. They may just have been trying to help me improve myself. But, whatever their motivation, the reality for me was that I never felt I was good enough. I'll never forget my mother asking me 'how could you *lose*?' when I failed to win for the first time in years. It cut me to the quick at the precise moment I was looking for reassurance that it was okay as long as I gave 100 per cent. Her reaction might be explained by her own past. Mum had been a very talented dancer in the Australian Ballet Company until becoming pregnant with Michael. It ended her dancing career prematurely and it's conceivable that she transferred her dreams to me. But, hey, I'm no psychologist. We'll have to leave that one for the couch.

Look, our family wasn't perfect. There's no such thing, is there? I'm sufficiently removed from my childhood now to see that much of the love I received was reward-based. Conditional love, they call it. I don't remember being loved in a physical way. Instead, love came in the form of gifts when I won medals. At eleven I had my first electric shaver, at twelve I got a sewing machine. It was never me the person, it was always what I did. I thought the only way I was going to be loved was by winning races. Even though I really enjoyed swimming, I felt at times that I was really swimming for my mum and dad. For their approval, to be precise.

Naturally, it's had its consequences in my adult life. I feel I still expect credit when I win a race or set a record. If I don't get that credit in the correct proportion, whether from approving friends, media exposure or sponsorship support, I feel very disappointed. It's a Pavlovian kind of thing, only I'm the one ringing the bell. When I don't get the anticipated response to my achievements, the whole pattern is disrupted.

Back then, it meant I had my spats with Mum over what I saw as the pressure she was placing on me to constantly win. My father was a different matter. Whatever our shortcomings as a family, it didn't stop me worshipping him. In many ways he was the first of my mentors. A larger-than-life character who could do no wrong. I dreaded the thought of ever letting him down.

He'd led an adventurous life. Born into a strict Baptist family, he'd been a Sunday school teacher before joining the navy. I vaguely remember looking at postcards from all the exotic places he visited around the world. Much to the horror of his family he strayed a little from the faith during his years at sea. He called it 'seeing the light'. Still, I was raised a Baptist.

On the occasions he docked at Perth, Dad worked as a taxi driver to keep the money coming in. It was crucial to him to be a good provider and, presumably in a bid for greater security, he was soon applying to join the police force. There certainly wasn't any problem with meeting the size requirements. At 192cm and a shade over 100 kilograms, he had the sort of presence that made people take notice when he walked into a room. He got the job.

As you would expect with someone raised in a strict Baptist household, he was a strong-headed man with a very traditional view of the world. He saw things in black and white and was in no doubt as to the difference between right and wrong. By the same token, he was very compassionate and generous, the type who would give his friends his last dollar. He was also a man with an unquenchable thirst for life. He loved his home brew and hated to miss a party. He wasn't going to be cheated out of a minute of life. And if things weren't happening to his liking, he'd go out and change them. He had both the determination and discipline to see the job through. I think I've inherited a lot of his qualities.

Dad was always very caring and nurturing towards me. If he was at home when Mum was at work he would cook for us. He cooked a mean scrambled eggs for breakfast after training. Of course, he wasn't around all that much during the years he was posted to the country. But it was during those years that I got to see the strength of his character up close when he and two other policemen faced a Royal Commission. They were accused of assaulting an Aboriginal while putting him in the back of a police van in Narrogin. They were ultimately cleared, but the whole episode caused him an enormous amount of pain. Nevertheless, his attitude was to take what was dished out to him in life and get on with it. I remember him saying that it's easy for people to kick you while you're down, but at the end of the day what everyone else thought didn't matter. It's what *you* believe that counts. And it's up to you to get back up on your feet.

The other man in my life at that stage had a similar attitude. Mal Brown, the legendary West Australian footballer now heavily involved with Richmond Football Club, ranks as my second mentor. Mal was the hero at the East Perth football club in those days and a good mate of my father's. Dad was often the duty policeman at the ground on match days and was close to most of the players. With Mum working behind the club bar it was a real family affair. I'd spend the game sitting with Mal's parents and cheering my head off. When the match was over I'd wait in the tunnel to collect the players' autographs before going upstairs to the club, where Dad would be on the door.

Like most East Perth fans, I just idolised Mal. I used to sit on his lap and tell him I loved him and that one day I was going to marry him. Meanwhile he'd be in the paper for thumping someone who'd antagonised him in a restaurant. But as far as I was concerned I wouldn't hear a bad word about him. He was always such a genuine person.

The thing about Mal was that, from the time I first made the state team, he was the one who would tell me it didn't matter where I finished as long as I gave 100 per cent. He'd ring me every year before I went off to represent Western Australia and say the same thing: if I gave it my best I was a winner regardless, and he'd still love me. I needed to hear that, because I was so caught up on love being dependent on success. He couldn't possibly have known how much those words meant to me. Indeed, they've stayed with me since. On the occasions I've tasted defeat, I've been quick to ask if I gave it everything I had. And if I can answer that I did, I'm satisfied. Not happy, perhaps, but satisfied nonetheless.

Mal's words were put to a severe test in 1976. This was to be my year. The year when the pay-off was due for all the hard work, the long hours in the pool and the sacrifices. The Olympics were nearing when I went to Melbourne and won the national title for 14-year-olds in the 200-metre backstroke. The final selection trials were to be held in Sydney the following week and I was right on track. One more good swim and I'd be off to Montreal. The job might have been made harder by the decision to take two swimmers from the event to Canada instead of the usual three, but I was still confident. First or second place would see me on the plane.

Both my parents had been in Melbourne to see me win the national title. Now we all headed north with the rest of the West Australian team for our moment of truth. The trials were held at the North Sydney Olympic pool, in the shadow of the Sydney Harbour Bridge. As I settled into starting position in the pool I knew that just 200 metres of water separated me from my dream. The starter's gun went off.

I came in third behind two Queenslanders. I went numb as the realisation sunk in that I'd missed out on the Olympics. Mal's words offered little comfort at a time like this. I might have given it my all, but the stark fact was that I wouldn't be marching out into the Olympic Stadium behind the Australian flag. I thought I'd failed miserably. It's what I had been working towards for almost three years. Suddenly, at fourteen, I felt as though my whole life was over. I no longer had a sense of direction.

It can all seem a bit melodramatic now. But that didn't make it any less real at the time. Fortunately any descent into self-pity was arrested when I found out shortly afterwards that the Olympic swimming team would be holding its final training camp in Perth mid-year. With Dad's role as one of three organisers we were up to our elbows in helping to arrange billets, food, transport and facilities. We took in a billet ourselves, freestyler Jenny Tate. It helped take my mind off my own woes and before I knew it I was slipping back into my training routine. There were always World Championships and the Commonwealth Games, after all. Besides, what choice did I have? My whole life revolved around swimming. I don't know what I would have done if I wasn't training my guts out for the next meet.

When the Australian team flew out from Perth I went to the airport and waved them off. I cried that day, but they were ambiguous tears. They were for me in part. But they were also tears of happiness for the team members I'd gotten to know over the previous two months. In a way I felt I'd become part of it all. And now they were going off to swim against the East German girls, with their deep voices and broad shoulders. Later on I got postcards from Jenny saying they sometimes wondered whether they were in the right changerooms!

I had my own concerns by then. Before the Olympic swimmers had even left Perth, Dad had started to get sick. He was a heavy smoker and we thought he had the flu. When it didn't improve he went to the doctor for a series of tests. Meanwhile, by August I had been selected to contest a number of events in the winter nationals in Brisbane. This time I travelled on my own. I don't know whether not having Mum or Dad there affected my enthusiasm, but after a tough swim I called home to say that I wanted to withdraw from the 1500-metre freestyle event. Queensland swimmer Tony Byrne was standing next to me when I made the call. I could have done with his support. Mum was having none of my protestations.

'Who cares anyway?' I asked her.

She handed the phone over to Dad.

'Look, Shelley, I'm not well. I *really* want you to swim this one for me.'

That was enough for me. I walked out of the telephone box and turned to Tony.

'My Dad's dying of lung cancer.'

He told me not to be ridiculous. But instinctively I knew.

A • SHORT • COURSE • ON • • MARATHON • SWIMMING

MARATHON SWIMMING. Bit hard on the knees, isn't it? Ha ha. Fair enough. Sure, it isn't one of the sports Mr Murdoch has gone chasing with a chequebook yet. You might even lump it in with obscure sports. But that is no reflection on its athletic merits or its dramatic appeal. I'm sure anybody who has seen footage of the sport will agree with that.

No, the sport of marathon swimming is another one of those unfortunate victims of the maxim that you ain't the genuine article until you've got a seat at the Olympics. And while we continue to lobby the world swimming body, FINA, to recommend a 25-kilometre event to the International Olympic Committee, athletes are forced to battle for recognition. It can get very frustrating, to say the least. Not only do individual marathon swimmers constantly have to get on the soapbox for the sport, but the trailblazers have to live with the knowledge they may be too old when it comes time to enjoy the fruits of their labours.

With Atlanta gone, the 2000 Olympics in Sydney loom as my last, remote chance to represent Australia at the Olympics. The irony is that 25 kilometres is by no means my best distance. In fact, it's not even strictly a marathon. The precise definition of a marathon is anything over 25 kilometres. Strictly speaking, from 1500 metres to 25 kilometres is called open water or long distance swimming. Yet, while my reputation has been built on swims over 30 kilometres, when it comes to representing my country I'll take whatever I can get.

We're inching closer. The 25-kilometre event was included for the first time in the 1991 World Championships in Perth. And the previous year FINA representatives told me that the event was fourth in line for an Olympic berth after the women's 4 x 200-metre relay, team synchronised swimming and women's water polo. Priorities may have changed since then, but it's nice to know we're on the agenda.

So where did this sport come from? Like most people, when I first heard the term marathon swimming I immediately thought of the English Channel. Truth be known, I couldn't have named anything other than the English Channel. Not until I first went to America in 1982 did I learn that there was more to it. By then there was what could loosely be called a worldwide circuit offering a modest amount of prizemoney and prestige to a group of semi-professionals. Not that these were money-making extravaganzas. But I was flabbergasted to find out there was *any* money in the sport.

Without wishing to get too bogged down in historical detail, it transpires that some of the swims on the circuit have been there for nearly 40 years. It was these races which formed the basis of world rankings. After decades of following this practice it was then decided that the sport needed a marquee event to lift its profile. The World Cup, a 25-kilometre event to be staged every four years, was born. It was to be marathon swimming's Olympics.

The first World Cup was held in England in 1984, with medals going to the first three placegetters and the winning male and female being crowned world champions for that year. Two World Cups on, the concept is faltering in the wake of dramatic changes to the sport's structure. The changes date back to 1991, when the men behind the five principal swims on the circuit gathered in Perth on the occasion of the World Championships. The races they represented were the two from the Canadian province of Quebec, Lac St Jean and Lac Magog, America's Atlantic City swim, Italy's Capri to Naples event and Argentina's Rio Coronda swim.

The fabulous five had travelled to Australia to meet with FINA representatives and discuss a proposal for a formal circuit. The so-called World Series was the brainchild of Englishman Roger Parsons, who believed that if all the races came together under one umbrella the sport would get the boost it needed to get into the Olympics. Until then there had been little co-operation between the various race organisers peppered about the planet. It was really no way to promote a sport. Together, who knew what could happen?

The meeting was a success. With FINA's encouragement, the five swims became the founding members of the World Series, to be administered under the International Marathon Swimming Association. The World Series kicked off in February 1992 with the Rio Coronda swim in Argentina. After completing all the races on the circuit, the World Series returned to Rio Coronda to stage the final. The following season then began with the next race on the calendar, that race then taking over as the venue for the final. And so the baton is passed on.

Going by the calendar year, the first races are in South America in January and February. After a break, the World Series resumes in Europe in June before shifting to Canada in July and America in August. The schedule has changed over the years as races have come and gone. I've swum as many as seven World Series races in a season and there are now up to a dozen races on the circuit. They range from the four remaining foundation swims (Capri to Naples having sadly gone under) to the latest generation of races in Mar del Plata, Argentina, New York's Long Island Sound and Lake Ohrid in the former Yugoslav state of Macedonia.

The World Series winner is decided on a points system. Each race gets the same weighting, while less points are awarded for performances in World Championships, Pan Pacific Championships (Pan Pacs) and European Championships. At the end of the regular season the top twenty ranked men and top ten women are invited to the final, where double points are up for grabs. The world champion is then crowned after the final. It stands to reason that the World Series winner and the world champion are one and the same.

Well, that explains how marathon swimming has evolved to its present state. But it doesn't really convey the flavour of the great races. Especially the big five, each with its own character and challenges.

• ATLANTIC CITY •

THIS SWIM WILL ALWAYS hold a special place in my heart, for several reasons. It was the setting for my first tentative step into the world of professional marathon swimming. The year was 1985 and the outcome was hardly world-shattering, an anonymous thirteenth place overall. But it *was* my first payday! Six years later I made amends when Atlantic City was the venue for my first outright win in a professional race. I surprised everybody, myself included, by leading home the field in 1991 and then repeating the dose the following year. Both wins were in record times. In my most recent swim in 1993 I finished as first-placed woman and third overall.

Atlantic City is the chief gambling city of America's east coast. A short drive south from New York, it is famous for its piers, its boxing contests and its nightlife. Being put up in casinos for the race always adds to the atmosphere. The race, held on the first weekend in August, has been staged most years since 1958. The concept for swimming the 35 kilometres around Absecon Island, on which the city is situated, dates back to the early 1950s when a local entrepreneur offered two lifeguards $100 if they could perform the feat. They did, and legend has it that they spent their entire takings in one wild night.

The race itself is wonderful. It's a one-man show and the guy is totally disorganised, but that doesn't stop everyone enjoying it, even when you might not find out about the programming until race day. The race is given a unique touch by the use of lifeboat crews from Atlantic City Beach Patrol to lead the swimmers around. They really help make the race. Everywhere else you swim with motorboats. Believe me, the crews work bloody hard. Two guys rowing a one-tonne boat for 35 kilometres, a lot of it into wind, waves or current. Try it some day.

Depending on the tides, the race gets underway at Gardner's Basin somewhere between 7 a.m. and 10 a.m. You start in an inlet before entering the ocean for three hours. Once out there the conditions are very changeable, with the water temperature having been as low as ten degrees. With the ocean leg behind you, you swim into the back bays and follow them back to the starting point. After the ocean breezes, the back bays are often hot and muggy. Horseflies can have a real field day chomping on the boat crew. It's one of those rare times I thank God I'm the one in the water. Meanwhile you're passing under bridges and alongside houses. It's a great race for spectators, because there's so many points to stand and cheer. They can really spur you on as you come into the finish line. And afterwards there's no shortage of places to have a celebratory drink. The toughest part is making it to bed before dawn.

• LAC MAGOG •

ABOUT AN HOUR OR so east of Montreal is the quaint French-Canadian town of Magog. Its main claim to fame is as the original source of maple syrup. In the third week of July they stage a race called Le Traversee du Lac Magog as the culmination and highlight of an annual festival. I don't know how long the festival has been going for, but they've been hosting the swim for about twenty years and I've been going on and off since 1985.

As much as I don't like to single out races, this one must come close to being my favourite. And it's not just because I've won it six times and come second overall on three occasions. It may have something to do with the fact that, along with Atlantic City, it's the only race which offers equal prizemoney to men and women. It certainly has something to do with the warm reception I always receive there, particularly from the women. Add the glorious scenery and you've got a winning combination.

It's by no means an easy race. When you swim in a lake that's frozen for half the year, you know you're going to strike some pretty icy stretches. And in order to finish at Magog you're forced to swim into a headwind nine times out of ten. The wind throws up short and choppy waves more difficult to contend with than the regular sets you can experience at sea. Apart from the wind, I've had to swim in hail and fog so thick we needed a compass to find out where we were heading. A real three-seasons-in-one-day place.

This isn't a fly in–fly out sort of race. Swimmers are paraded through the town and a couple of days before the race we take part in a two-kilometre demonstration sprint race. In preparation for the race we then have to travel across the Canada–US border to the starting point in Newport, Vermont. Someone inevitably has trouble with customs on the way because they've forgotten their visa.

Once in Newport we face a 42-kilometre swim back to Magog along the length of the sweetwater (freshwater) lake. The race starts at 6 a.m. and we don't finish until 3 p.m. or 4 p.m. I've already mentioned some of the challenges provided by the conditions. What I haven't mentioned is the challenge provided by spectators in boats. If it's a nice day and they've been on the grog, they're in no mood to go slow. You've got to be on constant alert for drunks in speedboats. And the further you get into the race, the more the boats crowd around you. It makes for a great atmosphere, but it can be terribly hard to police. All of which can make a swimmer very nervous.

Still, the positives generally outweigh any negatives. It's a tremendous thrill to approach the finish with a personal flotilla of 50 boats around you. Inside the harbour the moored boats add to the cacophony by tooting their horns above the noise of the thousands of people lined along the shore.

I got perhaps my biggest reception there in 1991. In the week before the race multiple world champion Diego Degano said he'd quit the sport the day he was beaten by a woman. Come Sunday I had a really good day and beat him. The cheers from the women were deafening!

• CAPRI TO NAPLES •

THIS RACE WAS THE BABY of one of the real characters of the sport, Lello Barbuto. Lello was a sportswriter with the *Il Matino* newspaper in Naples and for 30-odd years he oversaw a well-organised and flamboyant event which attracted the top distance swimmers in the world. I first entered the swim in 1989 and managed to win three in a row before missing what was to prove the last race because of World Cup commitments.

The Capri to Naples swim was always held in early July, which in those days made it the first race of the northern hemisphere summer. Swimmers hungry for news since South America would catch up during training swims in the blue Mediterranean surrounding Capri. There couldn't be a better place to do it. High above us on the top of the island was the town of Anacapri, home to some of the wealthiest people in Europe. And below the island were its famous grottoes. We'd occasionally swim into them, explaining to the poor attendants demanding admission money that we could hardly be carrying our purses or wallets.

The race itself, with up to 60 high-calibre swimmers involved, was always memorable. The course ran 32 kilometres from the island through open sea and into Naples harbour. Competitors hit the water about 9 a.m. and swam alongside fishing boats into the Gulf of Naples. The water temperature was never a problem, sitting somewhere between 21 and 23 degrees, but you risked getting seasick in the rolling waves. Tides and currents also played a part.

Once you'd traversed the gulf you knew you were approaching the city when the water changed colour from a gorgeous blue to a grim black. It was just like crossing a line. The pollution followed the shipping lane and once you got inside the bay it was just putrid. No wonder I never saw any fish the whole time I swam there.

The finish was a real production number. The crowds were vast and there were always cameramen from national television stations running about frenziedly. As soon as you got out of the water you received a huge bouquet of flowers before being bundled into the back of an ambulance to be rushed across to the changing facilities, lights flashing. It was the only way they could safely get you across the manic Neopolitan streets. Then, the following night, they would hold a special presentation dinner at the governor's residence. Everywhere you turned there were dignitaries dripping with jewels. If you'd won the race you'd leave with armfuls of trophies. There'd be one from the organisers, one from the mayor, one from the governor, one from the nation, one from the council, one from the people of

Capri, one from the people of Naples. From beginning to end, it was a wonderfully crazy event.

Unfortunately, neither Lello nor the race is with us any longer. Lello died in 1992 and that proved to be the final year of his race as well. It may be just as well. The whisper in the last few years was that the race was bankrolled by the local Mafia and, as they were being wiped out, so too was the money for the swim. True or not, it all added to the race's mystique.

• LAC ST JEAN •

THIS IS ONE RACE where there is never any shortage of drama, whether it be competitors suffering from hypothermia or dodging the mishmash of spectator boats. The race is organised out of the town of Roberval, to the north of Quebec City. It may be in the same province as Magog, but it can seem a million miles away. This is logging territory. And when the locals are in party mood, as they are over the last weekend in July, watch out.

The Lac St Jean swim started life as a single crossing of 30 kilometres before spending six years as a 64-kilometre double-crossing challenge. During the double-crossing years a select group of swimmers would be invited to compete for a winner's prize of about US$20,000. The race then reverted to a single crossing of 40 kilometres from the town of Peribonca to Roberval. One side of the lake to the other. But this is no Sunday stroll. Even though the race is timed for the height of summer, the water remains perishing cold. Lac St Jean can be frozen for up to nine months of the year. Enough said?

At 4 a.m. on race day competitors gather in the hotel for breakfast. It's not the best setting. The partying is still going on and the smell of beer hangs thick in the air. Music is still thumping away in the background as you're trying to psyche yourself for the race start at 6 a.m. It's times like these you wish you could just throw your goggles away and join the festivities. You really get to wondering if you're in the wrong sport.

The race begins in the mouth of a river which is two to three degrees colder than the lake. It's a tough, chilling start. It can be as low as 12 degrees for the first hour. Once in the lake you're faced with the same sort of challenges thrown up by Lac Magog, only the water is colder and you've got to contend with floating logs into the bargain. You really rely on your trainer to guide you carefully on such occasions. They have to be particularly vigilant for the crazies who come out in droves on hot days to play on the lake. In 1990, my first time in the race, my trainer Nancy Schnarr and I were told off for raising our voices at the crowds of people in boats who were in our way. Some guy on a jet ski nearly ran over my arm that day. I thought he deserved every bit of abuse he got. He might not have spoken English, but I'm sure he got the general idea.

Jet skis and logs aside, the finish makes up for all your trials during the swim. Roberval puts on arguably the most spectacular finish of all the races. As you swim into the harbour you're greeted by hundreds of boats and thousands of people along the shore, all shouting and whooping. I've been fortunate enough to be greeted as women's winner on all four occasions I've swum there. No matter how bad you feel, you get lifted for the last two kilometres. The adrenalin rush is incredible and I invariably get goosebumps and teary-eyed. The thought of a nice massage and some hot packs provides a further spur. Then, when you touch the finish, you hear a huge roar. You have to climb some stairs and they present you to the crowd, there and then, in all your glory. You look like crap. You've got grease all over you, you're all blown up and you're covered in muck from boat exhausts. In that state you get onto the dais and accept the trophy. Makes for a great photo, I suppose.

• RIO CORONDA •

HOW CAN I BE diplomatic about this? Let's start with the positives. This 57-kilometre swim along Argentina's Coronda River is very well organised (for the men) and attracts the largest, most colourful and most passionate crowd on the circuit. It's a real celebration, with a mardi gras feel as men and women dress up in costume and shout encouragement along the length of the course from small craft and the shore.

However, there is no denying that this race has its problems. My main beefs are the treatment of the female competitors and the water quality. This is a race which is big on hype, but since it was first staged in the 1950s it's all been based around the men. That emphasis shows through in the sort of support the female competitors get during the race and the prizemoney split. Unfortunately, when you get to the finish all the attention is again focused on the men. The women are just window dressing. It can be a real shock after the way you're treated elsewhere. The last straw for me came in 1995 when the race was used to honour the memory of a former world boxing champion who'd been convicted for murdering his wife.

Then there is the water quality. The Rio Coronda is by no stretch of the imagination a salt water swim, but I wouldn't call it sweetwater either. With all the raw effluent and industrial waste that flows into the river, it can be a bit like swimming in a toilet. And if you want to know how dirty the water is, you don't have to go any further than me. Without fail, I'm sick within 36 hours of the race. We swim on Sunday and come Tuesday morning I'm vomiting and battling diarrhoea. I'm the one in bed with the drips coming out of her arm. I've written to the mayor of Santa Fe to complain about the water quality, but I've never received a reply. The only thing I got was a rap over the knuckles by World Series organisers for jeopardising one of their races.

The Rio Coronda certainly has the potential to be a great race for everyone concerned if they'd clean up their act. The swim really stirs the local populace, 100,000 of whom turn out on the day. It helps that the multiple world champion Diego Degano comes from Santa Fe, a small town where leather is the main industry. They are very parochial in this part of the world and just love to see hometown swimmers doing well.

The race starts around 8.30 a.m. when you first slide into the mud-brown river. The water is warm and the conditions are usually hot and humid. Helped by a current of about eight kilometres per hour you swim downstream, careful not to make a wrong turn at any of the tributaries. Those in your boat are also kept busy threading their way through the chaos on the water as recreational boats jostle for position. It doesn't always work. In 1994 my leg was cut by my own boat's propeller when they were bumped by another craft.

With everything going on in the water and along the shores, it's a real feast for the senses. I may have had my bad moments there, but the joyous participation of the fans goes a long way to balancing the ledger. They undoubtedly played a role in my debut swim in 1991 when I won the women's section and came fourth overall, an unheard of result for a woman there. They thought I was a freak. I've swum there a total of five times, winning the women's section three times, coming second in 1994 and fifth in 1995 after having my shoulder kicked at the start. As you may have guessed, it's questionable whether I'll be returning.

SO, THAT'S A BRIEF SKETCH of the world of marathon swimming. Against all the history, the World Series is really still in its infancy. Races come and go in the somewhat elastic calendar according to sponsorship, community support and the wits and perseverance of promoters. With its regular nucleus of races, though, the World Series has all the ingredients to be a fantastic vehicle for the sport.

No doubt you want to know how much the top swimmers make out of the sport. How much loot have I got stashed away from my highly successful years on the circuit? Well, I hate to disappoint you (believe me, I *hate* to disappoint you), but there are no rivers of gold out there. Or lakes or seas for that matter. Only one swimmer has actually made money out of the sport and that's Argentina's Diego Degano. He hasn't made it through prizemoney, either, as is apparent from the average of just US$5000 for the first placegetter and US$3000 for the first woman. He's just been very smart at marketing himself and attracting sponsorship.

For my part, I'm almost wholly dependent on sponsorships of airfares and equipment just to cover the costs of competing on the circuit. Swimmers are still responsible for getting themselves to and fro between races, with no financial support from the World Series organisation. Promoters will provide accommodation for the top swimmers on most occasions, but as the swimmers' representative I'm still pushing for basics like meals and transport.

In the end, whether you can make any money out of the sport at all largely depends on whether you get financial support from your country's swimming federation. The difficulty here is that there are some inconsistencies which make it very hard for a marathon swimmer to fulfil their commitments to the federation *and* maintain the ranking upon which their funding is based. Although illness intervened to avert a crisis in 1995, just such a clash was looming had I been selected for the Pan Pacs held on 9 August. Under the federation's rules, I wouldn't have been allowed to swim any marathons in the month preceding the Pan Pacs. As it happened, that would have kept me out of the World Series final, a crucial component in assessing my world ranking. The same world ranking the federation uses to judge whether I'm worthy of their support. Go figure.

Finally, it's worth putting professional marathon swimming in perspective. While competent social swimmers can churn through many kilometres, only a relatively small number of swimmers can sustain the necessary speed over long distances in varying conditions to make a fist of the professional circuit. It's a very elite club, with just over 100 swimmers registered with the World Series. And that's the way it should be in a legitimate sport.

In the meantime, room always remains for those adventurous types who want to tackle the likes of the English Channel and the 'round Manhattan Island swim. These swims will always stand apart as personal challenges. Far and away the majority of people who attempt them aren't even looking at records. It's their personal Everest. Go climb it, I say.

THE • LOST • YEARS

DAD'S LUNG CANCER was confirmed the morning after Father's Day, 1976.

You could hardly miss it. All of a sudden this great bear of a man was losing weight. And yet we decided not to tell Lizzie at first. We felt she was too young to cope. It was probably one of the worst decisions the family ever made. She didn't find out for months.

The dreadful news was the signal for the longest ten months of my life. While my brother arranged to be posted back from Queensland to be close to home, I threw myself into swimming and school. Outwardly, our routines didn't change a lot. But at home I became daddy's little helper. I helped Mum shave him and wash him as his strength diminished. He had set up his bed in the loungeroom so we could take care of him. The last thing he wanted was to go into hospital. If he was to die, he wanted to die at home.

Those months gave me a different outlook on life. When you watch the physical being deteriorate, the thing that advertisers highlight so much, you begin to realise that it's the person inside that really counts. And as everything else was deteriorating, my father's character was just growing and growing.

He continued to work and he was still driving eight months into the illness, although it would take him five minutes to walk from the front door to the car. It was heart-wrenching to watch. Finally, it couldn't be avoided any longer. He had to go into hospital. By this stage he wasn't always coherent. After our daily visits Mum would find hospital spoons, knives and forks in her bag. I guess he never wanted his family to go without.

Early on the morning of 12 July 1977 we got a call from the hospital to say he wasn't going to make it through the day. After calling Michael we hurried over. When we got there we found him in a great deal of pain and barely intelligible. We gathered at his bed and I began to cry.

'Don't cry,' he said. 'Go and wring out your tissues and hang them on the line to dry.'

A couple of hours passed. Michael still hadn't arrived when the doctor came in and told Mum that they couldn't wait any longer. They were going to give Dad a needle to ease the pain. Dad didn't want it and we were adamant that they should wait until Michael got there. But the doctor wouldn't wait. Just before they gave him the needle I went to his side.

'Don't worry,' he said, 'you'll be a world champion one day. You'll represent Australia and win a gold medal.'

'Don't be crazy,' I said.

It wasn't what I wanted to say. I wanted to tell him that swimming wasn't important to me at the moment. I didn't want us to say goodbye like that. Soon afterwards they gave him the needle and he slipped into a coma.

My mother's brother-in-law had arrived by now and after a while he took Lizzie and me to the Subiaco shops to get lunch. It was while we were making a quick trip to the post office that I looked at the clock. At that precise moment, 2.18 in the afternoon, I felt something inside. My father had just died. He was only 49. Tragically, Michael never got a chance to say goodbye.

True to character, he had fought to the bitter end. He simply wouldn't let go of life. They pronounced him dead three times. At his time of death he weighed just 57 kilograms, a bag of bones. Curiously enough, he became the second policeman cleared of the Narrogin assault charges to die. The remaining policeman died soon afterwards. The case had clearly taken its toll.

I'll never forget returning home that night. His empty bed was still set up in the loungeroom. It was a terrible reminder of the huge hole that had just opened up in our lives.

His premature death also left a large hole in the broader community. That much was evident when 1000 people turned up to his funeral, including Mal Brown and the rest of the East Perth football team. Everybody felt the loss. Of course, no one felt it more than his family. None of us was coping and it became a question of trying to make it through from day to day. Our family was crumbling around us.

It's funny. I had always thought that it was my mother who ruled the roost. But once Dad died I realised he was the foundation of our household. He was really the leader, the person who made the decisions, the adviser in all problems. He always put everyone else before himself and, with his death, the family structure just didn't survive at all.

Mum was a mess. She just couldn't accept it. Not that we saw her much. She was doing even more shift work to try to make ends meet. In her absence my sister and I started to get into a bit of trouble. I felt as though I was expected to replace my father as the foundation of the household and, at fifteen, I just wasn't ready for it yet. And when my mother *was* around, we'd often end up fighting. I kept asking her what I had to do to be loved. Why couldn't she just accept me as I was? It's hard to say whether it was teenage angst or a justifiable question. My head was full of questions at the time.

I would lie in bed at night and wonder what life was all about. I mean, there couldn't be a god, could there? Why would the good people die if there was? Why would you take a good man like my father off this earth when there were all those bad people in jail? My father hadn't done anything wrong. I would just lie there and cry and cry. I couldn't believe a person I loved so much had been taken away from me.

I was mad at the world. I became so bitter I had to have counselling at school. I had thought that we all grew old together, that I'd have kids and my parents would have grand-children. I thought we all lived happily ever after. But no. It wasn't going to be like that. No fairytales.

To say it had a major impact on my life is an understatement. I was no longer the same person. You know what really got me mad? When I'd go to school and kids would complain about their Mum and Dad getting divorced. I would turn around and say 'wait until you lose them and never see them again'. I was grieving, with all those phases of denial, withdrawal and bitterness. Until you accept it and get on with life again. For me it was a matter of a few years.

They might aptly be called my lost years. I was working part-time to help bring some money into the household and although I was still swimming and competing at nationals, I didn't really have the desire any more. A lot of my drive had vanished with Dad's death. I couldn't see any reason to keep doing it. Somehow I made it to the age group nationals in 1978, but I don't even remember the 1978 Commonwealth Games. I was more interested in getting through school and getting tertiary entry marks. At seventeen, after swimming in the 1979 nationals held in Perth in February, I quit.

I had represented Western Australia from the time I was twelve and broken hundreds of club and state records. My medals, trophies and ribbons filled the loungeroom. Now I wanted to take them all down. To sweep away the past and move on. It upset my mother terribly. She thought I was making a bad decision by giving up swimming. But nobody could change my mind. I was stubborn and wanted to make my own mistakes.

I had grown up quickly in the period since my father's death. It had left me with a real sense of how precious life is and how quickly it can be taken away. I wanted to live life to the fullest from now on. Life's too short to do otherwise. And swimming simply didn't fit into the equation at the time.

Things moved quickly in 1979. I had finished school but wasn't sure what I wanted to do, ultimately deferring tertiary studies to take a job as a settlements clerk at a real estate agency. There was very little holding the family together now and soon both my sister and I had moved out to live elsewhere. I moved in with my boyfriend and we began to carve out a life together. In August, just after my eighteenth birthday, Greg and I became engaged. I had been searching for security and now I seemed destined for the life of a suburban wife.

All that changed on a wet Easter night in 1980.

The accident happened as I was driving along Scarborough Beach Road. It had just started raining when I pulled up 50 metres short of some traffic lights to turn right. I had my indicator on when I looked in my rear view mirror and saw this two-tonne truck coming up quickly from behind. With a horrible clarity I knew he wasn't go to stop in time. Instinctively I put my foot on the brake and braced myself for the impact.

BOOM! When I opened my eyes the entire rear end of my green Gemini had been crushed like a concertina. The boot was pushed in and there was a truck in my back seat. I couldn't help thinking that I should have been killed. But, miraculously, I didn't have a scratch on me. Not that I got off scot-free. A doctor later diagnosed whiplash and put me in a neck brace for five months. As it turned out, he missed the greater damage. My lower back had taken a battering in the accident and, without treatment, it soon began to trouble me again.

I became a regular visitor to the physiotherapist. There was nothing he could do for the next misfortune to befall me, however. Greg and I split up. My brief flirtation with domesticity was over. I returned home to Mum's and took on shift work as a computer operator with a pharmaceutical wholesaler to fill up my time as best I could. For some reason hiding myself away in a job with unsocial hours seemed the best way to help me through the pain of a broken relationship. Shortly afterwards I joined a health club to improve my fitness and found myself occasionally slipping into the pool to exercise my neck and back. Without the pressure of competition I actually began to enjoy the brief sessions.

Such simple pleasures were among the highlights of the next year. I was living the life of a virtual recluse, surrounded by banks of computers at night and keeping pretty much to myself during the day. On the rare occasions I ventured out at night I had to rely on a hairdresser friend, Peter Smith, to accompany me in the absence of a regular partner. There was no purpose or urgency in my life. Had I forgotten the lesson of my father's death, that you're here for a good time, not a long time?

After a year or so skirting the edges it was time to jump back into life. I was in the right frame of mind to listen when my family doctor told me that I should get a normal job, a nine-to-fiver, and start associating more with people with common interests. Swimming seemed the logical choice. It would be good therapy for my back, too.

Following doctor's orders, the shift work went and I got a new job working regular hours with Woodside Offshore Petroleum. Now for the second part of his prescription. It had been more than two years since I'd walked away from swimming, so it was a rather nervous young woman who visited Kevin Duff and his assistant coach Colin Raven at the City of Perth Aquaclub in October 1981. When I asked their advice on how I could get into coaching they pointed to the pool and suggested I have a swim with some of their kids. It was like a rebirth. To this day, I haven't got out.

Suddenly my old enthusiasm was rekindled. So much so that I threw myself back into full training under Duffy. This was my element. When I was in the pool, swimming against the clock, I had a sense of purpose. It wasn't as though I was dreaming of the Olympics again, but I could feel my bearings returning. And so was my old form. Only three months after getting back in the water I qualified to swim in the state championships. In January 1982, having spent three years out of competition, I won seven gold medals in the 400, 800 and 1500-metre freestyle, 100 and 200-metre backstroke and two relays. Yep, Shelley Taylor was back.

Unbeknownst to me, I was also on the verge of another great upheaval. My performance in those state championships was about to propel me into a new life as foreign as it was unexpected.

In Arkansas of all places!

'SO • WHAT • DO • YOU • • "THINK" • ABOUT?'

To describe the history, structure and character of marathon swimming is one thing. But what about the experience of swimming a marathon. How do I prepare? How do conditions affect a swim? What does the trainer do? What's it like swimming in polluted waters? And that perennial favourite, what do you *think* about?

Let's start with the preparation. Clearly, it's different for each swimmer. We each clock up the long distances in training, but every swimmer has their own way of mentally preparing for a race. In my case, for the best part of seven years I moulded my entire persona around thinking like, acting like and *being* a world champion. It wasn't a matter of just switching into gear in the lead-up to a swim. It infused and defined my life.

Every day was geared to preparing myself to race and to win. I had to watch what I ate and drank, get the right amount of sleep and rest, do the correct amount of training and discipline my mind. When you get to the top you're always trying to maintain that edge. The trick is to find the right balance. I always tried to enjoy it and think about the fun aspects. If it wasn't fun, why else would you endure six long, lonely and painful hours' training nearly every day?

I'd use training to solve a lot of problems. And because I love to compete, I could get the most out of each session. I'd almost be competing against myself. That meant I could go out at the end of the week and try to do a personal best in a 10-kilometre session. I'd think, 'What can I learn about myself today?'

About a fortnight before a race I'd change from being relaxed to being very intense. This was my livelihood and I had a job to do. I might not notice the change so much, but those around me certainly would. I'd become tunnel-visioned and I'd be in no mood for frivolity anywhere near the pool. Next, I'd start to visualise the race. I'd picture the setting, the trees, the smells, the people around me and my trainer on the boat. I'd imagine I was coming home in the race and I'd get goosebumps at the thought. As I'd touch the wall I'd want to go 'YEAH!'.

By the time I get on the plane to go to an event I'm very business-like. I'm at the point where I'm minutely examining what I'm eating and drinking and how I'm resting. Once at the swim location I like to ease into the environment quickly, whether it's Canada, Italy, Argentina or whatever. In the lead-up days we have press conferences and debriefings to attend. In between I get a feel for the water and reacquaint myself with the course.

The day before the race I'm room-bound except for meals and a training session. On the evening beforehand I sit down with my trainer and work out feeding times. It usually means an energy drink every twenty minutes and a chocolate drink on the hour. We then go through the list of equipment from chalk and grease to binoculars and a stopwatch.

SHE SEEMS TO CHANGE IN THE WATER. SHE BECOMES VERY FIERY AND VERY *determined. From joking with her out of the water, as soon as the race begins it's like a day at the office for her. She's ready to knock over anything that stands in her way.*

TAMMY VAN WISSE

Come race day I have a meal, a strong coffee and listen to calming, inspirational music like Tommy Emmanuel or the theme from *Chariots of Fire*. At the water I stretch, get my number and make numerous nervous trips to the bathroom. When it comes time to pump myself up I can generally be found behind a tree dancing away to Jimmy Barnes or John Farnham. At some stage I'll probably shed a tear or two from the sheer thrill of being there. And to release a little of the tension. Finally, I get myself greased with wool fat to stop chafing, especially in salt water. Wool fat is also reputed to retain body heat, but I doubt whether it would stand up to scientific tests.

The start is often anarchic. Swimmers refuse to get in line and by the time they fire the gun most are taking their first stroke. Then it's a mad scramble to get position and find your boat. I'm so pumped up at this stage that my stroke rate is going through the roof and I get frantic if I can't find my boat immediately. It's really a matter of your boat driver being aggressive enough to get in position for you. I'm not happy until I've got my boat and am up the front with the men.

Once the race is underway you have to adjust to the conditions. It's not like it is in the pool, where you can pretty much expect the same conditions every time you swim. Every time I swim I encounter a different combination of conditions. The most obvious difference is whether you're swimming in lakes, rivers or the open sea, each with their varying water flows. Water temperature is another telling factor, ranging from the frigid waters of Lac St Jean to the tepid flow of Argentinian rivers. Then there is the weather. Steamy, stormy or freezing sleet, like the postman we've had it all.

Each swimmer has their favourite conditions. Certain swimmers excel in the rivers where there is no buoyancy provided by salt. It means your body sits a lot lower in the water. That, in turn, means it's harder to propel yourself through the water. Some swimmers love the cold water because they carry extra fat. There are swimmers who prefer it to be rough because it suits their style. And there are others who like it hot and flat like a pool, which doesn't happen too often.

As for me, I don't really have a preference. My motto is that you should never concern yourself with things beyond your control.

SHELLEY SEEMS TO BE ABLE TO ADAPT TO ANY CONDITIONS. SHE PROBABLY EXCELS *in the rough because it's mentally tougher. And anything that's hard is where Shelley shines.*

TAMMY VAN WISSE

By the hour mark I'm looking to be in a groove. It should be another day at the office, barring mishap. I want my stroke rate to settle at 86 per minute. It's once I've found that rhythm that I begin to look for ways to occupy my mind. And believe me, it never gets boring.

Far from it. There are a million things to think about. It can be a bit like switching channels. One minute I might be doing a body check, using my senses to detect any fatigue or pains. If I'm hurting I might let my mind take me away to a tropical island. Or I might tune into the crowds to feed off their encouragement. Oftentimes I take in the environment, whether it be the temperature of the water, the roll of the waves or the sight of trees or buildings along the shore. And at times when I'm swimming freely, I revel in the 'rightness' of being in the water. People say I bloom like a flower, that I just flow. Bing! Just add water. I feel like a dolphin. The yin and yang just come together. In between these quiet periods I'm interacting with my trainer, keeping them up to date on how I'm feeling while they keep me informed about my progress.

Then there are the times that I feel so relaxed that my mind appears to leave my body. It's like I'm out there watching myself. I'm totally remote from myself. It's almost as though I dissolve in the water. Then, as usually happens, my trainer will interrupt my reverie to remind me that it's time to have something to eat or that I'm swimming too close to the boat. Heathen.

In truth, my trainers have to take a large slice of the credit for my success over the years. No explanation of marathon swimming experience would be complete without outlining their critical role in the equation.

SHE'S NOT COMPLETELY DEPENDENT, BUT LARGELY DEPENDENT ON GOING THE WAY *the boat takes her and being fed at proper intervals to maintain energy. It's a great encouragement to know there is someone there alongside you taking care of your needs and, while they're not going through exactly the same thing, they're certainly living every stroke.*

NANCY SCHNARR

The person who sits in the boat can be called a lot of things (during the race they can be called a lot of *unprintable* things!). Trainer, handler, coach. They may indeed be your coach, in the sense that they train you and have a coaching certificate, but that is neither common nor necessary. For most swimmers, their trainer during a race is ordinarily a friend, a family member or another swimmer who is not in the swim for some reason. Spouses or partners are also employed in the role, although some swimmers are more imaginative in their choice. I recall being at a bar in Magog two nights before race day and watching male competitors hunting for the best looking women to act as their handlers (as it were). One of the guys told me the next day that he'd found his handler. She was the singer the night before! But that was around 1990. It's become a far more serious business since then and I doubt whether any entertainers have taken on the job for some time now.

The point is, you don't need someone out there saying that your stroke looks shocking, lift your elbows and follow through. The coach's duty is to prepare you for a race, not to be there to critique you while you're actually swimming the race. It's not at all important for the trainer to know technical aspects of swimming. It *is* important, however, for the trainer to know their swimmer. And while your coach might have a headstart in this area, they aren't the only ones who can develop an intimate understanding of the workings of a marathon swimmer. Anyone with a fair dash of common sense and an aptitude for organisation can pick it up. As they complete more races with you they'll soon learn if you can handle cold water, if you fall away in rough conditions or get sick from boat fumes. They'll come to appreciate the swimmer's psychology. When to feed you, for example. You might not like being fed at exact intervals if you're about to pass someone. They might know to withhold feeding as a kind of reward once you've passed the other competitor. Without such an understanding, the swimmer's competitiveness and health can suffer. As you'd imagine, it could potentially be very scary if you've got someone on your boat who you met at a bar the night before. Especially if you're about to go into the frigid waters at Lac St Jean.

I took no such risks. From the moment I started taking the sport seriously I tried to ensure some continuity by inviting my trainers to travel with me. Nancy Schnarr, a feisty New York native, was the first and, as it turns out, the most enduring of my trainers. We first teamed up in Manhattan in 1987 and she was there again when I returned to New York in 1995. In between we've done countless swims together from Atlantic City and Perth, to Argentina and Italy. Nancy had swum competitively for fifteen years before we joined forces, but had no experience of coaching. Between 1988 and 1990 my husband, who had no experience whatsoever in the sport, travelled with me. He did at least get some tips from Nancy when we went to New York in 1988. Then, from 1992, I struck up a partnership with my coach, Graeme 'Grub' Carroll. Together with Nancy he was responsible for guiding me through some of my most memorable swims.

It's no exaggeration to say that the successful trainer–swimmer relationship is like a marriage. The trainer is your security blanket and your guide dog. You're blind in the water, so you're utterly reliant on them to guide you. That aside, they've got to know what you're thinking before you think it, they've got to understand what pain you go through. They must put your welfare before anything else and keep you as their sole focus. They're there to feed you, to inform you and to motivate you. It's a big mental game out there and they have to know how to keep you motivated. It can be an exhausting business yelling, screaming and scrawling messages for hour upon hour.

I KNOW THE THINGS SHE'S GOING TO GET UPSET ABOUT. FOR EXAMPLE, I PLACE *great emphasis on making sure the boat's in the proper position so that when she turns her head she can maintain eye contact. And after one of the Manhattan swims, I made a rule of never putting more clothes on during a swim. On this one occasion I put a jacket on because I was getting cold and, seeing this, Shelley began to suffer from the cold too. So I make a point of putting enough clothes on at the start and only ever taking clothes off, rather than the other way around.*

NANCY SCHNARR

In practical terms, my trainer is responsible for the little things that go into a good race. They must know the course, the tides and currents and what difficulties to look for. They, not the boat driver, determine the course I take. In the lead-up to the race they carry and prepare all my equipment, from the special drink I use to the particular whiteboards and chalkboards I prefer. During the swim they inform me about my stroke rate, my rhythm, my position, how far others are in front and behind and how far to go. Just as importantly, they do their best to humour me and take my mind off the pain I go through. That might take the form of jokes scribbled on the message board or various antics designed for a laugh. One thing they can't do is touch me during a race. That means instant disqualification. If I get a cramp during a race it's up to me to massage it out.

When all is said and done, a very dynamic relationship exists between the swimmer and their trainer. There is an enormous amount of trust involved and, from the swimmer's perspective, the trainer can make or break them on any given day. It can all make for a volatile atmosphere out on the water, and every swimmer has a different way of handling it.

When I'm out there swimming it's not play, it's work. As a result I'm a totally different person in and out of the water. There are times when I lose the plot and get a bit verbal, generally a sign that either my sugar levels are low, I'm frustrated, or I'm hurting. Whatever the reason, my trainer has to be able to absorb that. It's crucial for both parties to remember that whatever happens on the water, stays on the water. Nothing should be taken personally. To that end we always have a post-race chat and, if required, apologise for any abuse hurled during the race.

I'll admit that sometimes I have really lost my cool and have had to apologise profusely after the swim. I know I'm very demanding. I expect a job to be done and done right, whether it be mixing the right drinks or giving me information when I need it. Just as the person on the boat expects *me* to swim well and give 100 per cent. I've had a lot of people say that I give my trainers a hard time. That we're always having squabbles out there. And I agree, because if it's not done right we have a problem. If they're sitting back and having a chinwag with the boat driver rather than focusing on me, things aren't happening to my satisfaction. Conversely, there are races where everything's gone to clockwork. It's give and take.

I TALK TO SHELLEY THROUGHOUT A SWIM. EACH SWIMMER IS DIFFERENT. I'VE ONLY *ever been on a swim with one other person, and she was happy if no one spoke to her at all. I was amazed! There's another swimmer, a very successful one, who seems to function best by arguing the whole time with the people on his boat.*

NANCY SCHNARR

And, most significantly, my record shows that it works. I really think one of the main reasons I continued to be number one was that I was prepared to take my trainers with me and hang the expense. I've always believed that the person in my boat is a crucial part of the team. My victories are as much theirs as mine.

One thing they don't share in is the effects of water quality. Lucky them. Not that it's always a factor. The lake swims, in particular, pose no problems on that front. But there's no denying that some of the places World Series swimmers visit, particularly in South America, leave a lot to be desired. It's not so much a question of how water quality will actually affect your performance during a particular race. No matter how polluted the water is it's unlikely to prevent you from completing a swim, even if you're gagging at various stages. Sure, debris and logs can present a problem, and I would hardly describe it as a savoury experience to find yourself swimming past dead rats and condoms as I did in New York in 1984. At least I didn't swim past a dead body as Karen Hartley did in the same race the year before (mercifully she didn't see it).

No, the real impact of polluted waters is generally felt after the swim. That's when you find out how your system likes playing host to any number of indescribable nasties. And that's when it can affect your performance, in the following race and any subsequent races while you're recovering. Unfortunately, I'm eminently qualified to speak on the subject.

Not that I'm the only swimmer who gets sick. But there's nothing worse for me than that 36-hour period after the Rio Coronda swim. I've been sick after each of my five swims there. Everybody knows I get ill after that race. I'm the litmus paper as to how bad it is. Come Tuesday morning after the race on Sunday and I generally feel nauseous, have something to eat and then throw it straight back up. And so it begins. Within an hour the vomiting and diarrhoea arrive and I'm like that for the next twelve hours at least.

The first year, 1991, I'd left the morning after the swim and was on a plane home when it hit. In 1992 I was really sick before I left. I ended up stopping over in America to get some help. I was still sick the whole week. The virus stayed with me beyond that and for the next four months or so I continued to get attacks. I would be at speaking engagements and would have to run out in the middle to go to the bathroom. Sometimes I'd be gone for half an hour, much to my embarrassment. I realised then that this virus really liked me.

In 1993, after the Rio Coronda swim, they couldn't move me for 24 hours because I was so sick. Same location, same story in 1994, although I wasn't hit as bad this time around because we'd worked out where I should keep my mouth shut during the swim. My leg was cut by the boat propeller that year to make up for it. In 1995 it was the absolute worst. I was kicked in the shoulder at the beginning of the swim and afterwards had to be put on a drip in Parana. The doctors and nurses there know me pretty well by now. In the end I tried to swim the Parana race, but I couldn't complete it. I've never been that bad before and I was ill for a goodly part of 1995. And you wonder why I won't be going back there in a hurry?

I don't want to be seen to be South America bashing, but the pollution at one proposed venue was so great that it missed out on a World Series spot. It may surprise no one to learn that the offending site was Brazil's Rio de Janeiro. As the newly crowned World Championships gold medallist, I had arrived there with World Series organisers in early 1991 as the city was making a pitch for inclusion in the following year's calendar. As part of the schmoozing process we were taken up to the top of the famed Sugar Loaf, 1300 metres above the city. As I stood gazing down I commented on how beautiful the harbour was with the sun shimmering off its surface. Someone turned to me.

'That's an oil slick,' they whispered.

Sure enough, when I went down to the water's edge it was in a deplorable state, with froth forming in the waves from all the gunk. The mayor told us he would contribute a couple of million to help clean it up, but his offer was knocked back. It would have taken tens of millions to clean that harbour up enough for the swimmers to put their toes in it, let alone swim a marathon.

Such experiences have somewhat tainted my appreciation of the sport. I'm absolutely paranoid about Argentina now. I didn't even want to go in 1995. It wasn't very helpful when I did go to find that there were community protests about chemical waste being released into the river. If there has been a positive effect of my various experiences and ailments it has been to alert me to the issue of water quality and associated environmental issues, much in the same way solo yachtsman and Clean Up Australia founder Ian Kiernan became so passionate about water pollution as a result of his sailing. It means that I now wear another hat when I swim, that of a guinea pig and spokesperson for water quality. When I finish a race I will make observations about the state of the water, either to give authorities a pat on the back or to draw attention to deficiencies. If you're going to contribute to solving the problem, you've got to use the platform while it's there.

There is no doubt that progress is being made in some areas. New York is a good example of how environmental concerns in some countries have prompted authorities to make the necessary changes to improve water quality. I was delighted to find that the waters around Manhattan were much cleaner in 1995 than I'd ever seen before. And I said so. Unfortunately, the same can't be said for Argentina, where the poverty in some areas puts the environment at the bottom of priorities. I know it's a complex problem with its roots in social and economic change, but it saddens me all the same.

I've yet to mention the finish of a race. By the time I'm approaching the end I just want it to be over. I'm generally hurting, but as soon as I hear or near the finish I respond. That helps me surge to the finish. Once on land I'm in celebration mode, the adrenalin rush overcoming the exhaustion. This is the only time I get to truly cut loose. By the next morning my mind will be on the next swim, so I like to make the most of the hours before I hit the sack. It's like letting myself out of the cage for a few hours. That often means I can be found at a local bar dancing until the small hours with a smile plastered all over my face. Thankfully, the pain doesn't arrive until the day after the swim.

So there you have it. This is the sport I love. For better or for worse.

BORN • AGAIN • IN • ARKANSAS

I WAS TWELVE WHEN I MET future Olympic gold medallist and television whiz kid Neil Brooks.

We had come together in the same training squad under Kevin Duff. Neil was this tall, lanky kid who immediately stood out as the resident clown and larrikin. But boy, could he swim! He soon became my training buddy and, shortly afterwards, a fellow member of the state swimming squad.

As happens in swimming, the people you meet at the pool form your social circle as well. After all, you don't have much spare time to spend with any other kids your age. And swimming is a sport which quickly breaks down barriers. I don't think any other sport so regularly puts you in a position to see people looking their worst. There's no room for modesty at 5 a.m. when you have to spend a couple of hours right next to each other in the water, covered by nothing more than a thin film of nylon or lycra.

Neil was like a brother. We were both Leos, our birthdays were a week apart and our parents got on well together. His Dad, Mick, was a marshal and my Dad was a starter. They became really good mates and the two families began to socialise away from swimming. We'd go to each other's houses for barbeques. I vividly remember shaking the Brooks's fibro house in Doubleview as we all danced to 'Lady Bump' in the loungeroom. When Neil and I could escape we'd go out back and play pool. I have Neil to thank for my proficiency with a cue. He can also take credit for having taught me how to wolf whistle as we waited to be picked up from the pool after training.

We shared some great times. Who could forget Neil standing at the blocks before a race, pulling his tracksuit down and finding he'd neglected to put his bathers on? Then, over a three-year period in the mid to late 1970s, we shared the worst of times as I lost my father and he lost his mother to lung cancer. His mother had been diagnosed the year after my father's death and died in 1979. Both families were devastated. We now had a bond of grief. I knew exactly what he was going through. Unfortunately, I had no answers for him. I was still struggling to come to terms with my father's death and the disintegration of our family.

The timing was especially tragic for Neil. The following year he went on to win a gold medal in Moscow with the 4 x 100-metre medley relay team, better known as the Mean Machine. We'd lost contact since I gave up swimming in 1979, but I was ecstatic as I watched his golden moment. I rang up his Dad to congratulate him. There certainly wasn't any remorse that it wasn't me there on the dais. If I couldn't do it, I was just glad Neil could. I couldn't have known then how glad I would ultimately be. For, strangely enough, his success proved my passport to a whole new world.

I had returned to swimming with a bang by winning seven golds at the 1982 state championships. Yet, as pleasing as that was, I didn't have a clear idea of where swimming could take me. There's no question it had revitalised me. It was fun. But I didn't have any sense of destiny. The Olympic dream had burned low years ago. Luckily for me, others weren't about to let the flame die out completely.

One person who had noted my performance at the state championships was Neil's father, Mick. He was soon on the phone to his son in Arkansas, where Neil had accepted a university scholarship after his Moscow gold. Neil had a word to the head coach of the women's swim team and before I knew it Mick was asking me if I'd be interested in pursuing a sports scholarship at the University of Arkansas. Would I! Here was my second chance at life. I could swim *and* get a degree at the same time. It was perfect.

There was still a long way to go before it was sealed. There would be many phone calls yet between Arkansas and my coach Bernie Mulroy. In the meantime, I had qualified to compete in the nationals in February. But I had to say no. I wasn't remotely thinking of such things a few months earlier and had already booked a holiday to New Zealand. I couldn't afford to cancel it.

When I got back from New Zealand the phone calls and paperwork continued to fly between America and Perth. I just stayed out of the crossfire and concentrated on my swimming. I was jumping out of my skin about swimming again. The Commonwealth Games were on in Brisbane later that year and the prospect of a scholarship was brightening by the day. I figured I could continue to work towards one or the other. Either way, my life had regained its direction.

Then, the call. I had been awarded a full scholarship at the University of Arkansas! I would be joining the Lady Razorbacks swim team and studying for a four-year computer science degree beginning in August. They would pay for all my tuition, accommodation and meals. It was unbelievable. Neil and I were going to be teammates again, only this time it would be on the other side of the world.

I was really happy with my form in the pool at that stage. Then, around July, I started going backwards. My shoulder was giving me problems and nobody could work out what it was. It seemed that the oxygen flow wasn't getting through for some reason. I began to worry what effect this would have on my scholarship, but when I told the university they told me to come over anyway.

'If we have to operate, we have to operate,' they said, in true American fashion.

My eyes were now turned firmly to the east. Beyond Brisbane, all the way to the American Deep South. Others weren't so sure. I was repeatedly asked how I could quit my job, pack my bags, leave my family and head off into an uncertain world many thousands of kilometres away. But whatever doubts others harboured, I had no such qualms. Even when I spoke to Neil and asked him what was awaiting me.

'It's just like the television show *Dukes of Hazzard*,' he'd say. 'It's Hicksville.'

Coming from a Perth boy back then, you had to wonder.

My 21st birthday party doubled as my farewell bash. A few teary farewells later I was on the plane, destination Fresh Start. Little did I suspect I wouldn't set foot back in Australia for more than four years.

The journey was made easier by having another Perth swimmer for company. Breaststroker Jane Pole had also clinched a scholarship to the University of Arkansas and, green as we both were, it was a real comfort to be heading into the unknown together. Just how green we were we discovered during a stopover in Los Angeles. We'd been booked into a hotel in a seedy area of town, but that wasn't going to stop us taking a walk to look for the sort of burger joint you see in *Happy Days*. As we strolled about we marvelled at the cars, the accents, the different cultures on display. Not even television had prepared us for this. We were on our way back to the hotel when a police car pulled up beside us. They asked us what we were doing out and about in this area at this time of night. When we explained we were doing a spot of sight-seeing their jaws dropped.

'You're crazy,' they said. 'Head straight back to your hotel now and don't stop for anything.'

Welcome to America.

The next day we flew to Tulsa, Oklahoma, which was the closest international airport to the university (or college or school, as universities are called in America). We were picked up by the women's swim coach and driven to our new home, Fayetteville, Arkansas. It was a typical college town, full of tree-lined streets and lovely old homes. The campus reeked of old money. I've never seen so many 17-year-old girls driving Mercedes. It was, indeed, a long way from Yokine.

We were to be living on campus along with a host of other international students, many of them on athletic scholarships. My dorm was Reid Hall and my first roommate was a bona fide Californian 'Valley Girl', complete with a vocabulary consisting almost totally of the word 'totally'. At least I could understand most of what she was saying, thanks to Hollywood. Very few people seemed to understand what I was saying, on the other hand. True to stereotype, some even complimented me on how well I spoke English.

As it turned out, Neil and I didn't get to spend much time together because the men's and women's swim programs trained separately. He was living off campus, too, before leaving altogether in 1983. But he and his father had already played a large part in altering the course of my life. In later years he proved an unfailingly kind and generous friend and great adviser. I owe him a huge debt of gratitude.

Not even Neil could have spared me the bad bouts of homesickness I suffered in my first three months, however. I would just sit in my room and cry at the thought of years away from the familiar faces and places of Perth. It certainly didn't help when an uncle died in his sleep at the age of 31. I felt so distant and helpless. To compound things, my shoulder was still giving me trouble. After six weeks in town it was decided that I would have to undergo surgery. A doctor had found a blood clot and the proposed solution was to go in through my armpit and take out most of my first rib. The operation would alleviate the pressure on the muscles and nerves which was causing the clot and cutting off the oxygen supply.

Jane wasn't having a dream start either. Two months after our arrival she broke her ankle while 'mud' wrestling in chocolate pudding, an ancient campus rite of passage. We did not make a couple of very happy campers.

Things could only improve. And they did, for me anyway (Jane returned to Australia after an unhappy year). Six weeks after the operation I was back in the pool and feeling great. I was beginning to adjust to the Arkansas way of life, too. A large part of that was getting accustomed to the food, which seemed expressly designed for the purpose of putting on weight. They called it the Freshman 15, meaning you put on 15 pounds (7 kilograms) in your first year.

The first meal Jane and I had in Fayetteville was at the Hog's Breath Cafe, where we were introduced to a vegetable called okra. It was deep-fried, as were most things served up in that part of the world. Most of our eating was done in the school cafeteria and many athletes simply didn't appreciate how much fat went into the cooking of their meals. Breakfast options included pancakes, pastries, grits (the dictionary definition is coarsely ground grain) and hash browns. Then there were hamburgers and deep-fried chicken. To my knowledge the iced tea was not overloaded with calories, but it made a poor staple.

'Giggling Gertie' (a nickname Dad gave me), aged five.

Aged eleven, I had just won my first ever gold medal, in the
12-years 200-metre backstroke at the 1972 Western Australian
State Swimming Championships. *The Independent,* WA

Aged twelve, churning up the 400-metre freestyle championship title at the Western Australian Age Group Swimming State titles. *The Independent,* WA

Mum, Dad, sister Liz and me with Jenny Tate, our billet and a member of the 1976 Australian Olympic Swim Team, at Perth airport, bound for Montreal.

Dad, my Number 1 Hero, presenting me with a gold medal at the 1977 State Swimming Championships, not long after he had been diagnosed with lung cancer.

Mr and Mrs Peter Smith, 2 April 1988.

Victorious—1st overall—after my first ever marathon swim on 14 July 1984.

In no time you were putting on so much weight that it became an obsession. For our coaches as much as us. We had to weigh in before meets, and if you didn't make weigh-in you didn't go. With my scholarship on the line, I spent many an hour in the sauna in my first year. When I wasn't in the sauna I could be found lifting weights while dressed in green garbage bags, so as to sweat the weight off. I would not eat for days. The main challenge was to survive Friday and Saturday nights, which were usually party nights on campus, and Sunday evening's all-you-can-eat-for-$3.50 night at the local Pizza Haven. I was modestly successful on all three counts.

Otherwise, my days were pretty much dictated by swim team commitments. I was swimming 200 yards backstroke and 500, 1000 and 1650 yards freestyle for the Lady Razorbacks (all of the school's sports teams were known as the Razorbacks or the Lady Razorbacks). A typical day involved being up at 4.45 a.m. to walk over to the pool and be in the water by 5.30 a.m. We'd train until 8 a.m. and then, depending on your timetable, either go to class or go for breakfast. In the afternoon we trained from 5.30 p.m.

We competed in what was known as the South-West Conference against schools from Arkansas, Missouri, Oklahoma and Texas. Among our chief rivals were the University of Texas, Texas Christian University, Southern Methodist University and University of Houston. During the meets athletes and supporters would wear a bright red hog's hat and do the Razorback call. Unfortunately, 'pig soooeeee!' doesn't quite translate to paper.

I learned the American national anthem in no time, because it was played before each meet. I also learnt all about swimming as a team sport. Because all our performances counted towards team points there was great unity among us all. I must confess, I'd never really looked upon swimming as a team sport before.

By the end of the first semester I was feeling pretty comfortable in my new surroundings. We'd swum up to Christmas and now we had a two-week break (American college years start with fall semester from September to December, then spring semester from January to May, with a summer break between June and August). It was to be my first Christmas away from home. It was to be one I wouldn't forget, either, as my head coach invited me to join her family for Christmas at their home in Sacramento, California. On the drive across the country I saw snow for the first time. Now I *knew* I was a long way from Perth!

Back in Fayetteville I spent a lot of my time unsuccessfully trying to negotiate the ice and falling on my bum. I did manage to stay on my feet long enough to change my major from computing to physical education. I had found it increasingly difficult to get my work done around my training times, because the school's computer system was down so often. It was a good swap. I could never have hoped to get into such a popular course as physical education back in Perth.

It appeared the pieces of the jigsaw were beginning to fall neatly into place. I even gained another playmate when a fourth Perth swimmer, breaststroker Leith Weston, arrived halfway through the fall semester. But it was not to be the sedate semester I anticipated. Some radical changes were waiting just around the corner. The first to hit was the announcement that the school was planning to fold the women's swim program and send us all home. There was only one way to top that. I became a Christian. It happened something like this.

Arkansas sits in the middle of the Bible belt, as you may have guessed from the names of some of the schools in the South-West Conference. More specifically, this is Southern Baptist territory. I'd had some contact with the Baptist church because of my father, but my idea of religion was confined to putting in an appearance at church on Sunday. I had no concept of a personal relationship with Jesus Christ. Here, however, it was a way of life. You were faced with the choice of embracing it or actively rejecting it. Either way, you couldn't be passive.

My nextdoor neighbour and training partner, Kathy McCoy, was the one responsible for converting me. As I look back on it, it was probably divine providence that brought us together. Why should she turn out to be my training partner if I wasn't going to develop a close relationship with her? But I wasn't thinking that way at first. Truth be known, I thought she was a bit of a freak, albeit a very nice and sincere one. It was just that she was a strict Baptist. I found it very disconcerting when she took her Bible along to study at the pool.

My scepticism had no discernible impact on Kathy. Sweet as you like, she'd invite me to Bible study classes. I'd respond by asking her why on earth I'd want to do that? Until one night, when it didn't seem like such a bad idea. I was feeling very low about the uncertain future of the women's program when Kathy knocked on my door and, sweet as you like, invited me to Bible study. All right, I said. A couple of hours later I was asking what I could do next.

That night I prayed for Jesus Christ to come into my heart. I accepted him as my personal saviour. That was it. There was no big bang, but I must admit I felt a great weight lift from my shoulders. I went to bed knowing for the first time that I was going to see my Dad again. I cried tears of joy. I also realised that it wasn't an elite club, that there wasn't a qualifying age or status. It didn't even matter how many gold medals you won.

Later I began to think about the time I attended a friend's baptism when I was twelve or so. I went up to her afterwards and asked how I could do that. She told me that I'd know when the time was right. In hindsight, I couldn't help wondering why she didn't lead me to Christ. Why didn't she tell me when my father died that I would see him again? Instead, I'd bitterly rejected the notion of a God who would take my Dad away from me.

Now I was intent on making up for lost time. I read the Bible, went to Bible study and attended the First Baptist Church of Fayetteville. I learnt to look at people differently, to understand their strengths and appreciate them as individuals. The family ties were very strong in the church community, so I was taken in and nurtured. The whole swim team thought I'd become a nutcase, but it didn't bother me. God played a starring role in my life for the remainder of my stay in Arkansas.

If the swim team was worried about me, people back home were mortified. With the exception of Mum, they thought I'd lost the plot. They thought I'd been snapped up by some cult. Over time their fears were laid to rest. Nowadays I still pray to

God, but I don't preach it as openly. I'm not out there knocking on doors. It's just an ongoing part of my heart. Arkansas was simply my time of greatest need. I was being supported while a foundation was being built under me. It helped to know that someone was putting hurdles in front of me for a reason and that same person was leading me through the struggles. In early 1983 the hurdle confronting me was the prospect of losing my scholarship and an ignominious return to Australia. How could I have foreseen that it was the catalyst that would lead me into marathon swimming?

Not unexpectedly, the entire Lady Razorbacks team was in revolt over the threat to cut the program. And so the lobbying began to salvage something out of a disastrous situation. The uncertainty dragged over the spring break, during which I had more surgery on my left shoulder, this time for bicep tendonitis. Unkind cuts everywhere! Then, finally, some good news. The head coach of the men's program, Sam Freas, stepped in and offered to take over the women's program from the end of the school year. His assistant Kent Kirschner would become the women's coach. It was a godsend.

There was one minor drawback. As part of the deal, scholarship holders would have to accept a reduction in their financial support. I was to go onto a half-scholarship, which meant my accommodation and meals would no longer be covered. Plans were put in motion to billet out all the international scholarship holders from the beginning of the next academic year. From now on I would have to find a way of bringing in some extra income. My comfort zone had just disappeared.

So it was that I spent my first summer working as a swimming co-ordinator at the Lake Nixon day camp in the state capital, Little Rock. It was a Christian day camp which opened to the public in the afternoon, at which time the co-ordinators became lifeguards. I had a great time. Better still, I managed to shed almost 13 kilograms that summer by sticking to a strict diet with no red meat. And no donut breakfasts!

When school resumed I was billeted out. I was to be a nanny to three kids, in return for which I was given food and lodgings and use of a car. Money was tight, to the extent of not having enough money to buy toothpaste. But I *was* still here. Life wasn't too bad.

Sam Freas was doing his best to make sure it was kept interesting, too. He'd been coaching the men's world marathon champion, Paul Asmuth, over the summer and had decided it was time to introduce something a little different to pre-season training. His idea was to take both the men's and women's programs to nearby Beaver Lake and get us all doing some strength and distance work out in the fresh air. One of the little tricks he had up his sleeve was to sit in a boat and get us to pull him along using rubber tubes as harnesses. Someone told me that this guy had been booted out of West Point Military Academy for being too hard on the men. I wasn't about to argue.

One day Sam figured he'd vary the routine.

'See that point over there?' he indicated.

We all squinted into the distance, but couldn't make anything out in that direction.

'Look,' said Sam, 'just swim until you touch land and then turn around and come back.'

A bit over an hour later I stood dripping in front of Sam. As the men started arriving they looked at me and asked what I was doing there and where I'd come from.

'She got here first,' said Sam.

'No way!' they said. 'She must have run along the shore, Sam.'

'No, this wonder from down-under ain't bullshitting.'

Sam had noticed that I get faster the further I go. Intrigued to test his observation out, he suggested that I make an attempt on the American women's four-mile (6.4 kilometre) record. The following week he arranged to have the proper officials present at Beaver Lake and I was timed over the distance as part of a three-woman relay team. When I emerged I had clocked 1:22:44 and claimed both the individual record and a place in the new relay record. The date was 19 September 1983. To my knowledge, I still hold it.

After confirming the record I went to the boot of my car and took out a bottle of champagne. Kent Kirschner was behind me.

'Look, Sam,' said Kent. 'She *knew* she was going to break that record.'

The next time at training Sam asked to have a word with me.

'You know, I think you've got what it takes to be a world champion in marathon swimming.'

'There's a title in that?' I asked. 'What do I have to do?'

'Just keep swimming. I'll look after it from here.'

I was to wait almost a year before I got a chance to swim my first marathon. It wasn't just a matter of picking up a phone and booking a spot. There weren't that many marathon swims in America, for starters. And of those there were, most were swum in the hottest months of July and August. Not that the prospect was dominating my thoughts. It was more a case of curiosity.

My interest was fanned, however, by one of the assistant coaches. Richard Kersh had swum in marathons around the world and began to tell me captivating stories about people and places. He also believed I could do really well. I doubt I would ever have found out about or become interested in marathon swimming if it hadn't been for Richard and Sam. Let alone if I had never left Perth.

If things were looking up in the water, they weren't so rosy on the home front. A misunderstanding over responsibilities saw me 'expelled' from my billet. My punishment was to be shunted from a comfortable home in a nice part of town to a billet in a poor industrial area. They were good, kind people, but their diet alone was enough to drive me to despair. They virtually lived on fried chicken and anything else that *could* be fried. In no time I was putting weight on helter skelter. If for no other reason, I knew I'd have to get out of there soon for my health's sake.

Christmas 1983 was a vastly different experience to the previous year. Instead of putting my feet up in California, Sam took a group of swimmers to Fort Lauderdale, Florida. To train. We absolutely froze in the unheated outdoor pools. West Point knew what they were doing.

Back in Arkansas, Sam started making enquiries about getting me into a professional swim at Atlantic City. The organisers weren't interested. No experience, they said. Sam then contacted US Swimming to find out about *any* races that I might be able to swim. There was one, they said. It was a 16-mile (25-kilometre) swim along the Los Angeles coast, beginning and ending at Seal Beach on 16 July. Totally amateur. This was it!

It was also time to make a move out of my billet before the fried chicken got the better of me. At the end of spring semester I applied for and got a position as a residents' assistant on campus. Residents' assistants are older students who supervise the students on their dormitory floor and get free board in return. I took over an all-girls dorm, Humphrey's Hall, and, if I do say so myself, I was a natural. I was always good at playing Mum. Here it meant that I had to do everything from chasing guys out of rooms after open hours ended to cleaning up after girls who had too much to drink. You name it, I had to deal with it over the next two and a half years.

Summer also saw me take a job lifeguarding and instructing at the Fayetteville city pool. This way I could train for the swim, doing laps in my breaks and popping out to Beaver Lake for three-hour sessions on my days off. It helped that Richard was working there too. We'd train together as much as possible and he'd show me videos and advise me on technique in between regaling me with yet more stories about the world circuit.

I was as ready as any 22-year-old novice could be. It was a scorching Sunday when I stepped onto the sand in Los Angeles for the 16th Annual Seal Beach Rough Water Swim. I didn't have any wool fat, so I had to smother myself with white axle grease. Six other swimmers were greased up for the swim to Huntington Beach and back. My handler was a game young guy who was going to paddle alongside me on his Malibu surfboard, carrying food and drink in a backpack.

Once in the water, it soon became abundantly clear that grease wasn't going to spare us. It might have been 44 degrees on the beach, but it was a bone-chilling 15 degrees in the water. We were all freezing. As we turned around at Huntington things got really grim. My handler ran out of food and other swimmers around me were beginning to pull out. Next thing we were caught in a rip. No matter how hard we swam we barely moved. I can still see that damn 'Chicken in a Box' takeaway shop on the shore to this day.

'I want to get out,' I told my handler.

'No. You're not quitting.'

He was within his rights to refuse me. After all, he was hardly doing it easy himself. His wetsuit was chafing so badly that he was bleeding. Elsewhere, swimmers were being hauled out of the water one by one. The swim was supposed to take five hours, but we had well and truly passed that by now. Six hours. Seven hours. Still swimming.

Finally, after 7 hours, 19 minutes and 7 seconds, I dragged myself onto the shore. I could hear the announcer shouting over the blare of *Rocky* music.

'Here he comes, ladies and gentlemen! Here he comes! It's Shelby Taylor! Wait. Oh my god, folks, it's a *girl*! It's a girl!'

I had won. Indeed, only two other competitors, both men, completed the swim. And they were suffering so badly from hypothermia that they had to be carted off to hospital. I was left standing on the winner's dais by myself. Afterwards, Carol Lee-Hetzel, one of the top-ranked female marathon swimmers in the country, came up to me. She had pulled out mid-race.

'Anyone who finished that race can handle anything,' she said. 'You're going to be awesome.'

Awesome or not, after the back-slapping I was just another impoverished student back in Arkansas. Like many other students without rich daddies, I needed to find a way to supplement my meagre income. So I went out and got a job with the university's food and management department. It was my job to help prepare food, set up dining facilities and wait on tables at functions, something I had plenty of experience at from my days helping Mum at weddings and quiz nights. I became the hostie with the mostie, and since I was pretty good at it I ended up serving the food and drinks at the head table. That's when I got to meet Bill and Hillary Clinton.

As Governor of Arkansas, the future US president was a regular guest at functions in his capacity as patron of the university or somesuch. I served him and his wife many a meal and he'd ask what I was doing there.

'You got an *accent*, girl,' he'd say in his Arkansan drawl.

I couldn't resist.

'Excuse me, sir, I don't have an accent. *You* have an accent.'

We'd chat away happily after that as I served him. I guess he attended functions at the school about once a month. Not that he'd know me if he saw me in the street today. And no, for those of you with enquiring minds, he never asked for any servings on the side.

I had plenty on my plate as well. A free weekend was coming up in late August and Sam began making noises about an amateur race up in New York. My performance at Seal Beach and subsequent invitation to an international marathon swim (which I had to decline because of my residents' assistant job) meant I'd have no trouble gaining a start. At 48 kilometres it was a bit longer, but he was fairly vague about the rest of the details. Something to do with swimming around an island with a current to contend with and a few buildings to look at on the way. He'd find some accommodation and a handler for me. I just needed to scrape together enough money to get myself there and back and pay the boat driver. Was I interested?

Of course. While Sam took care of the paperwork I went door knocking around the business community to try to raise the necessary money. They gave generously and I was soon on the plane to New York, where I was met by a wonderful woman named Fran Schnarr. Although Sam's contact hadn't been able to offer me accommodation, he'd put him in touch with a woman in the local swimming scene he thought might be able to help out. Fran was only too happy to look out for a young Australian on her first trip to the Big Apple. The Schnarrs – Fran, her husband Joe, her daughters Nancy and Joanie and son Billy – were to become my second family in time. It had been confirmed in the meantime that Sam's sister-in-law, Trisha Coulter, would be my trainer for the race. Trisha was in personnel at IBM and knew nothing about swimming, but she possessed great common sense. That was fine by Sam and I trusted his instincts.

By now the truth had dawned on me. I wasn't so much swimming in New York as *around* it. Around Manhattan Island, that most famous part of it, to be precise. Along the Hudson, East and Harlem rivers. The buildings Sam had alluded to included such landmarks as the World Trade Center, the United Nations, the Empire State Building and the Chrysler Building. You could throw in the Statue of Liberty for good measure.

The Manhattan Island marathon may have been an amateur event in support of a children's charity, but it had attracted a fairly impressive field in its third year. The favourite was world champion Paul Asmuth, quickly followed by another professional, Steve Munatones. It was a long way removed from the Seal Beach swim. Up against these guys Trisha and I didn't really have a clue what we were doing. It would be a case of jumping in and swimming like hell. The closest thing we had to a strategy was Trisha feeding me chocolate brownies.

I was nervous as a kitten when we got in the river to start the swim on the morning of Sunday, 26 August 1984. But once we started I found the whole experience thrilling. I forgot about my fears and put my head down. Sure, the water quality was a bit off-putting, particularly the Harlem River section, but I was too busy drinking in the sights to worry. It was quite unbelievable, taking in one of the world's greatest cities from water level. Even more unbelievable was the result.

I finished the swim in 7:53:22, only sixteen minutes behind winner Paul Asmuth and about a minute behind second placegetter Steve Munatones. My reward for having easily won the women's division was a huge trophy. The only downside was my boat driver insisting I pay him more money as the media waited to interview me. New Yorkers sure know how to time things. It was a small hiccup, however, on an overwhelmingly successful day. Sam was ecstatic when I returned lugging my trophy.

If he was looking for a way to reward me, he ended up doing just the opposite. The rest of the swimmers had jacked up about training in the lake and Sam had to come up with a new torture routine. He couldn't simply make us do endless laps, because there were restrictions on the amount of time swim programs could require their athletes to spend in the pool. Something to do with the belief that we were at school to get an education as well. A minor obstacle for Sam. He would toughen us up by doing triathlons, aerobics and dry land training.

It was my worst nightmare. With my back, the last thing I needed to be doing was running, cycling, bouncing and the type of exercises best left at boot camp. But there was no room for wimps in Sam's program. So there I was, bouncing away to Jane Fonda. Cycling up and down hills. Jogging. Doing kangaroo hops, or crab walks with a bar on my shoulders. Piggy-backing fellow sufferers to the top of the football stadium. In humidity akin to Darwin, there was no shortage of people throwing up when they reached the last row of seats. At least then Sam would be satisfied you'd pushed the envelope and he'd give you an early mark.

It couldn't last. Should I say, my *back* couldn't last. One morning in October, after completing a triathlon around the hills of Fayetteville, I returned to my room for a quick nap before class. When I woke up I slung my legs out of bed and fell to the floor. I was partially paralysed from the waist down. I was in so much pain I was screaming. When I was carried to the infirmary they found that one of my vertebra had collapsed and was pinching down on a nerve. In medical terms I had a subluxed L5 S1, for those budding osteopaths out there. It meant that I had very little feeling in my legs and when I did feel them the pain was excruciating.

There was only one thing for it. They put me in traction, like a chicken on a spit. A chicken dosed up on Valium and codeine, to be exact, while its muscles wasted away. It was the first real test of my faith. *Why*, God? If you brought me here, as I believe you did, what am I supposed to learn from being flat on my back, unable to walk, let alone swim, with my family on the other side of the world? I'm 23, I'm single and I'm barely into the degree I want so much. Why me? What's the point? Can you send me a message?

No immediate answer was forthcoming. Instead, I was left to consider what this might mean for my swimming. The doctors had no such concerns. They were more worried about me ever walking again pain-free. The situation wasn't made any easier by Sam's refusal to believe that there was anything wrong with me. He thought it was all psychosomatic. Mind over matter would fix it.

Under pressure from Sam, I was deemed ready for release after two weeks. I had regained use of my legs and the drugs were warding off the pain, but it was not the best of moves. A week later my back crumbled again and I was re-admitted to hospital for a further two weeks.

Not to be denied, Sam decided once more that the quickest way to rehabilitation was to get me out of bed and into the pool. With the aid of intensive painkillers I shuffled back into the world, a pale imitation of the Shelley Taylor of five weeks earlier. I could only walk freely when I was doped to the eyeballs and I had to rely on Leith to carry my books to class. Once in the classroom I'd have to lie down on the floor on pillows, an appropriate position given that I was half-asleep through most of my lectures. It was a similar story in the pool, where I'd have to take a bunch of pills to compete in the meets. By all accounts I made it through the races, but I don't remember half of them.

Something had to give. The day finally came when I arrived at the pool to be buttonholed by Sam.

'Who have you been talking to?' he demanded.

'What do you mean?' I asked.

'Have you been complaining about me? The athletic director has just called to say that your professors are complaining about how drugged out you are in classes.'

'Well, *aren't* I?'

That got me a big blast. But I'd had enough.

'I'm sick and tired of the drugs, Sam. I don't want to become addicted. I'm taking myself off them.'

He looked at me.

'You know you won't be able to swim well without them,' he said softly.

I knew what he was trying to say. My scholarship depended on my performances in the pool. If I couldn't maintain my record of winning conference finals, my chances of gaining a degree would go up in smoke. Without a scholarship, I just couldn't afford the costs involved. Nonetheless, I was prepared to take the risk.

In swimming terms, it didn't come off. The misery would begin before we even got to the pool. If we were travelling to a meet I would have to spend most of the journey lying down in the aisle of the bus. And the unavoidable fact was that, without the help of painkillers, I couldn't tumble turn properly. While I was still reasonably competitive, it wasn't good enough. The crunch came when I failed to win at the conference finals in February. I knew then that an ill wind was about to blow. My scholarship renewal would be discussed after the spring break and the signs weren't good. Sam had resigned at the end of the season and, with his assistant Kent Kirschner taking over, the mood was ripe for change.

Not all was gloom and doom. When spring break rolled around I joined two vanloads of friends from the Christ on Campus group on a trip to Mexico. We were headed to a town just across the border to do voluntary work aimed at improving hygiene levels. It wasn't about preaching the Word. It was a tremendous time, apart from someone crashing into the back of the van I was in as soon as we crossed the border. Whether it was the accident or the hard work or the long hours on the road, the trip also resulted in my back doing its thing again. I had to spend fifteen hours flat on my back on the return trip and another week in hospital to get over it.

I'd only just got back on my feet when it was time to visit Kent's office. The words that greeted me were like a sledge-hammer. Going on my performances of the past six months, he explained, I could no longer be considered an asset to the program. Indeed, I was a liability. In such circumstances, they wouldn't be renewing my scholarship the next year.

I felt sick as I realised that at the end of my third year it was suddenly all going to be taken away from me. I tried to argue that he had to take my obvious misfortunes into account.

But they didn't have time to worry about that, he said. Results were all that mattered.

I was devastated. I *couldn't* just go back to Australia now. It would have all been for nought if I did that. There had to be another way.

There was. And it took Sam to point it out. Sam hadn't left town to take up his new job yet and when he heard that my scholarship was to be withdrawn he called and suggested we talk. He thought he might have the answer to my dilemma. Marathon swimming. Not the amateur stuff. No, on the basis of my performances the previous year I should be able to get into the professional swims coming up at Atlantic City and Magog over summer. I wouldn't have to tumble turn or dive, and if I could put in a half-decent showing I might make enough money to finance the remainder of my degree. Besides, he genuinely believed that my future lay in marathon swimming.

It was the best hope I had. I still had a semester in the Lady Razorbacks, but my mind was now firmly focused on the swims coming up in summer. When the news came through that I had been accepted into both Atlantic City and Magog I was over the moon. Here was my shot at rescuing my degree. As soon as the semester was over I hurled myself into training for my professional debut at Atlantic City on 14 July. After the success of my training regime the previous year, I was happy to be back working at the Fayetteville city pool with Richard.

It wasn't all sweat and pain. I was dating a guy, Greg, who turned out to have a rather spirited roommate called John Daly. John had a golf scholarship at the University of Arkansas and a liking for Jack Daniels bourbon. I'd be 'round at their townhouse all the time and John was the life of the party. He was a fabulous guy who was going through some rough times because of his unorthodox game and a weight problem. Neither met with the approval of the golf coaches and he struggled to get a regular game for the school. Such trials must have made his 1995 British Open victory all the sweeter.

Just as sweet for me in those days was the way in which the church community rallied around when I needed to raise the funds to pay my way to Atlantic City and Magog. Since I also planned to return to Manhattan to defend my women's title, I needed more than a few dollars. The church people opened their hearts and their wallets to me. I was finding cheques and envelopes full of cash shoved under my door. One friend, Jim Schoolcraft, even gave me a Christmas stocking full of quarters. There must have been about $250 in it.

Having put the Christmas stocking towards airfares, I finally made my way to Atlantic City. What a moment. Not only was I making my professional debut, but my academic career hinged upon my at least completing the swim. Perhaps the pressure got to me. Whatever the reason, I hardly covered myself in glory in finishing fifth out of the seven women and thirteenth overall. I *had* finished though, albeit in the unexceptional time of 10:23:50. Still, my share of the prizemoney was enough to brighten my mood and that night I started a tradition by partying the house down at The Irish Pub. I may not have won, but I was on the scoreboard!

A week later I gave a better account of myself at Lac Magog when I came second in the women's section and ninth overall. In hindsight I was really winging it out there among the seasoned pros. I still didn't have a clue what I was doing. But I did know that I enjoyed it and I did manage to win enough money to put me through school. That alone marked it as a success.

I was in high spirits by the time I arrived in New York to tackle my third marathon in two weeks. It had a comfortable feel this time. I was staying with the Schnarrs, and Trisha would be my trainer again. The only thing that had changed was my boatman. And whereas I felt under-prepared against the pros, I now felt as though I was one of the better organised swimmers in the amateur field. A lot had changed in a year.

When the swim got underway on the morning of 28 July I had a regular cheer squad on my boat. One of the swimmers from the pro circuit was there to give advice and Fran and Joe had come along as well. It was the first time Fran wore what was to become her lucky yellow and white striped shirt. Lucky for me that is. Every time she wore it, whether in New York, Canada or Australia, I won.

The race went like a dream. Despite banging into something in the water along the way, I beat 27 other swimmers to win the swim outright in 7:44:44. It was the first time a woman had won. I couldn't contain the tears at the ceremony afterwards. When I told people what I'd been through in the last year they were so happy for me. The guy who came second was in tears, too.

When asked by the *New York Times*, I attributed my victory to Vegemite and the good Lord. I made page three the next day above a story on Ronald Reagan's nose operation. An American poet, John Tynan, even wrote about the swim. It was eventually published in a book of his poems called *The Singer and the Ants* (published by Pathé Pictures International). The following is an extract from 'The Marathon Swim Around Manhattan Island, Sunday, July 1985'.

> The dawn like a quickened rose glows between the land
>   and high
> The little flotilla gathers like swallows in the brightning sky . . .
> One by one the hierarchy of the marathon unfolds; one by one
>   following a leader—the ultimate Leader *falters*! A mermaid
>   strokes relentlessly by—*stroke stroke stroke breath*—Victoriana!
> Victory . . . Ships horns, cheers, applause! . . . the mermaid
>   climbs out
> Of the debris, bone-chill, treacherous currents, speed-boat
>   waves, on
> To Terra Firma—no longer a mermaid but an attractive,
>   young woman
> Smiling before cameras, soon followed by her shivering,
>   exultant peers
> —Young and Old, Man and maid: Victors All!

This particular maid was approached by the president of the Manhattan Swimming Association after the presentation. Having watched the way I won that day, he'd decided I should have a go at breaking the women's solo record of 6:41:35 for swimming around the island. Maybe I'd even break the existing men's record which, at about ten minutes quicker, had a place in the *Guinness Book of Records*. Both records were substantially faster than the race times because attempts could be timed to take full advantage of tides and currents. Needless to say, the idea appealed. When I asked how I went about it, he suggested I keep up my training in Arkansas and he'd call me with the details. I was in.

If I had any doubts that things were turning around for me they were dispelled on my return to Fayetteville. Someone had put my name forward for an academic scholarship and, on the strength of my marks, it had been granted for the remainder of my degree. Suddenly the money I had won could be put aside to pay my airfare home. I was like a razorback in muck. I could now concentrate on getting even better marks to launch my career as a physical education teacher.

There was still some unfinished business, though. The record attempt. It got the green light shortly afterwards when a call came through to say that the swim was set up for Tuesday, 15 October. I had decided I really wanted this one. If I was to sign off from swimming (and who was to say what the future held?) I wanted to do it in style. An entry in the *Guinness Book of Records* seemed a nice way to do it.

I prepared as best I could by reading a book about a previous record swim and speaking to one of the past record holders. I also arranged for another ex-record holder, Karen Hartley, to accompany me on the swim. I'd met Karen during the Atlantic City swim and she was only too happy to come down from her Boston home to help. She'd join Trisha and Fran in my boat, along with an official recorder for the *Guinness Book of Records*.

The day arrived. The scene that greeted me, however, was far from ideal. Even though the start time of 1.16 p.m. would mean I'd have the comfort of mainly swimming in daylight, any advantage was balanced by a hurricane which had recently swept through the area. The thrashing wind and rain had left the waters around Manhattan crowded with litter and debris. Sections of old piers and bags of rubbish vied for space with all manner of human and animal waste flushed into the river by the rains. I'd be keeping my mouth shut as much as possible on this swim.

And what a swim it was! After I'd overcome the jitters about being in the water by myself, it evolved into a visual and emotional feast. As expected, I spent a lot of time avoiding rubbish, not always successfully. But my memories are dominated by more pleasant visions. There was the sight of the *QEII* coming in to dock as I swum by. That's one big ocean liner! Later in the swim it seemed that the ferry which travels between Staten Island and lower Manhattan would hold me up at a crucial stage. Instead, to my delight, the ferry threw its propellers into reverse and stopped to let me through. Passengers hung over the side cheering me on as I swam from the Hudson River into the East River for the final stretch. That was when I picked up the tide and began to fly along with this incredible rush of water. Buildings and cars were buzzing by as I surged towards the finish. People were tooting their horns in encouragement as the sun began to set and I watched Manhattan Island light up like a Christmas tree. It was the most glorious sight, real goosebump stuff.

As soon as I passed the finishing point a chorus of cheers went up from my boat. By completing the swim in 6:12:28 I had not only smashed the women's record but shaved almost twenty minutes off the men's as well. Good thing, too, because *Australian Women's Weekly* had come out to do a story on the attempt and it would have been a bit of a damp squib without the record. Naturally, I was elated. I was also stinging from all my collisions with debris. It wasn't until I took off my bathers later that I realised my neck was raw from all the banging against stray planks and suchlike. I looked like I'd been strangled. Worst of all, I found a noodle in my belly button! It grossed me out. All I could think was, 'Who ate this noodle?'

Given the state of the water, I guess I shouldn't have been surprised when I was struck down with dysentery within 36 hours. I'd never been sick in my life before from swimming. My plight obviously inspired some sub-editor back in Australia to dub me 'Queen of the Sewers', a far-from-regal tag which stuck much longer than I cared. I much preferred the local version, 'The Queen of Manhattan'. I certainly felt like royalty when I flew back to Arkansas the next day and all my friends turned up at the airport with a huge toy koala. What a homecoming. I was even more chuffed when I got in the car and heard the five o'clock news welcoming me home and saying how proud of me they were. What's more, when I arrived at Humphrey's Hall I found it festooned with congratulatory signs and green and gold streamers. It was a huge thrill, but not even a state reception could have kept me awake much longer in my condition. After dragging myself to Bible study, I fell asleep from exhaustion.

It didn't take long for me to come back to earth. As it happened, that Saturday afternoon I was due to make my usual appearance at the college football game. I had been making a little pocket money by selling food and drinks at the stadium and here I was again, doing my 'Peanuts! Get your peanuts here!' routine. Suddenly my name came up on the scoreboard screen to congratulate me on my record. Of course, no one in the crowd had a clue who I was. While they were applauding I was standing in the aisle with a box of peanuts slung around my neck, a somewhat anonymous and abashed world record holder.

The record behind me, my focus now shifted to my studies. After my false start in computing I still had the rest of the academic year to complete and another semester after that to gain my degree in physical education. Without the distraction of competitive swimming I was able to throw myself into practice teaching in the spring. My final summer was spent as an assistant camp director for Girl Guides in Buckville, Arkansas.

The camp was set deep in a forest which was home to numerous snakes, tarantulas and bears. The snakes, in particular, had little compunction about visiting the camp. As someone who is petrified of snakes, I never ventured far without a hoe in my hand, just in case. The kids must have wondered who was protecting whom. Inevitably, the day arrived when I was called upon to guard my group from a deadly copperhead snake. Shaking like a leaf, I dispatched the snake with my hoe and, following tradition, cut off its head and buried it in a coffee tin. Apparently their venom is still active no matter how long they're dead. Before the camp was out, I was called on to kill a rattlesnake as well. Enjoyable as the job was, I was happy to get back to my snake-free campus.

My last semester passed smoothly but for yet another car accident. I was returning home from a Thanksgiving dinner when another driver lost control on the ice and smashed into the car I was in, sending us into a ditch. My back didn't take too kindly to the unexpected detour and I ended up in hospital for a couple of days. I was beginning to feel like a magnet for car accidents by now.

Finally, the last exams behind me, I gained my degree. As is my way, I had been a diligent student and managed to graduate with honours. I was now a physical education teacher qualified to teach kindergarten through to grade 12. I had done it!

As satisfying as it was, my last day at school was tinged with trepidation. Arkansas had been my home for almost four and a half years. In that time I hadn't once been back to Australia because of financial constraints. I was about to leave people who, to all intents and purposes, had become my surrogate family. It wasn't so much that I was leaving America. It was the friends, the church community, the various people who had made such an impact on my life. It was *them* I was leaving.

Although I might not have fully realised it at the time, Shelley Taylor, the person, had been utterly changed by those years in America. I had built my self-esteem and confidence. I had gained a far greater understanding of the world and of people's worth. And my own values and beliefs were far clearer, thanks largely to the influence of the church. This was the Shelley Taylor who didn't really want to go home. The Shelley Taylor who cried when she boarded the plane for Australia. What was I returning to?

I landed in Perth on Christmas Eve 1986. I couldn't have felt more out of place if I was dressed as the Easter bunny.

THE • FIRES • WITHIN

WHY DO I DO IT? It's a deceptively simple question. Why *does* a person choose such a demanding and solitary sport? The simplest and most obvious answer is that I've always enjoyed the sport of swimming, whether pool or marathon. I thrive on the hard work that goes into training for competition and I absolutely love racing itself. To me, it's the best way to discover aspects of your character that might otherwise stay concealed. If you don't test yourself, how are you ever going to know your limitations? I hate the thought that I could die without having truly explored my capabilities. Not that swimming offers the only way to do that, but it has been a wonderful vehicle of self-exploration for me.

On a similar level, swimming has also provided me with a clear sense of purpose in life. The beauty of sport is that it allows you to set readily measured goals, whether it be time, height, distance or specific achievements. From the time I started out in swimming I could point to something and say *that* is where I'm headed. And when I got there, I could set a new goal and start over again with renewed vigour. For that reason, I suppose I've yet to find a compelling reason to stop what I'm doing. My life has always been one goal after another, especially once I became successful at marathon swimming. After my first world title in 1988 I felt I'd only just scraped the surface of my potential. Then the World Championships became a focus. Following on from the worlds, I could see the opportunity to make a career out of marathon swimming if I joined the circuit. And so on.

In recent years my outlook has changed to the extent that I have seen the benefit of broadening my goals. To win a third world title is a worthy achievement. To win a fourth is notable. To win a fifth is laudable. To win a sixth and a seventh . . . well, there comes a point when merely winning is not enough. You have to introduce new measures of progress and success. I still have my goals, but they have become more flexible as my priorities shift. One thing *has* remained constant: marathon swimming continues to present the best way for me to pursue the majority of my goals.

In that sense, two of the primary reasons I continue to swim are to raise the profile of a sport I love and to drive home a message of individuality to Australia's youth. If it wasn't for my achievements in the sport to date, I wouldn't have the opportunity to do either.

For some years now I've recognised the responsibility I have to promote the sport in Australia and internationally. In the same way that Wayne Gardner helped lift local interest in motorcycling by taking out the 500cc world championship, my successes can boost marathon swimming in the eyes of the Australian public. The fact is, we are attracted to our sporting champions and their achievements can help legitimise a sport where little interest existed before. That's where my world titles, my win in the Sydney Harbour race in 1991 and my Sydney-to-Wollongong swim in 1995 come in. They established me as a recognisable spokesperson for the sport and, without such people, fringe sports can quickly get shot down in the dogfight for space in the sports pages.

On the international front, I'm equally aware of the interest I've helped generate in some countries by challenging and successfully competing against the top men. It's just the sort of story the media flocks to, and that can't be bad for a sport with ambitions to be included in the Olympics. I've also devoted energy to being the swimmer's representative on the International Marathon Swimming Association. In that capacity I've waded knee-deep in the politics of the sport, from fighting for better conditions and safety provisions for all swimmers to campaigning for more equitable prizemoney distribution for women. I spent a lot of time at the outset being told to shut up and sit down. But when I refused to be intimidated, things began to move and people started to listen.

There have been times, I admit, when I've gotten tired of taking on such responsibilities. Regrettably, one of the realities of such a role is that you always feel as though you're not getting enough support from others around you. It's the curse of fringe sports that they seem to inspire the worst in-fighting and back-stabbing. I suppose that's a major part of the reason they stay minor sports. Thankfully I've been sustained by some notable successes along the way. It was very gratifying to play a part in the successful staging of the 25-kilometre swim at the 1991 World Championships in Perth, for instance. As a member of the organising committee I like to think that I had a significant input as to how the race was set up and staged, the result of which was to impress the FINA delegates who will ultimately determine if the sport takes the next step to the Olympics.

Away from my responsibilities to the sport, I feel a desperate need to communicate something to Australia's youth. Having travelled to so many places in the world where kids are denied a choice, I hate to see our own kids fritter away their opportunities through timidity or lack of direction. How can it be that when I see so much poverty and deprivation elsewhere, this lucky country can have one of the highest youth suicide rates in the world? What are we doing wrong? Young Australians are just being lost for some reason.

I see it in terms of the loss of individuality. This overbearing, homogeneous culture that we're being sold via the television is trying to squeeze all kids into the same holes. They've all got to dress the right way, talk the right way. There's no encouragement to act out your life according to individual tastes and talents. It means we're underrating our kids terribly. They should be told time and again that life is worth living and worth exploring *in their own fashion*. And, importantly in a country which still likes to cut down its tall poppies, anybody who succeeds should be applauded loudly. I just wonder sometimes whether we've become a nation that fears seeing anybody rise above the pack in any but the most self-effacing way. Egos should be nurtured, not trampled on.

My success in marathon swimming has given me the platform to try to pass that message on. I guess it's no coincidence, either, that I'm a teacher when I'm not away swimming. I want to contribute towards Australians believing in themselves. I want them to have the courage to get off their butts and take a few risks. If I can reach only a few kids, it will have been worth it.

So much for the altruistic reasons. What are the more tangible rewards for me, I hear you ask? Well, I could answer that personal enjoyment and a sense of purpose rate pretty highly when one is looking for things of value in this life. But I get your drift. Well, let's dispel one possible misconception right off the bat. I'm not in this game for the money, that much is for certain. The girlfriend of one of the Argentinian swimmers put it beautifully when she heard a bunch of us discussing the prizemoney for upcoming races. We were going on and on about it until she couldn't stand it any more.

'I can't believe you're all so worried about the prizemoney!' she huffed. 'You put yourself through all this training and the pain, and for what? The most any of you can hope for in any swim is US$5000. And that's only the winner. It just doesn't add up!'

She was right, of course. The numbers don't stack up. Yet, although no one's going to get rich on prizemoney, we still feel the need to debate the issue of a fair split. It's the principle, you know.

As for the prizemoney I have won, it gets eaten up pretty quickly by the costs associated with following the world circuit, mounting record challenges and day-to-day living. Sponsorships and grants help balance the books, although most sponsorships are in the form of services or equipment rather than cash. Finally, there's the relief teaching I do when possible and the occasional ad hoc job to keep the wolves from the door. I can be found babysitting and housecleaning in a pinch. Such is the enviable life of a world champion.

It's not a complaint. I'm just setting down the reality. It's not much different to a whole host of fringe sports. Marathon swimming is caught in the same bind as many other sports. Promoters can't put up large amounts of prizemoney unless they get sponsor backing. Sponsors won't back a sport unless they're guaranteed a certain amount of exposure. The media generally won't give an event exposure unless it already has the sort of prominence that can only come with sponsor and media support. And so we chase our tails.

WHAT KEEPS THE BEST SWIMMERS INVOLVED IS THE FAMILY ATMOSPHERE. *Everybody hangs out together, they eat together, they catch up like old friends. They travel week to week in different parts of the world and there's really little competition between them until the gun goes off. There was one occasion when our boat driver was so bad that I couldn't get in position to feed Shelley. For two hours other swimmer's handlers came over and fed her. Everybody looks out for each other.*

NANCY SCHNARR

Oddly enough for such a solitary sport, in the end it is the camaraderie which helps to keep me going. Again, it's not uncommon in fringe sports to find a sort of special bond through adversity. Nobody is doing it easy and we all know we must pull together as much as possible if we're to convince FINA the sport deserves a berth at the Olympics. There's a selfish side to this, in that many swimmers still harbour hopes of one day representing their countries at the Games. I'm not any different. But there is a pioneer spirit which rises above even the selfish concerns.

I think there's a term for such sentiment. It's called the Olympic spirit.

THE • GOLDEN • WEST

I FELT LIKE AN UNOPENED PRESENT that Christmas Day, 1986. Here I was, fresh off the plane from four life-altering years in America, and it seemed that nobody had noticed the transformation. I spent the day waiting for my family to ask if I'd changed much, but the question never came. I felt I had so much to tell, but no audience to relate it to.

The day only compounded my fears about returning to Perth. I knew everyone expected that I would slot right back into life at 'home'. The problem was it didn't feel like home any more. I felt totally out of place. I was no longer the Shelley Taylor who had flown out of Perth in 1982. That Shelley had been enlarged upon. And the difficulty for family and friends in Perth was that the growth had happened out of their sight. They hadn't been there to see either the gradual or the profound changes.

Perhaps the greatest legacy of my time in America was the self-confidence I developed. Not that I was ever an introvert. But America had taught me that if you didn't believe in yourself, nobody else would. I learnt that it was all right to have an opinion, to stand up and be counted. I found that when I got up in America and said that I *knew* I was going to do this or do that, people encouraged me. When I tried the same thing in Perth it was interpreted as arrogance. I was seen as being full of myself.

It was all so foreign to me. My natural instinct was to run back to the place I felt comfortable in. I'd really only come back to Perth because I'd graduated. I wasn't necessarily thinking that I'd be back for long. Increasingly, returning to America to do a master's degree seemed like a good idea. Particularly when I got together with Leith, who returned at the same time I did. She was experiencing the same problems. We just didn't feel that we fitted in.

My identity crisis was to persist for months. In the meantime I had to make an effort to construct some sort of a life in Perth.

I had a vague notion that I'd like to get back into marathon swimming, but it was no more than a distant prospect at first. My more immediate concern was the attitude of the Department of Education. Far from welcoming me into the state system, they told me that my American degree meant I would have to do twelve months' further study to qualify to teach. While that little argument raged, I had to find something to make ends meet.

In an oblique way, long-distance swimming came to my aid. I had heard that someone was planning to attempt a swim between Fremantle and Rottnest Island at the end of January 1987. I contacted the people involved, asked if they needed any help and they welcomed me on board. When the day came for the swim I suddenly found myself surrounded by like-minded people. For the first time since returning I felt in my element. As it happened, I actually got into the water with the swimmer, Peter Blackmore, during a particularly sticky patch. Despite being in a bad way he made it to Rottnest, establishing the precedent for what was to become an annual race.

After Peter had recovered I got talking to him and it turned out he was the state manager for the Munich Re-insurance company. I mentioned I was looking for a job and he said he needed a clerical assistant. Just like that, I had a job. It wasn't as though everything instantly fell into place for me. But I'd stumbled upon the first pieces of the jigsaw.

The next piece arrived courtesy of a chance visit. Shortly after starting work at Munich Re-insurance I went shopping with Leith and we found ourselves in a familiar arcade. Peter Smith, my hairdresser friend from years before, had worked in a salon there. I decided to pop in. When I couldn't see him I asked if a Peter Smith worked there. A voice came from the back of the salon.

'Yeh, I'm Peter Smith.'

He walked towards me, stopped and stared.

'Shelley Taylor?'

Must have been the haircut. Anyway, we chatted away nineteen to the dozen and parted agreeing that we should catch up again soon. A month later we met and attempted to cover everything that had happened over the previous five years. By the time we'd talked ourselves out that night it seemed that, at the very least, we still had enough in common to become friends again. When we began to see each other more regularly I started to get other ideas. By Easter I was flippantly telling some people we'd get married.

I was still working at Munich Re-insurance and finding the education department less than accommodating. Once it had been settled that I wouldn't have to do an extra twelve months' study, they told me I'd have to start out in teaching with a country posting. I tried to explain that I could hardly train as a marathon swimmer in an isolated town, but they weren't budging. I should have been a football player.

If I was still being stonewalled by the education department, there was at least some joy elsewhere. Whispers had begun to filter through that the 1991 World Championships would be held in Perth and that a 25-kilometre event would be included for the first time. It was like manna from heaven. Could it be true? Could this be my chance to win gold for my country, as my father had predicted? And in my home town! I daren't hope that it would turn out that way, but it was enough to start me dreaming.

I had already resumed pool training under Bernie Mulroy and his assistant Colin Raven at the City of Perth club. Apart from keeping me in shape, it provided me with a routine I understood. I was accustomed to a structured life and, in what was still a period of adjustment, I needed that routine to help ease me back into Perth.

Now, with the faint prospect of the World Championships to aim for, I was a woman on a mission again. I won at the AUSSI [Australian Union of Senior Swimmers Inc.] Masters nationals, held in Perth in April, and then set my sights on returning to Manhattan. I had kept in contact with the Schnarr family and it didn't seem that far away. Admittedly, the cost was a thorny issue until I put in a call to my old mate Mal Brown. With him banging the drum for me I was able to set about raising the money to pay for the trip. I also had another great supporter by this time. Peter and I had started living together mid-year and, come weekends, we would sit on the balcony and discuss our dreams and goals. We even got around to talking about how many children we wanted, such was our belief that we would share our futures together.

For the moment, however, I would be going to New York by myself. I was extremely relaxed in what had become familiar surrounds by now. And it showed. With Fran's daughter Nancy acting as my trainer for the first time, I won the race outright again and set a race record of 7:24:54 ahead of 40 other competitors. I was also seen on television in Australia for the first time thanks to Ronald Reagan Jnr, who did a story on me for *Good Morning America*.

The exposure did not generate the response I anticipated back in Perth, though. While my family and friends and the media were happy for me, I found that others had trouble swallowing it. It seemed that some people could not deal with what they saw as my cockiness. They seemed to be queueing up to knock me. The confidence I'd been encouraged to express during my years in Arkansas just didn't wash in Perth.

I didn't get long to dwell on the negative reactions. Right in the middle of a phone call with my mother, who was now living in the country town of Norseman, Peter slid an engagement ring under my nose. Despite some debate over the next few hours as to whether that actually constituted a proposal, we agreed we were now engaged. It only remained for Peter to ask my mother's permission, seeing as I'd virtually cut her off mid-conversation. The opportunity was presented by an invitation for me to do a lap of honour in an open car at the West Australian Football League grand final. My mother was to travel from Norseman and, with Peter, accompany me to the game as guests.

Whether it was nerves or the closeness of the footy, Peter still hadn't popped the question by half-time. I was beginning to get a bit fidgety by now, throwing him meaningful glances at every opportunity. Finally, as we juggled our tea and scones during the third quarter, he blurted it out. He needn't have worried. We may have only been going out six months, but Mum was delighted that her wandering daughter was getting betrothed. I was pretty happy myself. I'd begun to feel that I was lagging behind my peers, most of whom were already married or in the process of doing so. And I figured I'd found a good partner. It helped that I got on really well with his family, especially his father Leewood.

And so the date was set. I would become Shelley Taylor-Smith on 2 April 1988. There were still six months to go, however, and what a six months! In that period I swam in the state championships, finally got a teaching job at Swan Christian High School and had to abandon optimistic plans to swim the English Channel because of insufficient funds. I then got an invitation to represent Australia at the World Cup, to be held on Lac Leman (also known as Lake Geneva) on 14 July. The 25-kilometre swim was to trace a route from Lausanne, Switzerland, on one side of the lake, to Evian, France, on the other side. There was only one problem. I couldn't get official sanction from Australian Swimming, so it would be up to me to fund my own way there. That little poser would have to wait until after the wedding.

As it should be, our wedding day was one of the happiest days of my life. Radiant bride and all that. I used the occasion to pay special tribute to Peter, who had already been called on to prop me up as my training schedule became more and more onerous. His willingness to cook, clean and make allowances for my anti-social hours were integral to any ideas I had about pursuing marathon swimming.

It wouldn't be getting any easier for him, either. Especially once it was confirmed that there *would* be a 25-kilometre event in the 1991 worlds in Perth. The way I saw it, everyone would be relying on me to win in my home town. There would be huge pressure. From that moment on it became my primary focus. I would go to sleep dreaming about it.

I now had my answer as to why I'd fallen out of bed in Arkansas all those years before. By literally falling into marathon swimming I now had a shot at what would, for me, be the equivalent of an Olympic gold medal. Not only that, but I would have the rare opportunity to win in front of a home crowd and write myself into the record books as the event's inaugural gold medallist into the bargain. God does, indeed, work in mysterious ways.

Knowing what impact such a goal would have on our lives, I asked Peter if he could handle it. I told him it was going to be hard for both of us, real hard. Elite athletes are never easy to live with. *I* don't even like living with another athlete. Peter was great. He said he was prepared to back me up. Our first shared challenge was finding the money to pay for my trip to the World Cup. I wanted Peter to travel with me as my trainer, so it was going to take more than rattling a few cans.

Ultimately, I owed my World Cup trip to wonderful media and community support and the resourcefulness of school kids enlisted in my cause. Between raffles and stalls and goodness knows what else, the kids at Swan Christian High managed to raise $2000. Now I truly felt as though I was representing Australia.

Evian was looking gorgeous when Peter and I arrived there to join 50 other competitors from twelve nations. The warm sun was shining off the unruffled lake and the next few days of training were a joy in the still-cool lake. We should have guessed. As the night before the race descended, the clouds began to gather and the wind began to whip across the lake. As we lay in bed that night we could hear shutters banging and rain lashing the hotel. When morning arrived we were greeted with a mid-winter's day and by the time we boarded the ferry for the trip across to Lausanne the lake was in turmoil. Swimmers and officials were racing to the rails to be sick. On reaching the other side we were *all* sprinting, as we sought cover from the elements. By any measure, it was a thoroughly miserable day.

It was a long-faced group of 50 shivering swimmers who greased down. With Peter otherwise occupied, Berry Rickards had the dubious pleasure of applying the wool fat to me. As a FINA delegate, board member of Australian Swimming and chairman of the Australian open water swimming committee, Berry ranks as the most distinguished greaser I've ever had. Any levity in the situation disappeared, however, when they got us in the water. Thanks to the howling wind and crashing waves, it was a freezing 15 degrees.

This was no time to paddle around. We were all anxious to get started. When the gun sounded we were off in a mad thrashing of arms. But hardly had we got 300 metres when there was a similar waving of arms on the boats. The race had been stopped. It was the signal for a virtual Babylon of abuse. Swimmers were going off in half a dozen languages. When the organisers finally succeeded in getting their message across we were directed to swim back into the harbour and get into our boats. Once I was on board my sympathetic, but impractical, boat driver offered me a shot of whisky. Regretfully, I had to decline.

After much rushing about and gnashing of teeth the word came around that we'd been stopped because the Swiss police were worried about our boats sinking. Are you getting the picture now? In the end a compromise was reached, whereupon the race was to be shortened from 25 to 15 kilometres. We were to be taken out into the lake and started from there. Fine in principle, but when we arrived at the 'start' it quickly degenerated into farce. Before everyone was in position a number of swimmers set off. The cry went out that we'd started and the remaining swimmers just jumped in and started swimming. There was nothing for it but to follow suit.

After the inglorious start the swim settled down into a fiercely contested race. Just how fierce I was to discover when I found myself in position to overtake an Egyptian swimmer. I had moved into third place overall and was closing on the second-placed Egyptian. The thought of being bettered by a woman was apparently too great a shame for the guy to bear. Just as I was poised to pass him I heard my crew shout 'duck'. I dived instinctively and felt the Egyptian's boat pass right over me. They had intentionally tried to cut me off! I came up speechless.

If I needed any additional incentive to push on in those atrocious conditions, that was it. I got the guy in my sights and powered past him into outright second place. Fired up as I was there would be no hauling me in now. I went on to finish second overall and claim the women's gold for Australia. It might have been the euphoria of the moment, but I didn't lodge a protest against the Egyptian. Maybe I just figured he'd had enough disgrace for one day.

Besides, I was too busy rejoicing in my first gold medal for my country. Sure, it might not be making the back pages back home, it might not even have the full support of Australian Swimming, but as far as I was concerned I had been out there swimming for my country. That it also clinched my first world No.1 ranking was almost incidental.

When the time came to climb onto the dais to accept my medal, Berry came to my rescue once more. I had no official gear, so he lent me his Australian Swimming jacket for the occasion. When they played the national anthem I swelled with pride. So what if I had to mumble my way through it because I was a bit vague on the words? I'd be sure to learn it by 1991.

Buoyed by my victory, I went on to New York with Peter and won the Manhattan swim outright again in 7:24:44. The only letdown was our visit to Arkansas. Peter didn't enjoy his trip down my memory lane at all. It had played such a huge part in my life and yet, as I saw it, my husband couldn't grasp it. It reminded me how, in the eyes of the people I knew in Perth, I may as well have been on another planet for those four years. There were no common points of reference at all.

Back in Perth, I decided I'd use the next two years to have a good look at the competition I expected to face in the Swan River on 10 January 1991. My first stop in 1989 was Magog and the result did nothing to shake my faith that I stood a good chance of winning gold in Perth. With Peter as my trainer, I managed to win a tough race despite suffering carbon monoxide poisoning from the boat's exhaust. The price was hours on the toilet and a visit to the hospital. I barely knew what day it was at the presentation. Still sick, I flew across the continent to compete in a 25-kilometre swim in California. I had diarrhoea for the entire second half of the race and virtually crawled up the beach to finish second behind fellow Australian Susie Maroney. Then it was back across America again to take part in the Manhattan swim. This one, at least, passed without incident and I won it outright for the fourth time.

Back home, the various organising committees for the World Championships were being put together. I put my hand up to help organise the 25-kilometre swim and soon found just how much I'd bitten off. There were very few people about with experience of marathon swimming and our job wasn't made any easier when the championship organisers forgot to budget for us. We were considered so peripheral at this point that they didn't even bother to negotiate any television rights for the event.

With resources stretched so thin, the preparation threatened to turn sour when the organising committee decided to host an international event in January 1990. The swim was intended to act as a test run for the Swan River course but, on a choppy day, most of the boats sank! I was left with a sinking feeling myself when I came second to American Karen Burton, the swimmer expected to present the greatest challenge to my hopes of winning gold. When Australian Swimming president Tom Brazier tried to console me afterwards I assured him that the outcome would be different in a year's time. But first I had to stand down from the organising committee. It seemed that I was so worried about all the issues surrounding the swim that I'd forgotten to concentrate on the most important thing. My own race preparation.

With that responsibility behind me, I quickly got back into my stride a couple of months later when I won the Australian nationals at Sydney's Manly Dam. Having finished as the top Australian woman in both the January swim and the nationals, I safely assumed that I had clinched my spot in the squad for the World Championships and started planning the rest of the year. I wanted to use the northern summer to get some more experience on the professional circuit under my belt.

I had one major job to attend to first. I needed to raise the money for an English Channel record bid. I had been thwarted by lack of funds in 1988. It wasn't going to happen again.

The English Channel is the swimmer's equivalent of Mt Everest, and I was no different to any other swimmer. In fact, after meeting the likes of Channel legend Des Renford, who'd swum it nineteen times, I'd come to believe that you weren't really anybody in marathon swimming until you'd swum 'The Ditch'. And so the dream grew in me to the extent that I decided to go for both the one-way and double-crossing records in the one hit. But how to pay for it?

The answer arrived on a bus in late 1989. The bus was carrying a group of FINA delegates who were in Perth to go over the 25-kilometre World Championships course. When I took my seat I found myself next to a gentleman called John Whitehead, a Perth mover and shaker who was trying to raise sponsorship for the West Australian Swimming Association at the time. We got to chatting and John asked me what I was up to. I told him I was hoping to swim the Channel the following year, but that I had little more than hope as yet. He asked me what I needed, and when I said sponsorship he suggested I have a fund-raiser. By now my profile in Perth was such that a fund-raiser wasn't too bad a notion at all. We kicked the idea around a bit and came up with the idea of calling it Cocktails and Dreams. Getting people *on* the drink seemed the best way of getting me *in* the drink!

John took on the project with gusto. He helped form a committee which included Peter and my father-in-law Leewood, and together we worked frantically to make the whole thing a reality. I called in every old contact and supporter I could think of and gradually the night began to take shape. Everything was donated, including the food. One wonderful woman even volunteered to cook the lot, with the aid of her mother and her husband. The main money-raising part of the night was to be an auction. Once we'd done the rounds we had a huge variety of items, ranging from alcohol and furniture to stoves and paintings. The most generous contributor was Domestic Appliances, through their general manager Jim Smith. Apart from whitegoods, Jim managed to conjure up one of the real lures of the evening, a door prize of a trip for two to England.

With all the goodies on offer and some serious spruiking we managed to sell an amazing 500 tickets at $25 per head. That presented us with one last problem. With a week to go we discovered that the food donated for the night would only feed about 50 people. In a mild state of panic I put in a call to Gary

Carvolth at radio station 6PR. Gary had long been a champion of my cause and he excelled on this occasion. He hit the airwaves with a call for donations and before we knew it we had enough grub to feed an army. It helps to know miracle workers.

The hype by now was incredible. It was not as though I was the first Australian to go for the record. Far from it. But I was the first *West Australian* to attempt the Channel crossing, and in a parochial town like Perth that counted for a lot. It became a West Australian thing, to the extent that I had schools doing projects on my attempt, set down for 14 August because of favourable tides.

Amid all the hoo-ha, the Cocktails and Dreams night was held at the Fremantle Overseas Passenger Terminal three months before the swim. I was like a cat on a hot tin roof, and not just because it was such a momentous evening. No, I was worried sick that one of those sheep carriers would dock and stink the place out. I'm grateful to say that it was quiet on the wharves that night.

Except, of course, for the happenings *inside* the terminal. Well lubricated by cocktails with names like Shelley's Manhattan Midori and Shelley's Blue Lagoon, the crowd had a rip-roaring time of it. So did the auctioneer and by night's end we had raised an astonishing $25,000. Together with fund-raising efforts by school kids at Swan Christian High, the record attempt was now a definite goer.

Once I'd recovered from the night, I plunged back into heavy training. Neil Brooks became my training buddy as we'd plough up and down the Swan River, Peter alongside us in a borrowed dinghy. Peter was in training, too. Paddling beside me, he planned to become the first person to cross the Channel on a surf ski. The three of us formed a great team. Peter and Neil got on famously and, like two naughty boys, they never lacked for pranks to keep me amused. Jellyfish fights and bared bums were among their favourite routines.

There was more to it than clocking up the kilometres. In preparation for the cold water I had to start to pack on some weight. My diet and my waist expanded accordingly. Sunday night was the biggie, when Neil would come over to our place and watch wide-eyed as I demolished a roast and then polished off a whole apple pie for dessert. Besides the weight-gain program, I was now spending sessions with a sports psychologist. Steve Cohen reinforced my belief that my greatest strength was in my mind. He also helped prepare me for the actual Channel experience by tuning my senses. With his promptings I would make associations with the sensation of cold water on my back, visualise the landing in France and imagine the sights, sounds and smells that would greet me. He was trying to take me there before I even arrived, so that I would immediately feel comfortable in the new surrounds.

The time came to board my plane. Since I had three marathons to swim before I headed for England, I had to say goodbye to Peter. We would be meeting again the week before I swam. My first stop was Italy for my first appearance in the Capri to Naples swim on 5 July. It was a winning debut, significant also for meeting a young Melbourne swimmer who was to become a great friend and supporter. Tammy van Wisse, coached by national long-distance coach Dick Campion, was on her first trip overseas and looking for a start in the race to boost her claims for a spot on the Australian team for the worlds. Things didn't quite work out the way she wanted.

First, she got off to a horror start when her luggage was lost in transit. Being the mothering type, when I heard of her plight I took her under my wing and got on the phone to track her luggage down. Having done that, I let her stay in my room and introduced her to everyone. Just when she was settling in she had her second setback. There was no place for her in the race. There were already two women competing from Australia and that was our quota for this swim. It wasn't a complete waste of time, though. Tammy ended up helping out on the boat of the overall winner, American David Alleva, and gained a valuable insight into the sport in the process. Before parting ways I invited her to come to Perth and train with me later in the year, an offer she gleefully accepted.

From Italy it was on to New York to train up for the two Canadian swims at Lac Magog and Lac St Jean. It was while I

was training at the Long Island Aquatic Club near the Schnarrs'
home that I took the bold step of changing my stroke. I had
been training under coach Dave Ferris at the club during my
stays in New York and he took me aside on this occasion and
suggested a few basic adjustments. The main thrust was that I
was to go from a bent arm recovery, where the elbow is high,
to a straight arm recovery called swinging. The primary benefit
was that the back of my hand wouldn't be caught by waves
when I swam through choppy water. It was also more relaxing
for my shoulders and allowed me to throw my hand way forward
and take up big scoops of water. It was an altogether more
economical way of swimming in open water.

The first test of my new style came in Lac Magog on 22
July. It was an overwhelming success. Not only did I easily win
the women's section of the race in a record time of 9:31:44,
but I came second overall behind men's world champion Diego
Degano. The following week I repeated the dose at Lac St Jean,
Diego once more leading me home. I think it's fair to say that,
with my new weapon, there were some increasingly nervous
men looking over their shoulders.

After my two successful swims I was in a buoyant mood as
I rushed to England on 1 August, arriving just as Susie Maroney
became the fastest Australian to swim the Channel. I hoped to
make it an even better month for Australia. I set up base at
Weymouth on the south coast and was immediately swamped
with well-wishing calls, letters and telegrams from home. At the
home of my Channel coach Tom Watch and his wife Sheila
they couldn't believe all the fuss. After all, countless people had
swum The Ditch before. Indeed, during the prime 'season', up
to six swimmers could tackle it each day. In some ways, I realised
that the Channel had more of a mystique in Australia than it
did in England because of the efforts of people like Des Renford.
Then again, the blasé attitude of the locals might have something
to do with the fact that most of the Channel records are held
by other than English people.

For the next ten days I couldn't have asked for more
auspicious conditions. England was in the middle of a heatwave
and the sea was benign. Not that it wasn't still freezing by my

standards. I couldn't get over how the locals would happily splash about in water which had my teeth chattering by the end of training. I clearly needed to put on some more padding. Potatoes, potatoes and more potatoes was my answer, with apple tarts and custard tarts to follow. I was inflating before my very eyes!

On 11 August I moved along the coast to Folkestone, a short hop from my starting point at Dover, where Peter and I were reunited after six weeks apart. Everything was now in readiness. There were just three days to go and the expectation level was growing daily as more and more messages of support arrived from Western Australia and the Perth media kept tabs on my progress. All eyes were now on the sky and the sea.

And well they might have been. After an uninterrupted stint of perfect weather the sky began to fill with clouds, the wind picked up and the sea began to darken. I was jumping out of my skin to get underway, but I was at the mercy of the elements. It was a killing wait. Then came the night before my early morning start on 14 August. Our worst fears had been realised as we stared out into a stormy night, the wind-whipped rain hurling against the windows.

As the hours passed we monitored the weather forecasts and talked anxiously with our boat driver. Bleak as it was, we still considered going out until we consulted the local fishermen gathered at the pub. The Channel was their workplace and they knew its ruthless and unpredictable ways better than anyone. Tonight was no time to be out in those waters, they said. The attempt would have to be delayed.

It was a huge anti-climax. This was no ordinary swim. I wasn't only swimming for Shelley Taylor-Smith this time. I was swimming for Western Australia. It made the disappointment infinitely harder to bear. And it would be ten days before the next set of favourable tides was due. With my return flight booked for 29 August, there wasn't much margin for error.

Frustrating as it was, it was out of my hands. I couldn't do much other than train and keep my fingers crossed that the weather had done its worst. They were long, long days. The tension built as we approached the 24th and then lifted another notch when that attempt, too, had to be abandoned because of foul weather. I was now wound up beyond belief. It was incredibly stressful to go to bed having psyched yourself up to swim in the morning, only to find upon waking that you had to do it all again the next night. The same thing happened on the 25th and the 26th. There were only three days now separating me from an inglorious return to Perth. I felt sick.

I must have said a very loud prayer before I went to bed on the night of the 26th. When I woke up in the wee hours of the 27th I got the news I was longing for. The stormy weather had abated and we had the green light. Thunderbirds are go! As you can imagine, I was just itching to get in. We all assembled at Dover's Shakespeare Beach and, after greasing me down with specially prepared fluorescent pink wool fat, I finally headed towards France at 4 a.m.

For the first few hours I was travelling like a steam train in the calm water. Peter was stroking away merrily beside me in his custom-made yellow and blue neon wetsuit (so I could see him clearly in the dark) and my boat crew's main challenge was to try to get me to slow down. Tom Watch, a Channel veteran, was delighted with my progress by the halfway mark. I was right on record pace and looking strong. The only reservations held by anyone at this stage were those of the Australian television crew whose sea legs had failed them before we even left the harbour. It was going to be a long crossing for them.

Altogether, we couldn't have wished for a better first half of the swim. In hindsight, we could scarcely have been dealt a worse second half. Up to this point the wind had been a bit blowy, but it was nothing untoward. Then, as if orchestrated by the collective wills of existing record holders, the wind suddenly threw off its happy airs and lifted from a Force one to a Force five. What had been shaping as a red-letter day in the water was instantly transformed into a survival quest. The sea began to churn and the Boxing Kangaroo flag hoisted proudly on the boat began to flap wildly. I continued to beat my way eastward, but I could feel the records slipping through my fingers. The only hope was that this front might pass through quickly enough to allow conditions to revert to their prior, obliging state.

Fat chance. The wind kept up its roaring, the sea kept up its churning, and I was left to keep flailing France-wards. The television crew was reduced to a convulsive mess, Peter was suffering badly on his ski and the flag was in shreds. To make matters worse a real pea-soup fog descended on us. We couldn't see much further than 50 metres. When a monstrous tanker loomed out of the fog, too close for comfort, we knew we really had to keep our wits about us. Meanwhile, the tide was going one way, the wind was going the other and I was trying to swim through the middle. It was like swimming through molasses. I knew by then that the records were beyond my reach. The trick now was to stay positive. I needed to re-set my goals.

I decided that the real challenge now was simply to complete the crossing. I knew that would be no mean accomplishment in these conditions. Importantly, it would also show that I was no quitter. Not that the thought didn't occur to me. As the hours slowly ticked by, the pain and cold increased. Towards the end it was apparent that the weather wasn't about to change so the boat captain decided it would be foolish for me to try the double crossing. All efforts were now directed towards getting me on to French soil. Or sand, to be more accurate. After discussions with former Channel swimmers I had mentally prepared myself for landing on jagged rocks. But as we inched closer to the coast all I could see was a white blur on the horizon. Was I hallucinating? No. Thanks to the currents I would be coming ashore on a gloriously soft beach. What a lovely sight for a weary soul.

After nine hours and 27 minutes I struggled ashore at the resort town of Wissant. A horde of people came rushing over to me and, in true Gallic fashion, someone produced a bottle of champagne and began spraying it over me. I must have looked a treat. Next thing I knew there was a policeman striding towards us and I was told in halting English that I had to get back in the boat or I would need to produce a passport. Just what I needed after a swim of more than 50 kilometres!

And so I returned to England. Obviously, it had not turned out the way I would have wanted. But I was not as crestfallen as some might expect. Sure, I'd become merely another ordinary person who swam the Channel in a shocking time. But I knew that the Channel, more than any other waterway, was a lucky dip. In my case, it had proved an unlucky dip. After all, swimmers I'd beaten by more than two hours at Lac Magog had crossed the Channel in around eight hours. Given the right conditions, I knew I could have given the records a shake. My conscience was clear.

That didn't stop me feeling that West Australians would be disappointed in me. But I got an agreeable surprise when I got back to Perth. I might not have broken any world records, but I *had* become the first West Australian to complete the crossing. Everyone I spoke to said they were proud of me. They understood the situation and appreciated that I had done my best.

Comforted as I was by the response, there was one unpleasant surprise awaiting my return. It was a letter informing me that a trial would be held on 28 October to decide the members of the Australian World Championships team. The first two male and female swimmers would form the long-distance team. I was ropeable. I thought I'd met the selection criteria twice already. The last thing I expected was to have my spot at the worlds under threat at this late stage. When I calmed down my coach, Bernie Mulroy, explained that there was no point kicking up a fuss. I would just have to go out there and do the job.

I must admit, it made for a fascinating situation. My sternest challenges would come from Susie Maroney, who had beaten me in California the previous year, and, quite possibly, my new training buddy, Tammy. The unknown factor was swimming legend Tracey Wickham, who was making a bid for the event under coach Laurie Lawrence. David O'Brien and Peter Galvin were expected to fill the men's spots (they did).

The trial took place on the Swan River and I couldn't have wished for a better outcome. I stormed down the familiar course to take first place and then watched as Tammy surprised everybody by claiming second place. It was the signal for a

joyous riverside celebration. Unfortunately for Susie, she wasn't
able to do herself credit. Still only in her mid-teens, I don't
think her body had a chance to recover fully from her record-
breaking Channel swim in August. As for poor Tracey, she was
never in the race after too much grease was applied to her suit.
It created such enormous drag that she wasn't able to complete
the swim. Her coach, Laurie Lawrence, was especially gracious
afterwards, telling the media that whoever beat me on 10 January
would be the world champion.

SHE'S LIKE A BULL TERRIER. WHEN SHE LOCKS ON, SHE JUST DOESN'T LET GO . . .
*When Laurie Lawrence came over here late last year, I said to
him 'you're going to see what tough is'. He coached Tracey
Wickham and no one could ever doubt her toughness in the
pool, but Shelley would swim through a tidal wave to get to
the line.*

NEIL BROOKS 1991

The 25-kilometre swim was now just two months away. All
in all, 1990 had been a good year and I felt comfortable with
the favourite's tag for the event. I was feeling less comfortable
by the middle of November, though, when my body began
playing tricks on me. Every time I tried to tumble turn I was
in agony. After a visit to the doctor it was discovered that I
had an ovarian cyst which had attached itself to my bladder.
There was a lot of yanking going on inside. I was quickly
admitted to hospital and the cyst was summarily removed. As
the swim was still eight weeks off there was no major drama.
The only problem was of my own making when I rushed back
into training 48 hours after the operation. To the surprise of
no one, I collapsed in the showers afterwards. It was a classic
case of overdoing it. I really need to be monitored sometimes,
because I've never been able to do things by half.

Once I was back on my feet, my preparation went smoothly.
My in-laws were wonderful through this period, bringing round
meals whenever they could, and others were offering support
ranging from free massages to free step aerobic classes. Neil
Brooks bobbed up to help me again and Peter was an absolute
champion throughout, backing me to the hilt and paddling

alongside me on the Swan on weekends as I familiarised myself with every aspect of the course. The only part of the course I stayed clear of was the last 200 metres. I wanted to save that for the day.

I was saving a lot for the day. It was as though all the years of training, all the hurdles overcome, all the people who had urged me on were pointing to this one day. And always there were the dying words of my father sounding in my head: 'You'll be a world champion one day. You'll represent Australia and win a gold medal.'

I wanted *so much* to win this for my father.

Christmas passed in a blur. I had far more important things on my mind. It was with relief that I finally checked into the team accommodation at the Orchard Hotel on New Year's Eve. I didn't want any more distractions. I didn't even allow Peter to visit. Nothing could be allowed to disturb my focus.

The Schnarrs—Nancy, Fran and Joe—were in town by now. They had come all the way from New York to be there for my big day. Nancy, who moved into the hotel with me, would be my trainer and Fran had packed her lucky shirt. The signs were good.

As if it were possible, my focus sharpened even further on the night of 3 January when I recited the amateur oath on behalf of all the swimmers at the championships' opening ceremony. I was in seventh heaven as I read the words aloud in front of 8000 people at the Perth Entertainment Centre. I no longer needed to pinch myself. It was really happening!

The only thing that remained was for Steve, my sports psychologist, to fine tune a few details. One of the unforeseen events which had emerged as a factor in the swim was the incredible number of jellyfish populating the river. Their numbers had swollen since the New Year, so Steve sat me down and devised a strategy whereby I was to consider the jellyfish my friends. They would worry the other swimmers, but every time they stung me they would be kissing me. Stinging me was their way of showing affection. And the more jellyfish there were, the better. There would be thousands of them coming out to cheer me on!

The days passed slowly. But it was well worth the wait when I woke up on the morning of 10 January and looked out on a beautiful Perth Thursday. I was positively buzzing when Neil picked me up at 5.30 a.m. to take me to Beatty Park for a warm up. I've never been more ready for anything in my life. As Jimmy Barnes was singing to me down my earphones, 'there ain't no second prize'. Too right, Jimmy.

The scene at the river for the 7 a.m. start was like a private reunion. Peter was there with his family. My family was there. Mal Brown and his family were in a boat for the day. Even my Arkansas coach, Sam Freas, was there in his capacity as the executive director of the International Swimming Hall of Fame. Sam had told me I'd be a world champion one day. Now I guess we'd find out. Ironically, the event was expected to come down to a race between me and the Americans, with Karen Burton my main competition for the gold. I suspect Sam had divided loyalties that day.

The course was a straightforward 12.5 kilometres downriver from the Burswood Casino and the same distance back. If I had one concern it was that 25 kilometres was a short race, a virtual sprint, for me. Nancy had never been with me on such a short swim, either. Rather than wearing competitors down over a distance as I usually did, I would have to set the pace from the start and hope that nobody had the speed to catch me at the end.

From the moment the gun sounded I made it my objective to get out in front and swim my own race. I'd let the other women worry about trying to chase me. Once in the lead my goal was to try to catch the men in front of me. I wanted the top men to be my pacemakers, and as soon as I passed one I wanted to overtake the next. If I could do that I would have the women's race in the bag. For most of the race the other coaches could barely hear themselves above Nancy's battle cry of 'Go get him, Shell! Get him now!'

I felt great. Everywhere I looked I could see banners exhorting me to 'Go well, Go Shell'. At some points people were only 15 metres away on the banks, cheering me on. On the water I had Neil close in attendance, wearing my Razorbacks hat while he filed reports for 96FM radio and Channel 10. As for the jellyfish, I took Steve's advice on board and they became a major positive reinforcement. I bit into one and had stings all over my body, but as far as I was concerned they were expressions of love. My competitors would no doubt be thinking otherwise. There was a limit to our intimacy, though. I was swimming in the new Australian team bikini, finally deemed 'morally acceptable' by FINA, and had drawn the bottom tight for fear of a jellyfish getting inside. Too tight, as it happened, because it was rubbing my belly button raw.

Sore navel aside, the race was going uncannily to plan. Not that it wasn't nerve-wracking. I just had to keep saying to myself, over and over, 'control, concentration, swim your race'. And I was. No one was making an impression on my lead. Then, as I approached the Causeway bridge on the home stretch, it began to dawn on me. They couldn't catch me now. I was going to win the gold medal. I could see people waving Aussie flags and hear them singing 'Waltzing Matilda' as I passed under the bridge. By the time I emerged from under the bridge my body was covered in goosebumps.

The emotions started to flow freely now. I could see tears running down the face of my boat driver, Noel Williams, as he sang along. Nancy had my Australian flag out and was waving it madly. I reacted by kicking my legs and I absolutely flew over the last stretch. Then, as I came into the finish, I started to think of my Dad. I had to choke back the tears as I hit the line in five hours and 21 minutes.

I'd done it, Dad! You were right. I'd won gold for Australia. Right then, I felt he was there in spirit. As I ran up the beach I was jumping up and down like an idiot. I was indescribably happy. I raced over and embraced Neil, who as a media representative was one of the few people permitted inside the finishing enclosure erected to keep the public out until after the drug testing. As Neil and I hugged I let the tears flow. He knew exactly what it was like to win a gold medal without one of your parents being there.

Amid all the tears, there's no denying it was one of the happiest days of my life. I was on an unbelievable high. No wonder they wanted to drug test me! I was high on life. The only downer was Tammy's sixth-placing, Americans having filled the two other medal spots. I tried to console her, but there's nothing much you can say at times like that.

When the testing and the media interviews were over I was finally allowed to see my family, Nancy and all the other supporters who had stuck by me through the tough times. They were still there two hours later when a medal presentation was held by the river. With the official presentation not due until the following evening, most people had wandered off. In fact, when it came time to make the presentation to Sergio, one of the men's medallists, he was nowhere to be found. The local Italian liaison officer had to stand in for him, which got a few laughs.

From there I put in a brief appearance at the Burswood Casino, where all the race organisers and volunteers were having a bash to celebrate the event's success. Later, the long-distance swim team had dinner with the rest of the Australian team at Pier 21 before returning to the Orchard Hotel. Still 'in camp', I had to kiss Peter goodbye at the hotel.

I wasn't ready to hit the pillow just yet, though. The adrenalin was still pumping through my veins and, with the aid of a magnum of champagne kindly delivered by the hotel management, I intended to make this day last a little longer. The only problem was that when I went in search of Nancy I found her dead to the world after her exhausting day. Tammy was nowhere to be found, either. Suddenly I felt terribly alone. All the phone calls had stopped and I was left among the flowers and the telegrams. This wouldn't do. I called down to the national team coach, Dick Campion, and asked if he and his wife Jackie would like to join me for a drink. They didn't need much convincing and we spent the next couple of hours raising our glasses and watching *Pretty Woman* on the in-house video channel. Sometime in the early hours we parted company and I finally fell asleep with the gold medal around my neck. So ended my greatest day.

The next evening provided the icing on the cake. We were to be presented with our medals at the Superdrome during the night's pool events. While I was waiting I got a huge buzz when Lisa Curry-Kenny came up and hugged me, saying I'd done an 'awesome job'. I was still buzzing when it came time to walk out for the medal presentation. The crowd went wild. I'd waited twenty years for this moment. To stand on the dais, watch the Australian flag go up and hear the national anthem was the thrill of a lifetime. All the hard years of training and competing were put into perspective as soon as the medal was placed around my neck. The tears were streaming down my face and my whole life was flickering through my mind.

At that instant I realised that the medal wasn't just mine. It belonged to so many people who'd helped me along the way, whether financially, emotionally or spiritually. The beauty was that most of them were there on the day, watching and swimming every stroke with me. They felt my victory too. In a letter to them all afterwards, I wrote that on such days they didn't need to be world champions or have a gold medal placed around their necks to feel proud to be Australian.

I was light-headed as I walked off after the presentation. As I passed Neil on our victory lap around the pool I threw him my bouquet in honour of his friendship and help. Shortly afterwards we hooked up and together with Nancy made our way to the VIP room where all the sponsors, officials and dignitaries were. Sam Freas and Bernie Mulroy were there and it wasn't long before I was enjoying myself so much Neil couldn't pull me away. I suggested that he should try to get all my family and friends to join us, but he reminded me that Peter was hosting a family barbeque back at our place and I was guest of honour.

It took some convincing, but eventually Neil and Nancy shepherded me to the car. We drove back to my house and, just as I opened the front door, the booming sound of Neil calling the last 25 metres of the swim burst through the darkness. When the lights came on I found myself facing a packed room of family, friends and everybody who was anybody from the long-distance swimming world. It was magic! There were even Channel 10 cameras there for a story they were doing. We partied into the night as I relished the moment and Peter played the host with consummate charm.

I had a permanent smile on my face for the last three days of the meet. As a hometown girl and one of the three Australian golden girls (Hayley Lewis and Linley Frame were the others) I was swamped by people wanting autographs every time I went to the pool. I was determined to enjoy my time in the sun, because I knew that it would all be consigned to memory in a few days. It also shielded me briefly from the knowledge that not much had really changed. I was due to swim in South America in a fortnight's time and I didn't even have enough money to pay for my airfare. Sponsors weren't exactly scrambling to sign me up and I was hurtling back to earth at an alarming rate. The main highlight in the wake of the championships was probably the opportunity to swim with dolphins (and satisfy a photographer by feeding them with raw fish from my mouth) in my role as spokeperson for Clean Up Australia Day. But that was hardly going to pay the bills.

That's where Dawn Fraser came in.

THE • MOST • IMPORTANT •
• SIX • INCHES

M Y GREATEST STRENGTH in the water has never been my arms or my legs. It isn't my heart or my lungs, either.

No, my chief asset has always been my mind. Or, as my sports psychologist Steve Cohen put it, 'the most important six inches of your body is the distance between your ears'. He wasn't just referring to me. The same stands for any athlete. Any achievers, for that matter.

Steve showed just how potent a weapon the mind is when he helped prepare me for my Channel and World Championships swims. In both instances he was able to put me at ease with my surroundings before I dived in the water. There's no question that my mental preparation for the world championship swim, when I associated the jellyfish stings with the affectionate kisses of friends, played a central role in my success that day.

WHAT SETS HER APART FROM HER COMPETITORS? HER MIND. SHE'S THE MOST *determined person I've ever met. If someone else is physically bigger and stronger than her, it doesn't matter. She is going to finish the same way as she starts, whereas their physical advantage will fall away if they don't have the mental strength to go with it.*

NANCY SCHNARR

Steve might have helped take the mind games to new levels, but I had long known that my competitive edge resided in my head. Ever since starting swimming I've had that tunnel vision and been able to stay focused on the job at hand by shutting out external influences. And when it comes to the swim itself, I've been able to use my mind to overcome pain and shut down emotions. If circumstances prevent me from achieving my original goal, I employ my mind to re-set my goals. If I hadn't set my mind on getting to France once the Channel record slipped away, it would have been all too easy to chuck it in mid-swim. Instead, I can look back on that day and say that I did my utmost in the conditions. As a result, I'm left with no lingering regrets. It's really just a way of turning a negative into a positive.

I approach my life outside the water in much the same way. After all, you can't hope to flip over to a positive frame of mind on demand. It doesn't work that way. Either you have a positive approach to life or you don't.

BECAUSE YOU'RE SO ALONE IN THE WATER YOU GET A LOT OF TIME TO THINK TO yourself. So you have to play mind games all the time, to stop yourself from getting bored and to switch off from those signals of pain that your muscles and your shoulders are sending you. You go through quite a number of brick walls, so to speak, and from the halfway stage on you're starting to really suffer. Somebody who can convince themselves after halfway that they're still fresh, which is what Shelley seems to be able to do, has a huge advantage. It's a 90 per cent mental game.

TAMMY VAN WISSE

My positive thinking extends to the way I cope with the pain that inevitably accompanies every marathon. It's the nature of endurance events that they test not only your physical capabilities but your ability to withstand pain. And I've turned controlling pain into an art form. Indeed, my pain threshold lies at the heart of my domination of other women over the years and helps explain why I have been able to challenge the men over longer distances. The second half of a race is when Shelley comes charging home. I don't believe I'm a freak in that area. It's no doubt partly explained by the tools women have been given to cope with the pain of childbirth. In my case, that natural asset has probably been enhanced by decades of coping with sometimes-debilitating back pain.

From the five years I spent in a brace as a child, to the car accidents (I've had four in all—what, do I have a bumper sticker saying 'Hit Me'?) and the collapse in Arkansas, my back problems have helped harden me to pain. It helps explain why, when I look like I'm going to collapse, I can push through. Instead of

I'VE SEEN HER GO THROUGH SO MANY HARDSHIPS AND ILLNESSES, AND YET NOTHING
*seems to faze her. I know that if my preparation isn't going to
plan, or I've got a pain in my shoulder, doubts start to creep
in. With Shelley, even if she's been ill or she's had a sore back,
she's always been able to compete at a very high level. It's almost
as though she has this amazing capacity to switch her mind off
pain and push her body to extreme limits.*

TAMMY VAN WISSE

letting the pain undermine me, I work off it. I turn it to my
advantage. Because I've often had to push through the pain
barrier, I can ask myself 'how much more can I make it hurt?'
It's not masochistic. It's a way of stretching my limits and finding
out something new about myself along the way. It's a way of
growing. It's also proved a way of winning.It's not just physical
pain, either. If I'm suffering emotional pain from personal sorrow
I'll turn that into a positive as well. In 1991 I was able to surge
forward in Sydney Harbour when I turned my thoughts to a
close friend's terminal illness. I thought that what I was going
through was nothing compared to what she was suffering. Over
the years it has shown me that being content is not always the
best way to extract the most out of my ability. Contentment
can sometimes be a sign of staleness.

Over my career I've had lots of painful races which have
tested my mental strength, right from my first one at Seal Beach.
But if there's one that stands out as an illustration of what I'm
talking about, it is the Lac St Jean race with Nancy in 1991.

The beginning of this race, where you start off in a river, is
notoriously chilly. I'd handled it the year before, though, and
since then I'd swum in 14-degree water in the Channel. I
figured I could cope. On this day, however, Lac St Jean turned
on a shocker. The weather was bitter and the wind was playing
havoc with the lake surface.

I started out well and was in fifth position, moving through
the pack, at about the three-hour mark. Then, for no apparent
reason, my stroke locked up. It was almost as though I was
learning to swim all over again. I felt as if I was going backwards.
The fact was, I was frozen. I felt ill and before long the Red
Cross rubber duckies were beginning to circle me. My distress

HAVING NEVER RIDDEN A BRONCIN' BUCK, I COULDN'T SAY EXACTLY. BUT THE WATER *was so choppy that's how it felt on the boat. I was flying up and down and literally had to hold onto a rope because I thought I was going to fly overboard. And that was the beginning of the race.*

NANCY SCHNARR

was so obvious that everybody felt I'd be out of there pretty soon. I looked at Nancy.

'I'm really, *really* cold, Nancy.'

'I know,' she said. 'Look. See that buoy over there? It's real close. We've got to make it to that buoy. It's our goal. You can do it.'

It really wasn't that close at all. Truth be known, it was right on the other side of the lake. But I was prepared to believe her. Just as I believed her when she said that the water would start getting warmer soon. It didn't.

'It's not getting any warmer, Nancy.'

'C'mon, Shell, you can do it. You can do it!'

'I don't know if I can, Nancy. I want to get out.'

She was taken aback. This would be the first time I'd ever pulled out of a race. She was worried about how my psyche would handle it.

'But Shell, you *never* get out.'

'I'm just not feeling good, Nancy.'

'I don't care. You're not getting out. We're going to make it!'

She was screaming at the Red Cross boats not to come any closer. As far as she was concerned, because I was still coherent I wasn't in any danger. It was just another test of my mental strength. So I started to swim again. I had to convince myself time and time again that it wasn't hopeless, that it would get warmer, that I would finish the race.

After a total of six hours I reached the other side of the lake. There were still four hours to go and I was gripped by the cold. I was pushing myself like I'd never pushed myself before. The water was still rough and we were now swimming into a stiff breeze. But, finally, my reward arrived. The water began to warm up a little and my stroke and rhythm gradually returned.

YOU'VE GOT TO REMEMBER THAT SHELLEY IS A FIRST IN MARATHON SWIMMING, AND a first in terms of women athletes. Although marathon swimming isn't a big sport, she has shown that women can compete against men in long-distance events. As a result, she has a reputation as being the toughest woman out there. It means she carries the weight of others' expectations. She would not only be letting herself down, but she would be failing them too. It wasn't a case of not winning, it was a case of not even finishing when she's always been in the top ten overall.

NANCY SCHNARR

Over the last couple of hours I was stroking powerfully enough to finish as the first woman and fifth overall. I had taken it to the limit.

The following year, at the same venue, I found there were barriers other than pain one has to overcome. After being hauled out of the water semi-conscious, I woke up to find that I was suddenly scared of cold water. With a race coming up at Lac Magog a week later, I now had a belief barrier to break through. Again, I think it's a testament to my mental strength that I went to Magog and won. It's a conclusion even the experts agree with, as shown by this excerpt from an article written by Martin Warneminde which appeared in *The Bulletin* in 1991:

Head women's swim coach at the Australian Institute of Sport in Canberra, Dr Ralph Richards, has no doubt that Taylor-Smith is a freak—he prefers the word 'atypical'. He . . . mentions that extra fat provides women marathon swimmers with more flotation and a better mechanism for regulating body temperature, but he sees her mental toughness as a crucial factor. Senior lecturer in sports sciences at the University of Western Sydney's Macarthur campus, Dr Gordon Treble, also refers to Taylor-Smith as 'one out of the blue' and 'a one-off' but he hopes he could be wrong. He says she exhibits indications of a superior 'anaerobic ability'—producing energy not dependent on her oxygen intake. He also believes her body has the capacity to perform well while the blood stream is, in effect, poisoned with an unusually high amount of lactates—the waste products produced when muscle metabolises.

Hmmm. I think I prefer the word 'atypical' too.

A • YEAR • TO • REMEMBER

I'M HARDLY ALONE among Australians in having enormous respect for Dawn Fraser.

She had always struck me as someone who never had it easy, but was able to keep conquering new mountains nonetheless. She appealed to me as a real doer, a woman of words *and* action. When Dawn spoke, people listened.

I was listening intently when I first met her in January 1990 at a function to announce the 1989 Australian of the Year. I was a finalist and Peter and I were seated at the same table as Dawn. I was so nervous that I blurted out some nonsensical words before her natural warmth put me at ease. We ended up partying late into the night.

I next saw her at Neil Brooks's wedding in Perth in September. I'd just come back from swimming the English Channel and had the World Championships trial coming up the next month. When we found ourselves at the same table again, we had plenty to talk about. Although Dawn had media commitments the next day we all got a bit carried away with the occasion and by the end of the night she was leading us all in drinking rounds of B52 cocktails. Here was my kind of lady!

It wasn't until the time of the World Championships, however, that I really got to know her. I was touched when she came up to me before the 25-kilometre swim to wish me luck. She knew the pressure I was feeling and really took over the situation, keeping other well-wishers at bay so as not to disturb my focus. Then, during the swim, she was on Neil's boat, cheering me on to victory. She must have seen something she liked that day because the following night, after the presentation ceremony at the Superdrome and a few beers in the VIP room, she said she had a proposal to put to me.

Dawn had been chosen to be the frontperson for a new sponsorship and management group interested in providing funding for athletes in still water, surf and aquatic events. The so-called Lane 4 Sports Foundation (lane four in the pool is reserved for the fastest qualifiers) had been set up in Sydney and Dawn had been asked to select and manage the athletes. And I was to be one of the first chosen. As it had been told to Dawn, they would be able to do big things for me. What did I think?

What else *could* I think? It was scarcely the sort of proposal a cash-strapped world champion turned down. The next day we met again at the Perth Sheraton and talked about where my profile should go from there. I was planning to give the world circuit a real shake in 1991 and it seemed like the ideal time to capitalise on my World Championships gold medal. If I couldn't make a go of it this year, when could I? If there was any mileage in being a top marathon swimmer in Australia, this was the time to find out. As Dawn saw it, the only thing holding me back was the fact that I was based in Perth. All the major opportunities existed on the east coast. I would have to consider moving across the country at some stage if I was to attract a decent sponsorship.

After Dawn returned to Sydney I was left to chew over our conversation. I knew she was right about the move to the east coast. But it was foreign territory to me. And what about Peter? My thinking was then interrupted by a more immediate problem. I was due to swim in South America later that month and I simply didn't have the money to fund the trip. I wanted Peter to come along as my trainer, too. It was time to ring Dawn.

Not to worry, said Dawn, she'd just write me a personal cheque for $9500 to cover our airfares. I would be able to repay the money with sponsorships she would find for me while I was away. It was like having a fairy godmother. The image was reinforced when we met up with Dawn on our way through Sydney. The Schnarrs were also in Sydney at the time on their way home to New York and Dawn promptly arranged for all of us to have dinner with her old pal, advertising guru John Singleton. Not just any old dinner, either. We received the royal treatment at the magnificent Manor House restaurant in Balmain. It was an unforgettable evening and the perfect send-off for what turned out to be one of the most extraordinary years in my life.

The year had already begun in memorable fashion as I bowed to accept the World Championships gold medal around my neck. But it was only the beginning. Before 1991 closed I was to win every swim I contested, become the first woman to win a major professional international marathon outright (one woman had won Lac St Jean back in the early 1960s, but it was from an invitational field of only six), claim my biggest payday in front of cheering thousands around Sydney Harbour and decide on a move east which would ultimately hasten the demise of my marriage.

For now, all that lay ahead of me as I flew off to Brazil to compete in the All Saints Bay 20-kilometre International Crossing. It was a grand name for a shemozzle of a race. After first visiting Rio de Janeiro, where the local authorities hoped to win approval for a World Series swim, we travelled down the coast for the 26 January race. The signs weren't good from the start. At the pre-race meeting the organisers virtually told the swimmers that their chances depended upon being able to hire the best boats and pay a generous fee to the drivers. I walked out in protest. Then, come race day, we had to hop on a cramped public ferry for the two-hour trip out to the island from which we were to swim back to the coast. On arrival the start was delayed for an hour as swimmers sweltered under their grease in the cloying 35-degree heat. When the pistol did finally sound, it was the signal for chaos.

Nobody was precisely sure where the starting point was. Nobody could identify their boats easily. It was just a mad free-for-all as swimmers plunged into the tepid water and hoped that their trainers would eventually find them. One poor Italian swimmer probably wished he hadn't found his boat. The craft, licensed to carry about ten people, was bulging with nearly 30. It had been transformed into a party boat, complete with drunken revellers. As he swam along they would take turns at leaning over the edge and urging him on in, with more than one gentleman losing his balance and tumbling onto his back. Goodness knows how many spiked drinks he had on the way across.

Meanwhile, back at the ranch, swimmers were spread across two kilometres of ocean. There were no buoys and little direction from the boat drivers. I ended up giving mine a spray because he had me swimming against the current at one point. When I did land on the beach I had no idea where I'd finished. After some discussion it emerged that I'd won, but I left feeling as though I'd just played a role in some comic farce.

From Brazil I went on to Santa Fe, Argentina, for the eighteenth Rio Coronda 57-kilometre International Marathon Swim on 3 February. This race was certainly more deserving of its impressive title. Not only did it have a rich history, but it was immediately clear that it was a significant local event. For all that and the carnival atmosphere, the organisation, while professional, still left room for plenty of uncertainties. Particularly for the women.

I was on a roll, however. Nothing, not even the dysentery I picked up along the way, could stop me. I won the women's section comfortably and, in finishing fourth overall, became the highest-placed woman in the event's history.

After returning to Perth, I flew to Sydney for the launch of the Lane 4 Sports Foundation at the Manor House restaurant. Along with ironman Guy Leech, I was to be the first recipient of a Lane 4 scholarship. Sunspirit Oils were backing me as sponsors and immediately made good their pledge by covering my debt to Dawn. It was all looking very rosy, indeed. Perhaps I could make a living out of swimming after all. I returned to Perth in good spirits and kept in touch with Dawn as contracts went back and forth and the possibility of moving to Sydney was canvassed again.

Nothing concrete had been decided when I headed off overseas again in July. I was to be taking on my most demanding schedule yet, with five swims lined up over seven weeks, including the Pan Pacific Championships in Canada. It was to be an amazing seven weeks.

I began with a win in the Capri to Naples swim before coming second overall at Lac Magog, bettering my own record with a time of 8:59:24. I followed that up with another win at Lac St Jean, though not before Nancy had to push me to my limits in atrocious conditions. I couldn't have been more ready for my return to Atlantic City after an absence of six years. There was only one thing bothering me. Since arriving in North America I could see that Fran was not well. As the weeks went by and she followed Nancy and I to Canada, I could hear the all-too-familiar rasp in her cough. When she complained of an ache in her side I really began to worry. It was Dad all over again.

Not to be daunted, Fran was there again in Atlantic City, cheering me on from shore with Joe and her son Billy. With Nancy in my boat I set out with the express intention of enjoying myself. My birthday had fallen the day before the race, so I was in celebratory mode.

I had plenty to celebrate, as it turned out. After negotiating the ocean leg I entered the back bays in fifth position overall, marginally behind eight-time winner Paul Asmuth. In short time I had passed him and moved into fourth place. This was feeling good. I moved up on and then passed men's world champion Diego Degano and James Kegley. With three hours to go I was in outright second place. Only American Jay Wilkerson was ahead of me now.

I don't think it had occurred to me yet that I was on the verge of making history. It was one of those rare days where I was enjoying the experience and feeling great. Ain't it always the way. Relaxed as I was, I soon found myself pegging back Jay's lead. All of a sudden I was alongside him and we were going for it. All Nancy could hear from Jay's boat was his trainer shouting 'Be the man, Jay, be the man!'

We were about two hours from the finish and it was stroke for stroke. Jay would go and I would catch up, I would go and he would catch up. And so it went, for kilometre after kilometre. Any time Jay would drop behind I'd shout to him to come with me. I knew we would produce something special if we continued to push each other. Then, with about three kilometres to go, Jay fell off the pace. I put my head down and swam away to win by 59 seconds in an outright record time of 7:12:34.

I had just become the first woman to win an open professional marathon. And broken the existing race record to boot.

In doing so I had clinched the No.1 women's world ranking for 1991 and moved into second place in the joint rankings. But I don't really think it had sunk in what I'd done. I *did* know there was a big buzz about the place afterwards. I ended up being taken to shows at all the casinos and one woman wanted my bathers for some museum. She hounded me so much that I eventually gave them to her. The night finished up at the local watering hole, the Irish Pub, where we partied until dawn. James Kegley and I were the last ones at the bar.

It wasn't all sweetness and light, though. Some of the male competitors wouldn't congratulate me after the swim and when we had a presentation breakfast the next day Paul Asmuth pointedly ignored me. That really hurt. The majority of men were fine. Claudio Plit, an Argentinian who is one of the old campaigners of marathon swimming, even came up with a special plaudit.

'You know, Shelley,' he said, 'you are very dangerous when you are wet.'

The tag stuck.

It even followed me across the Canadian border to Sylvan Lake two weeks later. The town, 120 kilometres south of Edmonton, was the venue for the 25-kilometre event of the 1991 Pan Pacific Championships. And it was here that Shelley Taylor-Smith t-shirts emblazoned with 'Dangerous When Wet/The World's Greatest Marathon Swimmer' first began appearing. They were the handiwork of one of the administrators who wanted to stir up some interest in the 25-kilometre event. He certainly stirred up a hornet's nest for me, as I'll explain later. Suffice to say for the moment that, after I won gold, Jay Wilkerson gave me a far-from-complimentary forearm salute. I'm glad to report he earned an official rebuke for his actions.

I got a rebuke of sorts myself on my return to Australia. Fresh from my gold-lined plunge into the world circuit, my marriage effectively collapsed.

The signs had been there for some time. From very early in the piece Peter wondered why I lived such a frantic life when, to his mind, no one cared about the sport. Whereas I was accustomed to waiting until the last moment to find out if my plans would come off (cashing cheques on the way to the airport to pay departure tax, that sort of thing), he found it all very tiresome. Why on earth did I put myself through so much pain for so little reward, particularly with all the struggles that went on over even the smallest grants? He simply couldn't understand. But to his credit, he continued to support me as best he could.

There was a limit, though. It wasn't his fault. As a non-athlete, it was very difficult for Peter to appreciate the sacrifices I needed to make in order to do what needed to be done. In fact, I didn't even see them as sacrifices. They were a necessary by-product of the choices I was making. When we originally moved in together in 1987 I'd told him that it wasn't going to get any easier if, as expected, there was going to be a 25-kilometre event staged at the 1991 worlds. I desperately wanted to be there and, in pursuit of that, I was going to get more tired, my sex drive would disappear, I would become more and more focused and be an ogre to live with. I wouldn't even have the energy to cook or lead a social life. I warned him that he'd want to kick me out on the street. And yet he still took me on.

It was for that reason that I toasted him on our wedding day as my No.1 supporter. He was the man who cooked for me, cleaned for me and loved me when no one else would. He was wonderful. His loyalty also meant he defended me, too, when others questioned what I was doing. Over time it became a different matter behind closed doors, however. He began to express his frustration more often and soon our disputes were spilling out of the home and into public. It's something I really regret, but if two people are incompatible it's probably inevitable.

Inevitably, Peter came to the conclusion that my swimming had taken over our lives. He was right, and it all wore a bit thin for him. The first signs that he was cracking came during our time in England for my Channel crossing. When he first arrived it was fine, but as the pressure mounted in the wake of several postponements we began to fight over the smallest things. It was tough, training day after day and waiting for the green light. Peter struggled to come to terms with my demands on him as my trainer. It's always a volatile relationship between a swimmer and their trainer and Peter couldn't handle me yelling at him. He'd say 'don't talk to me like that, I'm your husband', and I'd say 'you're not my husband right now, you're my handler and I'm the swimmer'. It was not a distinction he could grasp. Not to say that he didn't do his job. He was a great trainer. But it really took its toll on him.

The most obvious indication that he wasn't prepared to support my swimming forever came after the 1991 World Championships. Obvious, and yet I didn't really take serious note. It was at the surprise party at our house after the medal presentation. Peter was cooking at the barbeque when he was asked by a television crew what he thought of my success. He said it was great. Now he was really looking forward to life getting back to normal. Hopefully I'd quit swimming after this and we'd have children. The warning light was flashing.

At least now the debate was out in the open. We went off to South America together and batted the issue around between swims. Nonetheless, it was unresolved when he returned to Perth and I stopped off in Sydney for the Lane 4 Sports Foundation launch. He must have begun to wonder if I would *ever* quit. He was still puzzling over the situation when I flew out in June to chase the world circuit and swim in the Pan Pacs. Our phone conversations during that period became more and more strained as it became clear that our goals had diverged. I didn't know what I was doing wrong and I'm sure he felt the same. It was sad.

As far as Peter was concerned, it was also time for an ultimatum. Shortly after I walked through the door from Canada he told me he wanted us to have children. *Now*. I said I wasn't ready, and you could almost hear the straw breaking the camel's back. We'd run out of middle ground. Oh, we tried counselling and various other ways of reaching a compromise. But we were both so stubborn. The perfectionist in me couldn't accept that I might be wrong. I believed I was being asked to do something I wasn't ready for.

The consequences of holding my ground were grim, I knew that. Before things started going wrong I had everything I wanted. A loving husband. Fantastic in-laws who gave me the close-knit, loving family I'd been seeking. Now I was going to jeopardise all that. Yes, my swimming meant even more to me than that. My swimming *was* me. Without it, I felt I would lose my identity. And I couldn't do that before I had found another way to shore myself up.

As all this personal strife was unfolding, the Lane 4 arrangement looked to be coming together. Told I would be getting a $25,000 sponsorship under Dawn's management, I handed in my resignation at school and began to gear up for Australia's first major international marathon swim. The 30-kilometre Sydney Harbour International Marathon on 10 November presented a gilt-edged opportunity to lift my profile on the east coast and show my new sponsors what they'd bought into. The event would show marathon swimming at its best. One of the strongest fields ever assembled would swim off in picturesque Sydney Harbour for an overall first prize of $12,000, with $4000 going to the first female finisher. The swim would have extra spice because it would decide the final rankings for the year and go down in history as the last major race before the inaugural World Series.

Against that backdrop, Peter and I decided to go to Bali for two weeks' holiday in October. To give it one last try. But, as had happened so often elsewhere in our marriage, our agendas clashed. Peter, quite rightly, was in holiday mode, while I tried to squeeze training for Sydney Harbour into the equation. We were at crossed purposes once more. Bali was not about to provide the magic solution. Our marriage was clearly teetering on the edge of a precipice.

Back in Perth, I sent my first invoice to Lane 4 and merrily banked the cheque when it arrived. This was almost too good to be true. Someone was finally paying me to swim! A few weeks later I sent off my second invoice and counted the days until my next 'payday'. And counted. And counted. Assuming the invoice had been lost in the system I sent off another one. Still no joy. I called the Lane 4 office and left messages. They weren't returned. By now we were due to fly to Sydney for the race, so I figured I could sort it all out once I got there.

Things were looking good when the Lane 4 people provided me with a car on arrival. The various men in suits behind the Foundation were showing me around and making all the right sorts of noises. Then, with two days to go before the swim, Dawn sat me down at breakfast and informed me that the whole Lane 4 deal was about to collapse. My jaw hit the ground. I'd quit my job, I had no other income, I, I, I . . . The fact is, said Dawn, that we've both been taken for a ride. There was no money for either of us and the Lane 4 directors were saying they knew nothing about my $25,000 sponsorship. Just what the game was she didn't know, but she'd sure as hell be taking someone to court. Her reputation was at stake here. Hadn't she been the one out recruiting athletes? She was very apologetic. But it wasn't her fault. Unfortunately, I knew I wouldn't have the money to take anyone to court. I'd just have to wear it. I left breakfast with a very sour taste in my mouth.

There was only one way to wash it out. I would have to swim the race of my life in a couple of days' time. There was another incentive. Fran had just gone into hospital. It had been confirmed that she was dying of lung cancer. This might be my last swim while she was alive. I would dedicate it to her. I knew I'd win the women's section. It just remained to be seen how much I could push the men, including the favourite, my Australian teammate David O'Brien.

All considered, I felt remarkably relaxed come race day. Especially considering I was as scared as the next person about swimming in the (shark-infested?) harbour. But Peter was great, and we had a cheerful new addition to the team, Graeme 'Grub' Carroll. I had known Grub as a fellow swimmer at national championships and we had met again recently through our mutual, regrettable, association with Lane 4. We had also bumped into each other during the worlds in Perth and I had established that he was now a coach on Sydney's northern beaches. When the Sydney Harbour swim bobbed up I contacted him and asked if he'd care to help out on my boat during the race. Sure he would, although he admitted to knowing very little about the job ahead. It showed. He turned up with a six pack of beer, a book and an umbrella. Hah!

The race started at Manly Cove and travelled to the city's Darling Harbour, where we were to complete three circuits before returning to Manly. Stroking smoothly, I found myself gazing in awe as we passed beside the Opera House and under the Harbour Bridge. What a beautiful day to be out in the harbour! By the time we reached Darling Harbour I was the leading woman and sitting in fifth place overall. David O'Brien was leading the field and looked to have the race sewn up. Until I began my charge.

Leaving Darling Harbour behind, I began to mow down the men in front of me. Dawn was on her jet ski next to me, urging me on. Every so often she'd pick up her mobile phone, dial and speak rapidly down the line. She was talking to Nancy and Fran, propped up in her New York hospital bed in her lucky shirt. Dawn would tell Nancy where I was positioned and she would relay back whether she thought I was in good shape. It was crazy, emotional stuff. As I moved into fourth, then third, then second place, the pain subsided as I thought of what Fran was going through. This was *nothing* compared to her pain.

With two kilometres to go I was closing on David. Grub was going wild on the boat, giving a convincing impersonation of a shark alarm as we moved up behind David. The people in his boat were frantically waving him on and I knew then that he was fading. He began to follow his crew's eyes back over his shoulder and I could feel his energy just flowing back to me. To the sound of Grub's booming voice we hauled him in and took the lead. Feeling strong, I just powered home over those final kilometres to win by four minutes in a time of 6:59:38. This one's for you, Fran!

I was in rapture. I'd beaten the best men in the world, and I'd done it in front of an Australian crowd. By winning both the overall prize and the women's prize, I'd taken the sting out of the Lane 4 debacle. And along the way I'd just become the *overall* world marathon swimming champion of 1991, the first woman to top the joint world rankings. My 1991 tally was nine out of nine firsts among the women, two outright wins and two gold medals.

How to relate the full joy of that day? Well, obviously I wasn't the only one it made an impression on. A little over a month later Jeff Wells, one of the top sports writers in the country, felt disposed to pen these kind words in *The Australian*.

Swimmer Shelley Taylor-Smith gets this column's award for the year. No trophy, no trip for two, no gift coupons. Just a piece of fish and chip wrapper stained with admiration. Not even any great research—just a pull of the poker machine handle on the side of my head. The world of sport spins on a hundred reels and images flash by—the Rugby World Cup, the glorious campaign of Les Scheinflug and his Young Socceroos, Ian Baker-Finch at the British Open, Bart's quinella in the Cup etc etc. But when the pieces of one image come together the wheels suddenly jag back into a jackpot and we get a picture of Shelley grinding down David O'Brien—a little 30-year-old Perth woman chewing up the prime hunk of Australian distance swimming—in the inaugural 30km, $70,000 Sydney Harbour International Marathon last month.

We had heard of Shelley's victories on the world marathon circuit but nothing had quite prepared us for this. Shelley would annihilate the world's best in both sexes, then come home over the top of O'Brien like Kiwi charging home to win the Cup in 1983, and find herself at the top of the world ratings. Soon it was made official in the rankings that the top athlete in marathon swimming . . . was an Australian woman.

But I'm not sure if the historical angle even enters into it—and neither is Shelley. For me it was the day, the ambience, the way she did it—falling back to fifth and then, after making the turn at Darling Harbour, allowing the toughness of her mind to dictate to her body, and that precise, killing rhythm never faltering. For Shelley it was much the same. Winning was nice, but only part of 'having a good time'. Mostly she was happy to be there, achieving her personal goals, and if she beat the men, so be it. Maybe she was entitled to stand on Manly Cove beach like a monument to female achievement, waiting for the bronze to set on her costume—a Statue of Liberation. But she was too busy helping the shattered O'Brien, and her other friends and competitors from that strange society of pain, out of the water. Throwing towels around them, comforting them, helping to make them feel part of an occasion which she found thrilling.

Indeed I did, not least because of the fantastic media and public response. Up until that swim I don't think most Australians comprehended what level I was competing at. I may have won Manhattan outright four times and just come from winning a professional swim in Atlantic City, but Sydney Harbour was like a coming-out party. After that day I could see the difference in people's eyes. I had swum against the world's best and won. And if so many people could take an interest in this one-off swim, surely my ambition to make a modest living out of the sport wasn't beyond the realms of possibility? Perhaps I could even help achieve one of my other goals, that of getting the sport into the Olympics.

The implications weren't lost on Peter, either. As we were walking back into our hotel after the swim he turned to me and said I was right to continue swimming. He'd just seen me put in one of the most powerful performances of my life. He couldn't make me quit right now, not after such a soaring accomplishment. There was a tinge of sadness in his voice. The die had been cast.

We weren't about to let the moment pass meekly, however. Now was a time to celebrate. That night we proceeded to party in my hotel room with a whole group of people, including some of the Victorian Sheffield Shield players who were in town and staying at the same hotel. Dawn was right in the midst of it all. At one point she took me aside. By now I looked upon her as my idol, my mentor, my adviser and my big sister all rolled into one. That's why I listened intently as she told me that the time was right for my move to Sydney. The $16,000 I had won that day, far and away my biggest payday in the sport, would finance the move and give me a few months' breathing space to get established.

By the next day I knew she was right. I waited until returning to Perth before sitting down with Peter. I explained that I was heading to Sydney for my career. I had to do it and I had to do it now. It was clear that we had different agendas at the moment. I would have to take my chances in Sydney and hope that, somewhere along the line, reconciliation was possible. Peter agreed.

There was one dissenter. Neil thought I was making a *big* mistake. He'd become good mates with Peter and he told me straight out that our marriage wouldn't survive the split. I said it would be okay. I suppose I knew he was probably right, but I asked him to let me make my own mistakes.

Having made my decision, I was happy to accept a number of speaking engagements in Sydney which had followed my win. It meant some flying back and forth, but it was a good way to make contacts and get a feel for the city I would soon be calling home. It was on one such trip in December that I received an urgent call from Peter at Dawn's place. Fran had just died.

I became hysterical. It was like my own mother had died. I had to be sedated for the next couple of days and just shuffled around feeling quite cold and numb. Dawn took over the situation and helped steer me through it. She knew how much Fran meant to me and was able to share some of my pain. It was a devastatingly tragic end to a memorable year.

And a prelude to the roller-coaster ride I was about to experience in my years in Sydney.

THE • FEMALE • UNIQUE

IF THERE'S ONE ASPECT of my swimming that the media has been quick to jump upon it's my ability to regularly finish among the top men. Sometimes even beat them all. Manslayer. Rose among thorns. They love that stuff. I guess there's not many female athletes out there able to compete with men with everything being equal bar a few kilos and an extra layer of subcutaneous fat.

Funnily enough, it means far less to me than it does to everybody else. I really don't think about it that much. If I can say this without sounding too pompous, I've been beating boys and men all my life. From the age of twelve I was coming first overall in two-kilometre races. In five-kilometre races, if I wasn't fastest overall, I was second fastest. I was always the fastest female.

SHELLEY BEATING THE MEN HAS JUST GOT TO INSPIRE OTHER WOMEN, PARTICULARLY *in some of the countries we compete in where women are considered second-rate citizens. It's not a political statement by Shelley, though. She just loves to race and beat anyone.*

GRAEME CARROLL

It was never something I thought to brag about. In my efforts to extract the most out of my talents, boys and then men were my yardstick. As I grew older and began to compete in longer swims I put it down to the fact that after a certain amount of hours in the water the pain barrier became a factor. And I knew I had a high pain threshold. That, and the extra padding a woman carries, means that the gap between men and women narrows in endurance events.

For all that, there's still no way I can match it with men in any distance under 25 kilometres. Five hours in the water is not long enough for those natural advantages to kick in. I haven't got the speed in 'short' races to match it with the men, some of whom are just outside Olympic times in the 1500 metres. Beyond five hours, well, that's a different matter. That's when I come into my own. And I like to think that I do it in such a way that the guys maintain their respect for me. There's no strutting up and down or rubbing it in.

That's not to say that the men have always accepted my successes as graciously as I would have liked. My Egyptian friend in the 1988 World Cup comes to mind. There have been other instances, too, some amusing, some not so humorous. There was never any drama in amateur events. Four outright victories in Manhattan between 1985 and 1989 and nary a problem, although I once received a ripper of a letter from a guy I beat into second place in 1988. Seeking advice on a Channel attempt, he opened the letter by asking if I remembered him. He elaborated: 'I'm the guy whose ego you crushed and humiliated when you beat me around Manhattan.'

It wasn't until I started to finish in the top three in the professional swims, however, that I really began to tweak some noses. Most of the 'incidents' took place between 1991 and 1992, when I won three professional swims outright and managed a batch of top-five placings.

DO THE MEN REALLY ACCEPT BEING BEATEN BY A WOMAN? DEFINITELY NOT. THEY *might do the gracious thing and shake her hand after the race if they've been beaten, but inside they're absolutely devastated. A couple of the Italian men I know said they would be disgraced in their own country if she beat them.*

TAMMY VAN WISSE

The fun really started at Magog in 1991. In the lead-up to the swim, multiple men's world champion Diego Degano declared that he would quit swimming the day he was beaten by a woman. It was a bold statement considering that I'd come second overall at the same race the previous year. This part of Quebec was fairly liberated, too, so there was no shortage of women (and men) willing me to beat him on race day. As you may have guessed I did, finishing second overall again and shunting Diego into third place. You should have heard the roar as I was passing him!

When the press surrounded him after the swim he defended himself by saying that he'd only made the comment on the spur of the moment to help drum up interest in the swim. Now,

Diego is a nice guy. I was prepared to believe him and he never did it again. Which is just as well, because he followed me to the wall again two weeks later in Atlantic City when I won my first professional race outright.

It was in the aftermath of that win that things got a little ugly. I had travelled to Sylvan Lake, Canada, to represent Australia in the 25-kilometre Pan Pacs event. When I got there I found that one of the sport's administrators, Roger Parsons, had arranged to have t-shirts printed with the words 'Shelley Taylor-Smith . . . Dangerous When Wet/ The World's Greatest Marathon Swimmer'. His intentions were pure. Like Diego, he wanted to stir up local interest in the swim. The only drawback was that it was like a red rag to a bull. Jay Wilkerson, who I'd pipped at Atlantic City, was still smarting from being beaten on his home turf. And fellow American Chad Hundeby, the world championship gold medallist who didn't swim in the World Series, was fuming. It made for an interesting day in the water.

SHE'S PROBABLY BEATEN MOST WOMEN BEFORE SHE EVEN GETS INTO THE WATER, *unless you're particularly strong-headed and able to ignore her past achievements. She's seen as a bit of a freak and a one-off. She's very different to anybody else who's ever been out there on the water, male or female. But women have still gained something from her performances. It does lift your own expectations and ambitions. You might think of finishing in the top ten, for instance. So it has filtered down.*

TAMMY VAN WISSE

It was a tough outing for me. This was my eighth marathon of the year and I had enough on my plate trying to win the women's section without having to worry about proving myself against the men. There was one very fresh swimmer in particular, American Amy Dunleavy, and she managed to lead me at one point in the blustery conditions. I had to dig really deep to regain the lead and, in doing so, I swam past Jay in the last kilometre to finish fourth behind outright winner Chad.

Once at the finish I did the right thing by waiting for Jay to come in so I could congratulate him. It seems he was in no mood for sportsmanship. As I went up to him he just turned his back on me and told me to take a hike, in not so many words. Then, as I turned away, he apparently swung around and gave me the big forearm salute, complete with clenched fist. I was looking the other way, but when some Australian officials saw it they immediately went up to the American head coach and let him know what had happened. Jay was subsequently reprimanded for his actions, but I never got an apology.

The next race on the calendar was the Sydney Harbour marathon. It was satisfying enough to win it outright. But what made it doubly satisfying was that it propelled me past Diego Degano into the No.1 spot in the combined rankings for the year. Not that I had a clue what I'd done until Roger Parsons called with the official world rankings. The men had known after the race, but none of them had bothered to tell me. That was okay. Who was smiling now?

There won't be any more moments like it. Three months after the Sydney swim the men's and women's rankings were separated after a vote at the federation's annual general meeting. I don't imagine it was entirely coincidental.

THE FIRST TIME SHE WON OUTRIGHT THE FEELING WAS THAT ALL THE MEN MUST *have had a bad day and that it wouldn't happen again. When she did it again and again they were a bit more on guard. A lot of the males became very worried about Shelley before races, asking how she'd been training and what her form was like, because they were genuinely worried about being beaten. I think the moment Shelley catches up with men during a race now they're defeated in their own minds, because Shelley's strength really gains after the halfway mark.*

TAMMY VAN WISSE

Presumably there were a few men who took quiet delight in my failure to finish the World Cup swim in Lac St Jean in mid–1992 (more on that later). That would burst my bubble! I couldn't give them the satisfaction, though. Coming into the next swim at Lac Magog I was determined to put the World Cup behind me. A fourth overall placing put me back on track, although I wasn't ready to go back to Lac St Jean the following week to face the freezing waters again so soon. I would take a break instead to prepare myself to defend the Atlantic City title I'd captured the previous year.

The Atlantic City swim fell three weeks after the World Cup. Despite my showing at Lac Magog I was still shaken by the effects of my first DNF (did not finish). It had rattled me and I was more than a little edgy about the expectations that would follow me into this race. The swim had received an enormous boost when I won outright in 1991 and the organisers were intent on capitalising on the 'Shelley Taylor-Smith phenomenon' in 1992. Only I wasn't feeling quite so phenomenal at the moment.

My salvation came from the unlikely quarter of Paul Asmuth, the eight-time winner of this event who had snubbed me the previous year. It was his voice I heard as Nancy and I walked into the traditional pre-race press conference at the Taj Mahal casino.

'We all know Shelley Taylor-Smith's win last year was a fluke,' he was saying to the assembled media. 'It will never happen again. She just doesn't look like she's in shape.'

That was rich. I'd just whipped him two weeks earlier in Magog. Without batting an eye I took my seat on the platform and looked around. The first question was a predictable one.

Had I just heard what Paul said about me?

'Yes, I did. I guess everyone's entitled to their own opinion. I'll just have to let my swimming do the talking, won't I?'

Later, as we left the conference, I turned to Nancy.

'Know what, Nancy? I think someone just fuelled my fire.'

MOST WOMEN GET OUT THERE AND SEE WHICH WOMEN THEY'RE GOING UP AGAINST. *Shelley doesn't see it like that. She competes against everyone. She's out there to beat the best, which is the men. Her philosophy has always been to train against the men as well. She will jump in the lane with the guys and try to beat the fastest one. That's the standard she sets. It's something I've never seen before and I really admire her for that.*

TAMMY VAN WISSE

My competitive nature ignited, I was back to my old self on race day. As with the previous year, I found myself in fifth place overall as we completed the ocean leg and entered the back bays. And just like 1991, it was here that I overtook Paul. It was too good an opportunity to miss. Looking up, I caught Nancy's eye.

'Déjà vu!'

'Yeh, some fluke huh?' shouted back Nancy, just loud enough for Paul's boat to hear.

And I wasn't done yet. As we wound our way through the back bays I passed David O'Brien, then Diego and then Jay. I had hit the front and there were still three hours to go. The dynamics were different this time, though. Jay was overtaken by Diego and he chose to sit about 25 metres behind me instead of going head-to-head. The mental game had begun.

For more than two hours I clung to my lead, Diego always shadowing me. With three kilometres to go my shoulders began to feel the pinch. They were killing me. But there was no way Nancy would let me off the hook. Remembering the exhortations of Jay's trainer the previous year, she tried to lighten me up.

'Be the man, Shell!' she shouted. 'Be the man!'

It worked. You couldn't help but smile at the appropriateness of it all. With the tension slackened I tried to work through the pain. As I searched around for positive images I started to think about the gold medal Kieren Perkins had won the day before at the Olympics, and how much I'd love to win gold for Australia. I picked up my stroke again. And Diego finally fell off.

SHE'S BEEN TRAILBLAZING EVER SINCE SHE BEGAN MARATHON SWIMMING. SHE *shows to other women that we can do better than we give ourselves credit for if we set ourselves higher standards. She's never had those boundaries to her thinking, and it's set her apart from everybody else.*

TAMMY VAN WISSE

I won by a couple of minutes and bettered my one-year-old world race record. It was thrilling enough to have beaten Diego under such testing circumstances. But more than that, I figured no more guys would take cheap shots at me again. Think again. At the presentation ceremony the next day a few were still saying I'd just had a good day. They weren't about to admit I'd beaten them on level terms.

The woman who'd pestered me for my bathers for her museum the year before had no such qualms. There she was again, pleading for my bathers as a reminder of a blow struck for womankind.

Make that a soft blow, would you? Some of my best friends are men.

HEADLINING • IN • SYDNEY

I PACKED MY BAGS for Sydney in January 1992, leaving my husband and security behind. I'd just kicked off a whole new ball game of my own making.

Despite the buffer provided by my Sydney Harbour swim winnings, I was heading into uncertain waters. After building a good relationship with the Perth media, so vital for athletes in minor sports, I would be starting all over again in Sydney. The Sydney Harbour win had given me a foot in the door, but I knew it would take a long time to foster the sort of contacts I enjoyed in Western Australia. I was unquestionably now a small fish in a very big pond.

There were other considerations, too. I needed to build bridges with the education department if I was to get relief work. And I would have to go knocking on strange doors if I was to get any financial support from the state's sports funding bodies. I did have one ace up my sleeve, at least. I had been among the finalists again for the 1991 Australian of the Year (having previously been nominated in 1989) and had picked up the award for the 1991 Australian Female Athlete of the Year. A small fish, yes, but one with a few calling cards.

My first priority was to get settled in. I'd been helped immensely in this area by Grub Carroll, who had proved a real white knight since the prospect of moving to Sydney had been raised. His part in my Sydney Harbour swim might not have quite been the joy ride he expected, but he was still willing to add me to his training squad at the Warringah Aquatic Centre on Sydney's northern beaches. Although he was the same age as me, he'd already been coaching for eight years. He had a host of athletes under his ample wing, including water polo players, ironmen, triathletes and swimmers such as Commonwealth Games representative Brooke Hanson. Now he had a marathon swimmer.

It was also through a contact of his that I was able to find accommodation in the beachside suburb of Curl Curl. When a grant linked to the nearby NSW Academy of Sport came through, I began to feel that things were falling into place. It now remained to be seen how the relationship with my new coach would evolve.

Grub knew he had taken on a huge responsibility in adding me to his squad. Because I was a long way from home he knew I would be leaning heavily on him for advice and support. On top of that he was taking on someone who, at that point, was at the summit in her field. A reigning world championship gold medallist and No.1 ranked marathon swimmer in the world. It would be a tough act to maintain.

Happily, the relationship clicked from the beginning. Whereas some might have seen our identical ages as a potential problem, coaches being expected to exert authority over their swimmers, it proved to be one of our prime assets. I knew and respected him from his days as a national breaststroke champion. As contemporaries, we had shared experiences. We thought along similar lines and were able to communicate easily.

In no time we found that we had built a healthy partnership based on trust and mutual admiration. Discipline was never a problem, because I've always been highly motivated. I wasn't about to start shirking training now. If anything, I probably helped to organise *him* in some areas. In return, he helped teach me how to loosen up at times when my natural intensity threatened to work against me. He was like Neil Brooks in many respects, always the clown and the life of the party. A big kid. It was refreshing and fun to have him around.

The other important connection between us was our emotional attachment to swimming. Like me, Grub is very emotional. And knowing the role of emotions, he never tried to suppress mine. It became a key ingredient in our success over the next three years, as Grub graduated from my coach to my trainer (Nancy continuing to do the majority of North American swims). As we travelled to races around the world he could often be found in a worse state than me afterwards. If it was a bad day we would rival each other for the number of tears spilled. If it had been a joyous day, the tears of happiness would flow just as abundantly.

Ultimately he became a coach I felt I could call night or day. He became both a friend and a confidant. We were even roommates on tour. He has a *very* understanding girlfriend, Estelle, God bless her.

In the early part of 1992, it was still a case of getting to know one another. Soon after unpacking my bags in Sydney I was off to Argentina to hook up with Nancy for the first race of the inaugural World Series. It was a poignant reunion so soon after Fran's death. Nancy had made a pillow out of Fran's famous lucky t-shirt and it became my new mascot. I'm glad to say it had lost none of its powers. I won the women's section of the race in fine fashion.

Clutching my new pillow I returned to Australia to swim in the nationals at Manly Dam, just a short hop from home. I duly won the national title and, in doing so, qualified to represent Australia at the 1992 World Cup, to be held at Lac St Jean in early July. I had a few months to prepare and it was in this time that Grub and I decided he should make his debut as my trainer at the World Cup. It was to prove a significant decision.

Before flying to Canada I went to the Italian Riviera for the first staging of a World Series event over six days. The six consecutive swims took us 66 kilometres down the coast and carried me to another win. I then had to skip what turned out to be the last Capri to Naples swim in order to finalise preparations for the World Cup. I admit to being a rather reluctant participant. My main concern, as I'd expressed it to Australian Swimming, was that the 25-kilometre event would be staged in early July in a lake that normally didn't host long-distance swims until the end of the month because of the water temperature. Australian Swimming was satisfied everything was under control and that was the end of the matter.

Others weren't so sure. There had been 50 participants in the World Cup in 1988. When I turned up this time I found that only fifteen had made the journey, of whom just six were men. There was no disguising the fact that the concept had bombed. The truth was that with the World Series now up and running, the money on offer in Naples and the

25-kilometre event's place in the World Championships, there was no compelling reason for swimmers to front up to the World Cup. Besides, where would you rather be swimming, the warm waters of Europe (following the Capri to Naples swim another race was staged in Lake Geneva) or the icy waters of Lac St Jean? It begs the question why I was there. Well, I was representing my country, for one, and I never imagined the day I'd turn down that opportunity. Secondly, I'd signed a form agreeing that I would represent Australia when called upon. I don't dishonour agreements.

For all the reservations, it wasn't as bad as I expected when I got into the lake to train. The water was about 17 degrees in most parts and the sun was shining. You'd have thought I would have seen it coming. Sure enough, women's race day dawned vile (the men were to swim the following day). It was 12 degrees and bucketing down when the organisers made the competitors line up for the official presentation to the sparse crowd. As they slowly announced the nations we all turned purple in the stiff wind. We were thankful when we could finally jump into the marginally warmer water.

I was fired up by now. Even if the event had been undermined by lack of interest, it still represented a chance to win gold for my country. So when the gun went off I shot away downwind towards the first turn. I was churning through the water at a great lick, but not so fast as to miss the fact that it really *was* cold. With the wind chill factor it was probably in the vicinity of 13 degrees. I tried to shut it out, though, as I made the first turn well ahead of my nearest female competitor after 6.25 kilometres.

It was like turning into a brick wall. The vicious headwind was throwing up waves almost a metre high and the rain was now lashing into my face. Then, as I pounded my way ahead, I suddenly had to take evasive action as my boat veered crazily towards me.

'What's going on?' I screamed.

'Don't worry about it,' called back Grub. 'I'll tell you later.'

As I eventually found out, Grub, poor sodden Grub, had drunk so much coffee in an effort to keep warm that he was dying to take a leak. In the end he couldn't hold out any longer. As the boat battered its way into the wind he grabbed a bucket and got himself set up to have a pee. At that precise moment the boat was thrown up by a wave and he had to grab for the side of the boat. It was out of his hands now, so to speak. Next thing the unfortunate boat driver is getting sprayed with friendly fire. His spontaneous reaction was to duck for cover and, in doing so, the boat almost ran me over. Just another one of the dangers a marathon swimmer must face, I suppose.

Relieved to still be in one piece (though not as relieved as Grub), I resumed my steady stroke. Everything seemed to be going along as planned until I stopped unexpectedly at about the 10 kilometre mark and asked for a drink. Grub handed me a hot drink and I began to swim again. Not for long. I pulled up after a brief burst and said I didn't feel right. Grub reached out, gave me another drink and after that it all becomes very hazy.

I do remember starting to swim again, but it didn't feel like I was going anywhere. Soon my body began to lock up and then my brain did the same. Next thing I recall is gazing up to see a distorted Grub leaning over the edge of the boat, his bloodshot eyes appearing to burst out of his head. It was like looking at Marty Feldman through a fisheye lens. I was definitely out to lunch.

I've since pieced together the rest of the story. As I blundered on I apparently began to turn blue. At one stage I began swimming into the side of the boat, banging my head as the driver tried to avoid a collision. Not long after that, at approximately the halfway mark, Grub made the decision to pull me out. I'd been in the water for a little more than three hours and was still leading, but America's Karen Burton was poised to pass. Grub had held two fingers up and asked me to tell him how many. When he couldn't get an answer out of me he decided not to risk it. The instant he leant over and touched me I was disqualified.

It was a decision that possibly saved my life.

Sister Liz and me with our hero Dad as a sailor.

My husband Peter and me on the Swan River, preparing for the English Channel. *WA Newspapers*

Richard Kersh (*left*) is the man responsible for starting me off on a career in marathon swimming. Will Howe (*right*) believed in me and my potential, and paddled by my side during training sessions in Arkansas, US.

After my 1990 English Channel swim, the French spectators crowded around, inviting me to their holiday homes to shower and celebrate with them.

Neil Brooks and me checking the Swan River temperature while preparing for the English Channel in 1990.

Doing my usual and expected 'jig' after I won the Inaugural Sydney Harbour International 30 km Marathon Swim on 10 November 1991.

Celebrating with Dawn Fraser.

I SAW IT AS A HUGE RESPONSIBILITY TO PULL SHELLEY OUT OF THE WATER. BUT WHEN *I saw her blue lips and heard her blurred speech, I knew she was risking deep hypothermia. She was unconscious during the 15 minute trip back to port and I did my best to revive her by wrapping a blanket around both of us and holding her close. It was a very harrowing episode. I understood the aura Shelley had built up around her. She was considered invincible. And when you carry that sort of a reputation in sport, it is both a competitive edge and a personal triumph. That day she became human again.*

GRAEME CARROLL

It was about 90 minutes before I regained full consciousness. I was in the hospital tent and could hear a familiar voice. When I looked across at the next bed I saw it was Anita Sood, a swimmer from India, with her coach beside her. Anita smiled at me.

'Shelley, it's nice to know you're human after all.'

I didn't say anything. I just looked around and suddenly it began to sink in what had happened. I was lying in a bed covered in hotpacks. There was a whole bunch of swimmers there. It seems I was the fourth female to be brought in. A couple of minutes passed before I turned back to Anita.

'That's not really what I want to hear right now, Anita.'

Anita's coach, Carol Lee-Hetzel, was quick to reply.

'At least you're *alive* to swim another day.'

That hit me. Anita's best friend had died while attempting to swim the English Channel in 1988.

I just lay there, my misery growing as it sunk in that the others were still out there swimming. The tears rolled down my face. I could only think that, under my terms, I'd failed. I felt unbelievably guilty. I'd let Australia down and thought that I might never get to represent my country again. It wasn't good for either my reputation back home or the sport's, particularly with Australian Swimming. How would they feel about dipping into their coffers to send me to international competition next time around?

On a more personal level, I tried to digest the shock of having my first DNF beside my name. I *always* complete what

I start. I felt an enormous sense of failure. People in the sport had come to think of me as superhuman. Of my past twenty major swims, I'd won all but one. I suppose I'd started to believe their expectations were justified. I *was* superhuman, wasn't I? That's why I'd reacted the way I did to Anita's comment. It had suited me just fine to believe that I wasn't a mere mortal in the water. It had become part of my winning psyche. It had served me well to think that I could overcome all odds, that I could ride over everything and punch through all pain barriers. I had to believe that in order to remain at the top.

While I was grappling with all these thoughts Grub kept walking in and looking over at me. He couldn't bring himself to talk to me just yet. I could see tears running down his face. It had taken an enormous toll on him (he still gets emotional when the day is recalled). His first major race as my trainer and he'd had to make the decision to disqualify me. In the midst of all the emotion it was difficult to stay focused on the key point here. He'd saved my life. As someone skilled in lifesaving through his association with a surf club, he'd been prepared to take control that day. Anybody else who didn't know the signs could have lost me. Even Nancy worried about what she would have done in a similar situation. Would she have tried to push me a bit harder? It's all hypothetical. Grub *was* there that day and his action created a lasting bond between us. I was very lucky.

But at the time my thinking was jumbled. I was mad at myself *because* I'd lost control. As far as I was concerned it was a sign of weakness to let others have control of your life. It's only been in recent years that I've begun to appreciate that asking for help can be a sign of strength, rather than a weakness. On that day I walked out of the tent like a Christian entering a Roman circus.

Although the race was still going, eyes immediately turned my way. Up they came, one by one, to ask what had happened. They knew I wasn't a quitter, so why had I got out? I told them I hadn't got out. I'd been *pulled* out. Then the real crunch came. I had to watch the other women come in. I knew I had to be tough. As it happened, only four of the nine starters completed the race. The tears were streaming down my face as I cheered the winner, American Karen Burton, to the finish. I had a big lump in my throat thinking it could have been me.

As I stood there in the rain, Roger and Val Parsons, IMSA officials and prime movers behind the World Series, came up to me. I'd come back, they assured me. It wasn't the end. And yet I felt I'd just lost all the confidence built up over years in a matter of hours. I was no longer infallible. And I had a new demon to contend with. Cold water.

A marathon swimmer's battle with cold water is another one of the key mind games. Some succumb to it far more readily than others. Some thrive in it, and it's not just a matter of how much fat they're carrying for insulation. Cold water strikes right at the heart of your mental strength. For my part, I'd always managed to absorb its challenges and come out the other end. In the Channel. In Lac St Jean the previous year. But not this time.

I knew I had only one choice. The Lac Magog swim was scheduled for the following week and I would have to get myself ready for that. The longer I left my fear unattended, the worse it would become. The next week was spent analysing where I'd gone wrong (no obvious answer to that) and rebuilding my brittle confidence. By the time I stepped into the water at Magog I was a picture of grim determination.

I won. Both the race and the mental skirmish. In finishing fourth overall I had repaired much of the damage done at Lac St Jean. And yet I wasn't quite ready to return to the scene of my demise for the following week's World Series swim. That could wait another year. It was softly, softly for now. It was more important, having addressed the central concern, to keep going forward. I was still shaken and I wanted to use the Atlantic City swim in a fortnight's time to really get my equilibrium back. As it happened, that's where Paul Asmuth unwittingly came to my aid. In questioning my ability to win the race outright again he really rattled my cage. With personal pride at stake I was able to repeat my 1991 performance and bury the ghost of Lac St Jean. Still pumped, I went to Sylvan Lake the following week for a World Series event and won the women's section.

I got back to Sydney with a sense that I'd at least partly redeemed myself for my World Cup disappointment. Whether I had or not didn't really matter to my family and friends across the Nullabor, though. They were more interested in the redemption of my marriage. The pressure to return to Perth was constant. Where was this golden rainbow that supposedly awaited me in Sydney, they all asked? Where were the big sponsorships, where were the fawning media? They figured that since I hadn't set the place alight in six months I wasn't ever going to make it in Sydney. They just didn't appreciate that it would take years to build networks in a city the size of Sydney.

They meant well. It's the nature of friends and family to try to draw a husband and wife together when they see them drifting apart. They still believed that Peter and I could patch things up. The odd thing was that, since my move to Sydney, we'd been getting on famously. I suppose the heat had been turned down. When family and friends saw that the anticipated fireworks hadn't eventuated, I guess they started to think a reconciliation was on the cards. Hence the calls to come back to Perth. And I have to say, our amiable phone conversations had got me thinking too. Not so much about returning to Perth, but maybe our marriage wasn't *entirely* beyond salvation.

It was in that frame of mind that I eventually flew to Perth, but only for the Christmas–New Year period. While there I sat down with Peter and spelt out my feelings. I thought we could still make a go of it if he was prepared to give me until the worlds in September 1994. After that I'd be ready for kids. He didn't exactly fall over in his rush to agree, but I left with the impression that the door was ajar. I was wrong. I didn't know it yet, but the death warrant for our marriage had already been signed. I'd left my run too late.

Speaking of runs, my next stopover was in Argentina for the World Series final at Santa Fe. This was my infamous brush with the sewage plant at El Vado, the full import of which was brought home to me the following week over 88 kilometres in the Rio Parana. It was on shaky legs that I sped back to Australia mid-February.

And it was with a shaking voice that I listened to Peter over the phone on my return. I was due to travel to Perth the following month for the national championships and before I got there he wanted me to know that he was dating someone. I knew her. Sue had announced her engagement at our wedding and had since split with her husband Greg. Was it serious, I wanted to know? About as serious as it can be in three weeks, he answered.

I was crushed. It had only been a month since we'd talked about resuscitating our marriage. In the intervening period I'd written to say how excited I was about the prospect of really blossoming into a woman and having children. Now it was all to be nipped in the bud. I was just deluding myself.

Swallowing my pride, I went to Perth in March. The nationals were to serve as trials for Pan Pacs later that year and, with the 1994 worlds in Italy in mind, I didn't want to relinquish my spot as Australia's No.1 female marathon swimmer. I had something to prove after the World Cup, too. It was obvious that Peter and I had effectively split by now, but we were still able to put that aside as he drove my boat with Grub on board. As at Sydney Harbour, they were a good team. And as at the worlds in 1991, my in-laws cheered me on from shore. I won the swim by about half an hour from Melissa Cunningham, with the nearest male competitor 52 minutes behind.

There was no malice when Peter and I said our goodbyes. As much as I was hurting inside, I couldn't blame him. Indeed, I thanked him for his support over the years. I had plenty to think about as Grub and I flew back to Sydney.

As always, however, swimming soon consumed my thoughts. In June I headed off to the Italian Riviera for the six-day World Series event and it was during the time there that I helped hatch a plan to rescue the Pan Pacs. The 25-kilometre event was in severe danger of being dropped from the Pan Pacs program this time around because of the absence of a suitable venue in the host nation, Japan. There had been talk of staging the swim in Hawaii, but the moment someone mentioned sharks we all got cold feet. I thought I had the answer. Sitting down with some of the top American swimmers, I suggested we try to talk the Italians into staging a swim to trial the proposed 25-kilometre course for the 1994 World Championships. If we could convince them to do that, then we'd ask if the same swim could double as Pan Pacs.

Having settled on our plan, we approached the right Italian officials and laid out our proposal. They'd think about it. Meanwhile, we had to follow the World Series to North America. I'd won the women's section of the Italian Riviera race and I backed that up with a win in Magog. Then it was on to Lac St Jean for the first time since the World Cup. I was ready for it now. Despite hurting my shoulder when I collided with a log, I went on to win the race and reclaim the piece of my ego extracted by the lake the previous year.

A third consecutive outright victory in Atlantic City proved beyond me, but I did finish a respectable third overall in winning the women's section. I secured the same result at my next race, a 30-kilometre charity swim across Long Island Sound from New York to Connecticut to raise money for free cancer screening. The word had come through by now that the Italians *would* stage a trial of the World Championships course at Terracina, south of Rome, in September. And yes, we could use it for Pan Pacs. Excited to be getting a foretaste of the worlds, I decided to stay in North America to take advantage of the training options. That meant travelling across the continent and into Canada with my good friend and fellow World Series swimmer Kim Dyke. Basing ourselves in her home town of Victoria, British Columbia, we kept ourselves in top shape by training under Canadian national coach Ron Jacks. It says something about the fraternal spirit of the sport when two swimmers soon to face off under different flags can prepare together, doesn't it?

Before August was out I took my leave and flew to Italy. I wanted to get an early feel for the accommodation, figuring if I found a good room I'd put my hand up for it the following year. I was rewarded for my foresight by finding a great room in a hotel which had an oceanside pool right across the road.

My smugness was dented shortly afterwards, however, when I began to hear of Australian Swimming plans to dump the open water swimming committee. If they did that we would have to form our own body to promote the sport, a disastrous proposition considering the scant resources available. Australian marathon swimming was in great danger of being catapulted into the void. And me with it.

I tried to put such gloomy thoughts aside in the days leading up to the swim. At least I had superb weather to lift my spirits. Until the day of the race, of course. As the swimmers gathered in the morning to head to the starting point, the sun had disappeared behind thick, grey clouds and the rain was squalling in off the sea. By the time we got to the beach we were wrapped in fog. The organisers finally managed to herd our sorry hides into some sort of formation and with a bang the majority leapt into the water.

I was still standing on the beach with a number of swimmers. That was no starting gun. It was a thunderclap, for goodness sake. I turned to Karen Burton and Chad Hundeby and asked if they ever swam in lightning in America. No way, they said. I didn't think so. But there seemed little choice. The others were getting away. So in we charged.

Lightning crackled all around as Grub led me out towards the first buoy. I hadn't even made it before I got tangled up in a huge jellyfish stinger. I could see this was going to be a fun day. Sure enough, I was soon fumbling about in the dark as the fog closed in even further and the rain thrashed down. I couldn't see a darn thing and, in the confusion, I contrived to lose my boat with Grub in it. For all I knew he could have been fried by the lightning. Although it was 10 in the morning it was now so dark that the lightning was like someone switching a light on and off. It was positively eerie. And here was I swimming about in all this, lost at sea. I couldn't find my boat and I sure as hell couldn't see any buoys to guide me. This *was* a fun day!

To my eternal good fortune Grub eventually loomed out of the darkness. He was madly bailing water out of the boat and having some kind of day himself. With some semblance of normality restored, we set off again and began to rein in the pack. On and on we went in the elemental chaos, Grub shouting 'Go, go, go!' as I overtook one swimmer after another. Amid all this I began to wonder if it was worth it. Australian Swimming really didn't give a fig, did they? Why was I putting myself through all this?

They were hardly the sort of thoughts designed to carry me to victory. Fortunately they lifted just as the weather relented a fraction. We had rounded a cape against which the worst of the storm was venting its spleen. We still had to fight our way against the current, so it was no doddle. But as I settled into my rhythm I gradually got my nose ahead and went on to win the gold medal from Kim. I was aching all over when I crawled onto the beach. The jellyfish sting had left great welts across my body and the pounding waves had given everyone a torrid time. Worse still, the organisers had not done their homework properly and had us swimming against the current all day. A race which should have taken the leaders five and a half hours had taken seven and a half hours. Stragglers were still coming in at 9 p.m.

I'd done what I set out to do. I had won gold for Australia and I had triumphed on the course which would decide the 1994 World Championship. Yet my satisfaction was tempered by the sword hanging over the sport's head back home. It wasn't until I got back to Australia that my mind was put at ease. Long-distance swimming was on notice, but still within the Australian Swimming fold.

My marriage was not to benefit from any such reprieve. It was time to face the glaring truth. Our marriage was over. I filed for divorce that same month.

In hindsight, we should probably never have married. Peter's family didn't give us six months, saying that we were too alike. They were right. We were both strong-willed people used to getting our own way and we had differences of opinion from the word go. And although my wedding day was among the happiest days of my life, I had my reservations even then. Deep down inside I was worried that I was marrying for the wrong reasons. I was concerned that I was listening to too many people saying that I was 26 and nearly over the hill. The old security trap. I suppose I also felt I was never going to fit back into the Perth scene unless I had a partner.

It's not like I went out on a hunt. But when Peter came along we seemed to share the same goals. We were looking for partners at the same time and really thought we could make it work. We probably didn't examine our motivations closely enough. I don't blame anyone. It takes two to tango and Peter gave it his all.

As fruitless as it is to point fingers, I accept I made some miscalculations. I believed that if two people loved each other a marriage would always survive. To my mind that meant I could afford to put the marriage on the back burner for a while as I pursued personal goals. I can now see that I put *too* much energy into swimming and not nearly enough into my marriage. I now believe I should have put my marriage first. I should have worked harder to save it. I didn't realise that marriage, like a garden, needs to be nurtured, fed and watered constantly.

Without wishing to labour the point, I suffered from a problem commonly found in successful people. The inability to find a proper balance in your life. I can say, with some authority, that trying to find the correct balance when you're world champion is bloody difficult. As a friend said to me sometime later, I got an A in swimming and an F in marriage. They figured that meant I had a C average, which wasn't too bad!

I didn't see it that way back in 1993. For some reason the act of filing for divorce (and the discovery that Sue was pregnant to Peter) was a catalyst for one of the bleakest periods of my life. I found it one of the hardest things I'd had to deal with emotionally since my father died. For all that I tried to rationalise it, I found I was very sad, very bitter and very angry. I plunged into a dark pit of self-loathing and despair. I learnt from it, but not before I'd endured six months of anguish.

After filing for divorce I went downhill very quickly. I was distraught and more negative than I've ever been. We're talking serious depression here. It wasn't like I was going to jump off a cliff, but I had no drive to get out of bed. No drive to *live* each day, when I ordinarily squeezed as much out of each hour as was humanly possible.

Oh, I was still swimming, but Grub had to come and wake me up to get me to training. And I was still teaching. But I couldn't stop crying. I'd cry while I was driving to school. I'd cry on my way to the pool. I'd cry in my home. It was very scary. It didn't help that I was diagnosed with chronic fatigue syndrome at the same time. Who's to say where one ended and the other began? I do know this: the combination of mental and physical collapse took me places I never want to go again.

All this time, whether I liked it or not, I had a life to lead. I went back to Perth for Christmas, but I didn't make the best of company. Then, in February, I made my annual pilgrimage to Argentina for the Santa Fe and Parana swims. I had a *Sixty Minutes* crew in tow and did my best to put on a brave face. I've always been accomplished at suppressing my emotions when necessary, so I carried it off with some aplomb. One thing I *couldn't* hide was the pain I felt when my left leg was struck by a propeller during the Santa Fe swim.

The accident happened in the early part of the swim as my boat, with Grub in it, tried to steer a course through the tangle of spectator craft. About the two-hour mark one of the craft got too close and, as the two boats bumped, my boat's propeller was knocked towards me. Thinking of my arms first I pushed the boat away, but my legs were sucked into the propeller. The propeller blade sliced through the flesh beside my left knee. Grimacing, I decided to soldier on and try to keep the injury hidden from Grub. I didn't want him fussing.

After another two hours, however, it was apparent I was in trouble. My body position was out of whack and a bewildered Grub was coaching me, something he never does during a race. My leg was thumping from the pain and I was no longer floating high on the water. Finally, I had to tell Grub what had happened. After a quick inspection we decided it wasn't serious enough to pull out, so I swam on and finished the race as the second-placed woman. Still nursing my leg I went on to Parana the following week and came second in that race as well.

Perhaps the drama of those races helped snap me out of my funk. Or maybe my depression had just run its course. Whatever the reason, I began to take an interest in life once more on my return home. Now I look back on that period and can't believe that was me shut away at home, crying in my cornflakes. I don't really recall the details. I *do* know it was a nightmare. And yet for all that, it was also a very enriching time. With the help of a psychiatrist I went back to my childhood and found all this stuff I never knew was there. It helped explain why I was the sort of person I was. Having identified the connections and patterns, I could begin to change my destructive habits. My habit of bottling up pain, for instance. My need to be in control of all situations. My association of dependence with weakness. All sorts of things.

It was a hard-won insight.

I didn't have too much time to reflect on the discoveries, however. My immediate concern was to weather the usual bouts of diarrhoea and vomiting Argentina had bequeathed me. It was not a good time to be feeling this way, not with the world championship team due to be picked from the Australian nationals in March. Although I didn't see any real danger of missing out on one of the two spots up for grabs, I had particular reason for wanting to win the swim this time around.

A pretender to my crown had emerged in the shape of Melissa Cunningham. I first met Melissa, a young Queenslander, at the 1993 Australian nationals in Perth, where she finished behind me to be selected for the Pan Pacs team. She had gone on to claim the bronze medal at the Pan Pacs and had since moved to Melbourne to be coached by national coach Dick Campion. Dick knew all about my recent personal problems and had seemingly decided that I was on the slide. His new charge was being touted as the heir apparent and these nationals represented her first chance to depose me as the country's premier long-distance swimmer. I might still argue that there was a difference between 25-kilometre events and the longer true marathons, but such subtleties would no doubt be lost on most people.

The nationals were held at a man-made lake on the Gold Coast. With a world championship berth and my pride at stake I charged around the course to win the women's section. Melissa came in second, while David O'Brien and David Bates made up the men's team. With Dick as the team coach, we would all swim under the Australian flag at Terracina on 8 September.

Having repelled Melissa's challenge for the moment, I returned to Sydney to train for the World Series final, to be held on the Italian Riviera on 18 June. Just when I could have done with an uncomplicated run-in, the next couple of months threw me into a spin.

It started when an issue of *New Weekly* magazine hit the stands around May. Inside was a story that was to drive a wedge between Peter and me that may never be removed.

The messy saga had its origins in a discussion with my new management agency. Shortly after signing up with Markson Sparks I was asked if I had any skeletons in my closet that could be dusted off to generate the sort of publicity that might attract sponsorships. I asked what sort of things they meant. That's when they raised the circumstances of my separation. Was there anything unusual there? I explained that it was an amicable split and that the only thing out of the ordinary was that my husband was now going out with a former girlfriend of mine. It seemed harmless enough to me.

Not to others, it seemed. The next thing I knew I had received an offer to do a story with *New Weekly*. Before agreeing I spoke to two of my greatest advisers, Dawn Fraser and Rome Olympics gold medallist Kevin Berry. I'd met Kevin at the worlds in Perth in 1991 when he was media liaison officer for the Australian swim team and, as a fellow northern beaches resident, we'd become close since my move to Sydney. They both said they could see no harm. Dawn, who'd seen a few headlines in her time, just told me to remember that what's news today is tomorrow's fish and chip wrapper.

A deal was struck. I sat down with the reporter in December and explained how Peter and I had originally separated following my decision to come to Sydney to pursue my swimming. I told them how Peter and I were talking about reconciling at Christmas 1992, before I found out he was dating someone from our social circle. I related how shocked I was when I found out Sue was pregnant. I was also a little dismayed when I was subsequently told that they'd named their baby Tyler Smith. It was a bit too close for comfort. End of story.

Or so I thought. I didn't even twig when I was asked to help shoot the television commercial for the magazine. After all, my story *was* one of the exclusives. I wasn't at all worried about the subject matter, because I'd told the whole story very straight as far as I could tell. I'd even said that life was too short to hold grudges and that I didn't point the finger at anyone.

My complacency evaporated when I saw the finished commercial aired on Sunday night prime time. The voiceover went something along the lines of 'world champion marathon swimmer tells how her best friend stole her husband!' I almost choked. Then Wendy Harmer came on and said, 'I wonder if he was doing the breaststroke?' I couldn't believe it. I never said she 'stole' my husband, or that she was my best friend. The colour draining from my face, I reached for the phone and called my agent. Yes, he'd seen it. He was delighted. Don't worry, he said, it was just a little bit of journalistic licence. I emphasised that I'd never put it in those terms, but he was unconcerned. It would all be fish wrappers soon.

The magazine was due to hit the stands the next day. On my way to a training camp I stopped off and bought it. It was far worse than I imagined. Underneath the headline they had a sub-heading along the lines that Sue had had the baby I'd always wanted. I was gagging by now. Meanwhile, back at home, a friend had volunteered to stand by my answering machine to monitor the reaction. It was running hot, and not a lot of it was complimentary.

I never listened to the tapes, and I'm not even sure who rang, but it was mainly people defending Peter and Sue. And rightfully so. I was upset myself about the way the story had been presented. The reporter received calls as well, and she confirmed that I'd never said Sue was my best friend or that she had stolen Peter from me. The misrepresentations were the work of sub-editors looking for a punchy headline.

It was a valuable, albeit costly, learning experience. I haven't spoken to Peter or my former in-laws since. But, according to my personal philosophy, it was not a mistake. There *are* no mistakes in life, only learning experiences. I had told the facts, without vindictiveness. Others had twisted my words. As a consequence I learnt that you don't sell off details of your private life. They are too easily sensationalised, and the end result is a lot of pain and anger. What had been a fairly amicable parting was transformed into a bitter divide overnight. And it hurt me as much as it hurt Peter and Sue. I had been made to look spiteful, whereas I'm not the sort of person to resort to such things.

I was still reeling from the whole sorry episode when I received my second crushing blow the week before my scheduled departure for the World Series final. In the space of just a few days what was left of my mental preparation was blown apart. It was the Sunday night before my flight on Friday. I was in the shower at home, conducting my regular monthly breast self-examination. With cancer having claimed my father, Neil's mother and Fran, it was always in the back of my mind.

There. What's that? There was a lump in my left breast. Nausea cascaded over me. My palms began to sweat. It was the first time I'd ever found one. A million thoughts leapt into my head. Could this be it? Forcing myself to stay calm, I got out of the shower, dried off and picked up the phone.

I called a couple of girlfriends, one of whom was a nurse. Get it checked out straight away was their advice. I didn't need any encouraging. After telling Grub what was going on at training the next morning, I went to the doctor. After a brief examination I was assured that it was quite normal to find lumps in your breasts and that it was probably benign. They'd do all the tests anyway. I explained that I was heading overseas on Friday, so I was quickly booked in for an ultrasound and mammogram later that day. Despite all the soothing words, my throat was dry as I sat in the waiting room before the tests.

The mammogram was incredibly uncomfortable, squishing your boob into the machine. As the medicos disappeared into another room to study the results, I found myself doing sit-ups and leg-raises to take my mind off the situation. When the woman came back in it was to say they couldn't see anything untowards. Now for the ultrasound. Again they said they couldn't really detect anything conclusive, so I was given the results and told to take them to a specialist the following day. When I walked out I still didn't have the answer I was looking for. I wanted someone to tell me that it was definitely benign. Until then I couldn't relax.

By the next morning's training the negative thoughts were beginning to creep in. I couldn't psyche myself up for my main set and had to get out of the pool. Right there and then I burst into tears and let all my emotions flood out. As usual, Grub was wonderful. He sat down next to me and let me talk it through. I had always succeeded in turning negatives into positives, hadn't I? Why not now? When I got back into the pool I told myself to treat the session like it was my last training session on earth. I did personal best times, with the tears washing off my face.

The specialist couldn't give me a definitive answer, either. While the lump was almost certainly benign, I could take my pick of three options. I could forget about it (some chance!), have a biopsy taken that would provide an answer one way or another, or simply have it removed. I decided on door number two. He suggested that we do the biopsy as soon as I got back from overseas. Agreed.

One thing in my life *was* laid to rest that day. After a series of administrative cock-ups, my divorce was formally completed.

It was a subdued Shelley Taylor-Smith who went off to the 36-kilometre Super Finale Italian Riviera race. Once settled in I spent a lot of time with Kim Dyke, whose best friend had breast cancer at 23. After countless chats and no signs of change in the lump, I reached race day with my motivation intact. But even I couldn't have predicted my performance in the circumstances. I swam out of my tree, winning the women's race and finishing fourth overall to claim my second World Series title. Kim was my nearest female challenger, and she was fully 20 minutes behind me. Among the others in my wake were Diego Degano and David O'Brien. I was rapt.

It was a reasonably cheerful Shelley Taylor-Smith who returned to Sydney for a 10-day interlude. I needed to be. The biopsy was the most painful thing I'd ever had done to me. The lump was really fibrous and it took some serious slicing before they could extract a piece. Unfortunately, the biopsy was still being analysed when it came time to head off overseas again for what would be a 10-week trip leading into the World Championships. With a strict policy that results not be given out over the phone, I would be kept in suspense for more than two months. I was given another assurance that it was probably benign, and with that I flew to New York.

The idea was to train up to the Lac Magog race, swim there, and then progress to hard training in Quebec City. From there I would return to New York before flying to Italy to begin my final preparations for the worlds.

My program got off to a great start when I went up to Magog in the third week of July and broke my own women's race record by 23 minutes. I had come third overall in a time of 8:37:46 to win the race for the sixth straight year. By the time I arrived in Quebec City I could almost taste the gold medal awaiting me in Italy. I had blitzed the opposition in my two races since detecting the lump. If anything, it seemed to help concentrate my mind. That was until it started to grow. I had been pushing myself in the pool for a week or two when I noticed that the lump was getting bigger. With each succeeding day it increased in size until it was about the size of a 50 cent piece. I could feel it with every arm stroke and it hurt whenever I bumped into a lane rope. What had been irritating at first was now getting to be a worry. I hadn't expected this. What was happening? I could feel myself getting a little more stressed day by day.

My worries multiplied on my way through New York, in the most unlikely fashion. It was the taxi driver's fault. Let me explain. I've never been one to travel light, mainly because I carry all my equipment with me. The obvious result is a host of heavy bags. Now, with my bad back, I cannot risk lugging all my stuff around, so I always rely on someone else to do the lifting and dragging. On this occasion, when the taxi pulled up to take me to the airport for the flight to Rome, I found myself faced with a dilemma. The frail old driver couldn't have lifted my handbag, let alone hoist my bags into the trunk. There was no option. I had to do it, and the inevitable happened. I put my back out.

I was a bundle of misery by the time I arrived in Italy. My back was shot and I was more than a little apprehensive about what was happening with my breast. My spirits only improved when I checked into my hotel room in Terracina. I hadn't lost sight of why I was here. To defend my world championship title, no less. There was certainly no lack of incentive to get my mind and my body back in shape. The back would just have to be nursed. Perversely, the grief it was giving me went some way towards helping me forget about the lump in my breast.

At first, the back pain only inhibited my training slightly, but then, a week before the race, it laid me flat out for almost a whole day. It was just like the bad old days in Arkansas. My lower back had swollen into a big knob. It wasn't until late in the day that I was able to climb out of bed and go across the road with Grub for a short workout in the pool. I grimly did my laps and then got out, the pain nibbling at me as I went for a shower. Just then I was intercepted by the team manager, Chris Guesdon.

'Shelley, I've got something to put to you.'

He didn't get much of a reaction. I was only interested in a hot shower, a massage and bed.

'I've had a phone call from Evelyn Dill-Macky (president of Australian Swimming),' said Chris. 'She wants to know if you'd like to carry the Australian flag at the opening ceremony.'

A smile burst upon my face.

'Really?'

'Yes. And you'll be leading all the countries out because Australia is at the head of the parade as the next host country.'

I said I would be honoured. It would be the thrill of a lifetime. It was also something I needed to hear right then. In one fell swoop it had swept away all the negative thoughts I was accumulating. I got another boost the following morning when Nancy flew in from New York. I now had both Grub and Nancy in my camp for this swim, although Grub would be the only one on my boat. Things were looking up. Was it purely coincidental that my back started to improve from that day? As for the lump in my breast, I felt a lot better after I had a heart to heart with Grub, Nancy and Kim Dyke. I decided to put my fears in a little black box and lock it away until the time was right. I'd always been good at doing that with my emotions and, as I saw it, there was no point in wasting energy over something I couldn't change. If the lump was malignant there wasn't much I could do about it at the moment. Besides, if it *was* malignant, surely someone would have made the effort to contact me. So I assumed the result was favourable, and focused on the job ahead.

I'll never forget the opening ceremony. We had to drive the couple of hours up to Rome in a bus, with me lying down in the aisle (my old Arkansas back-saving trick). When it came time to carry the flag out with water polo captain Ray Mayers, another member of Grub's Warringah stable, I was bubbling over with pride and excitement. It left me buzzing and extremely positive. Now I was ready to swim.

The 25-kilometre event was not for a few more days. In that time it became a ritual at our hotel for all the swimmers from the various nations who were staying there to crowd around the television after training and watch the events in progress in Rome. We'd all boo the Chinese women whenever they won (there were no Chinese long-distance swimmers). And every time there was a medal ceremony, Grub would nod at me, indicating that was where I'd be shortly. I'd get goose bumps at the thought and go to sleep dreaming about it. The night before the race we had our usual tactical discussion and I made my usual round of phone calls to family, friends and advisers. I reached my former coach Bernie Mulroy in Perth.

'Remember, Shelley,' he said. 'Most of the competitors will be with you for the first third of the race. Some of the competitors will be with you in the second third of the race. *No one* will be with you in the last third.'

I hoped he was right. The next morning I woke to look out on a gloriously clear, bluesky day. It was Perth all over again, even if Jimmy Barnes had given way to Tommy Emmanuel on my Walkman. I still figured they'd be playing my song at the end of the race.

The women had to wait around at the race start while the men were sent off first. Who would challenge me today? Kim was a threat. Hungary's Rita Kovacs was a chance. Ann Chagnad, of France, would be there or thereabouts. And then there was my teammate, Melissa Cunningham. What would she pull out of the hat today?

The familiar crack of a starting pistol and we were off. For the first two kilometres the pack stayed together before splitting into two distinct and parallel lines. I was leading out the first line and an American swimmer was doing the same to my left. As we rounded the first buoy the lines should have broken up under FINA rules designed to stop swimmers drafting behind other competitors. It didn't happen. I had Rita tucked in right behind me, letting me do all the work while she enjoyed my wake. Grub was spitting chips, but to no avail. The same thing was happening with the other pack ten metres to my left where Ann Chagnad had taken the lead and had another swimmer snuggled in behind her. Unless the organisers intervened, there was nothing we could do about it. 'Just black box it, Shell,' I kept telling myself.

By the time I reached the 10-kilometre buoy, Rita was still there on my feet. I had the outright lead by now, but over the next kilometre Rita made her move. She went past me, and I didn't have a response. By the 12-kilometre mark she had sprinted away to a clear lead. We still had half the race to go, though, and I figured if I kept my rhythm I'd come back at her. We had now turned around the cape and were heading straight down the coast to Terracina. This was where I had made my move in the Pan Pacs the previous year. Not this time. Rita held her lead and then extended it to 200 metres. For the first time it crossed my mind that I might not win the gold today. It was a bitter thought.

There was no time to dwell on it. The next thing I knew Grub was shouting out to let me know that Melissa had passed Ann and moved into third place. She was gaining. It was time to pull out all stops. Grub reached into his bag of tricks to try to humour me and I turned my mind back to the basics. Focus. Forget about the others. Maintain your stroke rate. Keep your rhythm. Suck in the pain and use it. Swim *your* race.

Melissa went past me, with her Australian flag flying high.

I had a lump in my throat as I realised I couldn't go with her. I could only watch as the silver slipped from my grasp as well. I was jolted back to my senses when Grub shouted out that Melissa was challenging Rita. Yes, that's right. Melissa was going to win another medal for Australia. I had to look upon my bronze as possibly contributing towards us winning the team gold. And I had to accept that I wasn't good enough today, that Melissa had bested me fairly and squarely. It wasn't easy, I admit. It had all happened so quickly. Now I just had to concentrate on staying positive about getting a bronze.

Melissa did the business. She passed Rita to win gold and I followed them to the finish in third place. After touching, I kept my head under the water for a long breath. I wanted to compose myself, acknowledge that the gold medal had eluded me and present a gracious face to the crowd. When I did look up I could see they were trying to gauge my reaction as much as I was trying to gauge theirs. I finally broke the ice by shrugging my shoulders, smiling and waving to the two Canadian coaches, Ron Jacks and Eric Isbister, who had been great mates over my years on the circuit. I don't think it was quite what they expected from a race favourite who had just been comprehensively beaten.

It certainly wasn't what the media expected. As I climbed out of the water the cameras crowded around me to ask what had happened. Yes, Shelley, what *happened*? I told them. Hey, I wasn't good enough on the day. I was really happy with my bronze medal and I was delighted that Melissa had won the gold for Australia. Together with the men's performances it meant we had won the team gold. And yes, I *was* pleased with my performance. I had given it my all. You can't do any more than that. I didn't tell them that, true as that was, it hurt like hell.

More particularly, I didn't give them the answer they were really searching for. They desperately wanted a *reason* why I hadn't done as well as expected. It would have been so easy to suggest that the lump in my breast was an unwelcome distraction. But I knew where that would lead. With the amount of publicity given over to breast cancer in recent years, it would have instantly been turned into a major theme. What I might have offered as a consideration *in* my performance, as opposed to an explanation *for* it, would read like an excuse. Worse still, it would be used to take some of the shine off Melissa's gold. That would be both unwarranted and unfair.

When the media scattered I saw Grub in the background, crying. I couldn't afford to let my emotions show just yet, though. Dick Campion came up at that point and I gave him a big hug of congratulations. His own swimmer had won gold and the team had done likewise. It was a great result for him. He responded by telling me how much my contribution to the sport had helped pave the way for the likes of Melissa and David Bates. I had to go off to drug testing soon afterwards and it was there that I found Melissa. I gave her a hug, too, and told her how happy I was for her. She had definitely earned her success that day.

Back in the safety of my hotel room, I finally let all my pent-up feelings flow out. It wasn't that I was critical of my effort. It was just that a bronze medal was never in the plan. I had really believed that I would be celebrating my second World Championships gold medal. Now that I wasn't, I could open my little black box. When I had dried away the tears I picked up the phone and dialled my doctor's surgery back home. I wanted to make an appointment for the moment I reached Sydney so we could discuss the biopsy result.

That same night I had to attend a barbeque put on for all the swimmers by the town. As I wandered from group to group, happily discussing the race, Kim came over and told me that the other swimmers couldn't believe how well I was taking it. I explained that I was genuinely satisfied with the bronze. I'd had a lot of trials over the past year and, under the circumstances, I had no complaints about my performance. The acid test would be the medal ceremony at the pool in Rome, but when it came around I didn't find it too painful either. I was really quite at peace with myself, knowing that I'd done my best. Under my definition of winning, that counts for as much as coming first.

Even so, I was anxious to return home. I was one of the first swimmers out of Italy, arriving in Sydney on a Tuesday morning. My doctor's appointment was on Thursday and it was then that I finally held the biopsy results in my hand. The lump was benign. Those were the words I had waited more than fourteen weeks to hear. Relieved as I was, the lump's growth was still a concern. The doctor and I decided it should be taken out as soon as possible, so I booked in for surgery the following week.

The reception on my return had been surprising, to say the least. There wasn't one phone call from friends. At first I was worried that people didn't want to know me because I hadn't won. Then I realised that they just didn't know what to say to me. On the Friday night I went to a testimonial dinner for rugby league legend Johnny Raper and everyone was tip-toeing around me. It seems I was declared off-limits because people didn't know whether to offer condolences or congratulations.

I was still being avoided like the plague when it came around to checking myself into the hospital the following Tuesday. The surgeon was fabulous. He kindly offered to make the incision where it wouldn't show above my bikini or bathers and assured me everything would be fine. It was. When I woke up I was told I could leave when I wished. Just like that. I promptly checked myself out and drove the five minutes back to home. It was official. I could now get on with my life again. I had conquered that hurdle and I was ready for my next challenge now.

I had to laugh the next morning as I watched the *Today* show. Liz Hayes was explaining how exercising three hours a week was supposed to reduce the chance of breast cancer by 30 per cent. Six hours' exercise a week was reputed to reduce the risk by 60 per cent. I could only think that, by working out six hours a day, I must have reduced my chances of getting breast cancer by more than 400 per cent! After my Argentinian experiences, it was nice to know that the sport had contributed *something* towards my well-being.

As was to be expected, in time word started to get out about my brush with the spectre of breast cancer. The story finally came out in Sydney's *Sunday Telegraph* newspaper. And, boy, did it come out! On the front page on rugby league grand final day, no less. It was weeks since the World Championships and everybody's mind was on the footy, but I suppose breast cancer was very topical. In no time the story was picked up by other media. When it went national on Channel 9 the cat was well and truly out of the bag.

I'd told the *Sunday Telegraph* that my bronze medal was as good as gold to me after everything I'd gone through. I also said that the experience had altered my outlook on life. My priorities had changed. I was no longer so worried about getting due recognition for my achievements. And I no longer had a feeling that I owed the world something. From now on I was determined to look beyond swimming for a sense of fulfilment. And I was truly overjoyed to be alive. I'd wake each day passionate about the hours ahead. I couldn't contain my enthusiasm for life.

The phone started ringing off the hook after that. Everybody just *knew* there had to be more to the story when they saw that I was happy with a bronze medal.

With my life now back on an even keel, I began to consider my next move. Despite missing out on the gold in Italy I had retained my No.1 world ranking for the seventh successive year. There weren't too many challenges left on the world stage. Perhaps it was time to start thinking about opportunities closer to home. It seems I wasn't the only one thinking along those lines.

The idea of swimming from Sydney to Wollongong was hatched by Des Renford and Kevin Berry. Both Kevin and Des believed I needed to boost my profile in Australia by swimming locally. It was all very well to be known as a world champion, but Australians hadn't seen me swim first-hand since Perth and

Sydney Harbour back in 1991. As Des argued, it would be good for the sport *and* Shelley Taylor-Smith for people to see me do battle with cold water and the elements.

The plan was hatched in November. After pondering it for a while, Des had decided that my best option was to take on his own Sydney-to-Wollongong mark of 27:30:42, set way back in 1974. I was game. It seemed like a great chance to start 1995 off on a good note after my rollercoaster 1994. But not everybody was so keen. One of my key advisers said he couldn't think of anything more boring than watching someone swim from Sydney to Wollongong. I patiently explained that people wouldn't look upon it as someone rolling their arms over for hour after hour. They would be swept up in the bigger picture. The scale of a woman against the open sea. The very *thought* of swimming between the two cities. To my mind, Des had hit upon a winning idea.

The idea was one thing. The cost and logistics involved in staging such a swim were another matter altogether. After a preliminary meeting with my management we began to get a feel for the magnitude of the project. We'd need a shark-proof cage, a pilot boat to tow it and rubber duckies to act as support craft. And those were just the core requirements. There would be a thousand other tiny considerations, from expert tidal advice and mobile phones to lighting and food for the support crew. All up, we would need to find in the vicinity of $30,000 before we could get the attempt off the ground and into the water. While the search for sponsors got underway, Des would research the building of a shark-proof cage and Kevin would liaise with the Maritime Services Board to find the best pilot boat. Lindsay May, navigator for Sydney–Hobart contender *Brindabella*, was also enlisted to investigate the tides and plot the best time for the swim. When Lindsay came back to us we pencilled in 10 January as our target date.

I felt like a target myself shortly afterwards during a stopover at Melbourne airport. I'd bought a local paper and found myself reading a diatribe from Melissa directed at yours truly. The gist of the story was that I had used the breast cancer scare as an excuse for my performance in Italy. I couldn't believe it. I'd said all along that she was the best on the day. There was obviously some bad blood developing here, and I didn't feel it was justified. It was doubly worrying for me knowing that Melissa was coached by Dick. After all my efforts on behalf of the sport in Australia, it didn't seem right that the national coach's swimmer should be taking a shot at me.

It was not much later that my agents received a phone call from Melbourne. Would I be prepared to go head to head against Melissa in Melbourne in January, with the winner taking $20,000? No, I wasn't. I was already committed to the Sydney–Wollongong swim. The idea was flawed, anyway. If it was a question of trying to settle who was the best swimmer, as far as I was concerned that had already been decided. Melissa was the best over 25 kilometres at the time and I was the best at true marathons, that is, every distance in excess of 25 kilometres.

The exercise did at least provide me with some proof of my changing attitudes. There was a time when I would have been upset by the presumption of a less experienced swimmer giving me only four weeks' notice of a challenge on her own turf. Now I was able to just brush it aside. That clinched it. As Grub observed, I really *had* changed.

What hadn't changed was the situation regarding sponsorship of the Wollongong swim. There was none. It had been a month since our first meeting and there was barely a month before the swim was meant to take place. We had made all the right contacts, but we lacked the money to fire the whole thing up. We would need a lucky break soon or we'd have to look at a postponement.

The lucky break came in the second week of December. I hadn't been intending to go to the Christmas function that night. A last minute change of mind and I was soon enjoying a drink with the No.2 man at GIO Australia, John Crawford. What was I doing with myself these days, he asked? I told him about my planned swim. Interesting. What would GIO have to put in to become a minor player? I threw out a figure and he nodded thoughtfully. Half an hour later John reappeared at my elbow. What would it take for GIO to be a *major* player? I stayed calm and tossed another figure at him.

'We're in.'

Don't you just *love* corporate heavyweights!

All of a sudden the flame had been lit. The cage was built to Des's specifications, a pilot boat was hired and the Kiama Surf Club agreed to provide two rubber duckies, complete with crew. The support team swelled. Kevin had put me in contact with an events organiser, Wayne Staunton, who proved to be a genius at taking care of all the details. Grub would be a key player. Tammy was to come up from Melbourne. Two of the guys I trained with, former ironman Graham Bruce and Warringah Aquatic teammate Ben Davies, would be there. A good friend, Andrew Goldrick, was also drafted into the team, as was the curator of Manly Oceanworld, shark expert Ian Gordon. That was a story in itself.

I had introduced myself to Ian after hearing him speak about sharks during a function at Oceanworld in November. As he was talking, I found myself looking over to the Heads and imagining swimming out through them on my way to Wollongong. My palms began to sweat at the mere thought. After explaining to Ian what I planned to do, I confessed that sharks were one of my greatest fears in life. People were always surprised that a marathon swimmer should be worried about them, but I always thought it was one of my few normal characteristics.

After assuring me that they wouldn't bite (sure, they all say that), Ian ended up saying he wanted to get involved in the swim. I was more than happy to have him along. A month or so later he made an even better offer. Just when we were scratching our heads for a publicity angle, Ian came up with the idea of me swimming with the bronze whalers and grey nurses at Oceanworld. At first I told him he had to be joking, but before I knew it I was preparing to join Ian, Grub and a photographer in the tank.

I couldn't believe I was doing this. They even made me sign a disclaimer just in case something went wrong! I was a mess of nervous giggles by the time I slipped into the tank and promptly forgot everything Ian had told me. My only solace was that Grub had a bit more meat on him. I figured the sharks would go for him first.

With a large audience gawking through the glass we got ready to do the shots. I had to dive down holding my breath, but the first time I bolted straight back to the surface. The second time I wrapped myself around Ian like an octopus as soon as a shark came near. Finally, though, I started to relax. It wasn't easy. Everything I'd ever been told about sharks suggested they'd tear me to shreds as soon as I came into view. Ian was re-educating me, however. They'd just been fed, so they weren't on the lookout for food. They were just minding their own business. In fact, the only time we got a reaction out of them was when we got face to face with one and eyeballed him. Suddenly there was a sound like a gunshot (it was the dorsal fin flicking) and he careered away. I kicked madly for the surface and the photographer dropped his camera in a similar dash. Ian joined us soon after.

'What was all that?' I spluttered.

'You just invaded his space,' laughed Ian.

By the time we got out I was buzzing. And ready to face the open sea alone.

We were still racing around madly a few days before the official press conference on 6 January. Phones and faxes were running hot and the to-do list never seemed to get any shorter. But it all seemed worth it when the press conference went ballistic. The media just jumped on the whole idea and blew everybody concerned away. Some people had severely under-estimated the swim's appeal, although I was never one of the doubters. Television channels clamoured to get footage of the swim, radio stations primed themselves to give regular updates and the print media was no less keen. The way it was shaping, people would get to follow the swim stroke by stroke. One of our main challenges now was to round up enough mobile phones to cater for all the interest.

As the storm raged around me, I tried to stay calm. It was one thing to find that you'd pushed the right button. We had certainly succeeded in turning eyes my way. But now I had to deliver. Record-breaking attempts are fine when you actually break the record. They often go pretty limp when you don't.

We were due to start from Watson's Bay at 3 a.m. It was a warm, still and starry night as our little circus set up outside Doyle's seafood restaurant. A lovely cocktail of nervousness, adrenalin and exhilaration was coursing through my veins. Then we were away. Wollongong or bust!

Bust. I had only been swimming an hour or so when the nausea began to strike. I wasn't even in the open sea yet! Although we couldn't be sure, the most plausible explanation was that I was getting poisoned by the exhaust fumes from either the pilot boat or the rubber duckies. As though that weren't enough, next thing I knew we hit a swarm of bluebottles. They were virtually flying through the front of the cage and hitting me in the face. I think I may have even got one inside my mouth. It was hellish.

I stopped. I just managed to tell Tammy that I thought I was going to be sick when I vomited. After a couple of deep breaths I started again, but it wasn't to be for long. A few minutes later I had to stop in a fit of vomiting. I wasn't at all cold, but I started to shake like a leaf. That was enough for those on the boat. A quick discussion and the signal was given. It was over. I was plucked out of the water and transferred to the pilot boat for the trip back to Watson's Bay.

When we arrived I was taken inside the local angler's club. I went straight to the toilets and got my head over the bowl. When my stomach was empty I stood under the shower for an eternity. I was in a daze. When I emerged I was given a cup of tea and promptly threw that up before finding somewhere to lay my head. I was out to it for three hours.

When I woke it was to face the press inquisition. I was drained. How could I explain it? Well, it was out of my control. Between the nausea from the fumes and the bluebottles my body had said 'enough!'. Would I be trying again? You bet, as soon as possible. There was no hiding my enormous frustration at the chain of events, but I was determined that it would only be a temporary setback. Plans were quickly made for a second attempt a week later and the build-up started over.

It was a very, very long week. With the level of expectation now cranked up through the roof, I found the pressure almost unbearable. What had begun as a venture to announce my rejuvenation was threatening to turn into my funeral notice. The thought of a second failure terrified me. So much so that every time I went near the sea I got anxiety attacks and felt like I was going to throw up. I had to be force-fed all week because my appetite had vanished.

The night before the swim I watched a film called *Iron Will*. A line from it stayed with me. 'When face to face with your fear, trust in your maker and He will guide you.' I figured I might need a lot of trust and guidance the next day.

Tuesday 17 January dawned clear and crisp. We were to be setting out from Watson's Bay shortly before 6 a.m. and, once through the Heads, would be searching for a favourable current to speed the way to Wollongong. We'd made a few adjustments since the first attempt. The tow rope from the pilot boat had been lengthened from 30 metres to 60 metres and the rubber duckies would only be coming close in to feed me. Grub had organised a kayak so that he could paddle close by. We'd also added some shade cloth to the front of the cage to keep bluebottles at bay. I'd taken the extra precaution of wearing stockings, too, so as to reduce the risk of stings and sunburn. Finally, I had only a light film of grease on because I didn't think water temperature would be a problem. How wrong can a girl be?

The early part of the swim went off without a hitch. We cruised out through the Heads and into the open sea, where my earplugs helped me keep my sense of balance in the rolling waves. What a sight it was, swimming through the Heads with the sun rising. This was one of those times when I felt merged with nature.

Heading south, I took in the familiar landmarks, from the lighthouse atop South Head to Bondi Beach and coastal suburbs. Our main priority now was to locate the current, and about the three-hour mark we hit paydirt. We were right on course. The only surprise was the water temperature. It seems that such strong currents draw up cold water from the ocean depths and

I was soon feeling the change as we hit patches as low as 12 degrees. Nobody had warned Lindsay about *that*, otherwise we might have been better prepared.

I had already put on some rubber booties to stop my feet being cut up by the back of the cage. It seemed I might need more than just booties to survive in this water. I stroked on, trying my best to shut out the growing pain and cold. By the fourth hour the cramps were starting to set in and the muscles in my legs, pelvis and stomach were playing merry hell with me.

Worse still, it was becoming increasingly tricky to co-ordinate signals from the cage to the pilot boat so that we could manage the feeding sessions in the strong current. I was being tossed around the cage so much that my stockings had been ripped to shreds. Andrew and Ian had to perch on the inflatable fenders just to try to stop me from banging into the back of the cage every time we stopped. The last thing I fancied was getting cut up and leaving a trail of blood in the water. Diving with the sharks at Manly Oceanworld and swimming along like human burley were two different matters altogether!

Of course, this was all great theatre for the television crew as they darted around in the rubber duckies. If Australians were ever going to get a sense of what it's like to swim in the middle of the ocean, this was it. Judging by the way the mobile phones were being tossed around, the whole venture was having an impact somewhere. The support crew simply couldn't cope with the number of calls flooding in from radio stations, friends like Dawn Fraser and Kevin Berry, family members and, at one stage, the Prime Minister. Swimming legends Murray Rose and Jon Konrads even took time out to offer their best wishes.

Back in the water, I was feeling the pinch. The water cascading over the front of the cage had been alternately warm and cold at the start, but it was now unrelentingly icy. It was like having a bucket of icewater tipped over my head every ten seconds. After thousands of buckets my head was aching horribly, my feet had gone numb and my chest had tightened considerably. My stroke lost all its flexibility and, with that, I felt like I was swimming on the spot. Then the images of 1992, when Grub had trawled me out of Lac St Jean, began to creep into my mind. I dreaded the thought of lapsing into a comatose state again.

By the sixth hour of the swim my body temperature had plummeted. Instead of taking Tammy's advice, I elected to keep swimming without a wetsuit. By the seventh hour I couldn't hold out any longer. I wriggled into a wetsuit and donned a thermal cap, but I'd left it too late. Hypothermia had already begun to play with my mind.

As I took each breath I could feel my subconscious beginning to play mind games. Look at them. There was Tammy, working on her tan. And Grub, chatting away loudly between large mouthfuls of pizza. I wanted to shout at them. Hey, what about me!? What am I, some sort of sideshow? Look at *me*! Watch out for *me*! Share *my* pain! I'm dying in this freezing water and you're treating it like a holiday cruise. Twice I had to be convinced to keep going as the sun disappeared behind steel-grey clouds. And all the while I could hear the support team singing '99 bottles, sitting on the wall, 99 bottles, sitting on the wall, and if one of the bottles should accidentally fall, there'd be 98 bottles, sitting on the wall' etc. etc.

I couldn't quell the crazy thoughts in my head. I figured everyone was getting a kick out of my misery. It wasn't fair. I wanted to be in the boat. Then the voice began to sound in my head. Quit now. You don't need to prove anything to anybody. You don't need their approval. Just tell them you've given as much as you can and you want to put an end to this torturous pursuit right now.

The carping voice gradually wore down my will. I can *do* it. I can *do* it . . . I *can't* do it!

We were more than four hours short of Wollongong when I stopped (not that I knew it at the time). I had been going for roughly eight hours now and I wanted out. There should be no argument this time. The way I saw it, Grub had to decide between my safety and chasing the record. It should have been straightforward. But he was stalling. Tammy and Graham Bruce jumped into the cage to talk to me. My lips were blue, my eyes were all puffed up and my teeth were chattering. My face muscles were shivering uncontrollably with the rest of my body.

Grub looked towards land, where he could see the escarpments which signal the start of the Illawarra region. He knew we were on course to more than halve the record.

'Look, Shelley, there's the hills! We're almost there. Can you see the hills?'

I turned and squinted towards shore.

'I can't see them, Grub. I can't see them. P-leeease, Grub, let me out. Why can't I get out?'

I felt like a small child asking why she couldn't have a lollipop. Grub was saying no way and looking at me like a stern teacher (hey, I thought *I* was the stern teacher!). I couldn't look at him any more. Someone here must see reason. I swivelled to Graham.

'Please Brucey, *let . . . me . . . out.*'

No reaction. I looked at Tammy. Surely she'd understand.

'Tammy, I want to get out. *Please* take me out, I don't want to do any more. I'm really hurting.'

Tammy looked back at me for a while, and then turned away.

IF YOU'D SEEN HER IN THE WATER SHE WAS A MESS, AN ABSOLUTE MESS. AT ONE *stage she was cold and crying and wanted to get out. I couldn't handle it. I ended up breaking down and crying, because I've been in that situation before. I knew exactly what she was feeling. My heart went out to her. I wanted to get her out, but luckily Grub was there.*

TAMMY VAN WISSE

Won't someone listen to me? My tears began to mingle with the seawater. By now I was bunched into foetal position at the back of the cage, Grub's eyes burning into me. I looked straight back at him.

'Okay, Shelley, if you want to get out, there's the boat. I'm not going to help you. You can *swim* to it.'

The pilot boat bobbed on the swell 60 metres away. I looked back to Grub. The anguish must have been written all over my face. He chose the moment to jump into the cage and hold me

With my Australian flag after I won gold at the 1991 World Championships.
John Fairfax Feature Bureau

With my mum Irene, who has taken up swimming recently and shows great potential in the pool and ocean.

With John Newcombe (*left*) and former prime minister Paul Keating (*right*), receiving an Australian Achiever award as a finalist for the 1991 Australian of the Year.

24 September 1993: that great morning when Sydney was told that it would host the 2000 Olympics, I was there as a Sydney 2000 Ambassador with other great mates from the Australia Day Council.

On the Sydney to Wollongong swim Tammy van Wisse feeds me while my cage-man expert Andrew makes sure the cage stays afloat. *New Weekly*

With legendary coach Graeme 'Grub' Carroll after I won gold at the 1994 Australian Nationals and the World Team trials.

With my 'sister' and handler-trainer Nancy Schnarr. We had a unique winning relationship. Nancy deserved the gold medals and credit just as much as I did.

close. He wanted to gauge how cold I was and I vaguely remember him feeling my face, arms, legs and back. Lifting my goggles, he looked hard into my eyes and then grabbed me by the shoulders.

'Look at me, Shell. Look at me! How many fingers am I holding up?'

My immediate thought was, 'Not again!' He'd done this at the World Cup. Not that I remembered it, I was so zonked out. But, hey, it did get me out of the water that time. Here was my chance. I only had to say three or keep mum and I'd be on my way home. It was so tempting.

'How *many*?' insisted Grub. He was getting anxious now.

Don't ask me why. But somewhere from the recesses of my mind a tiny, honest voice broke through.

'Two.'

There, it's done. I'd missed my chance. Now I'd just have to start swimming again. Grub pulled the goggles back down over my eyes.

'Goggles on, head down, butt up. Now go! Give me twenty minutes and I'll let you out.'

I forced my arms back into a stroke as the team all began to cheer and chant. They were with me stroke by stroke now and I could see on their faces that they were feeling my pain. There were tears aplenty and I finally felt that they were all on my level.

I KNEW I HAD TO HOLD IT TOGETHER. IT MADE IT SO MUCH HARDER THAT I COULD *feel her ice cold skin and her pain. It's not easy playing God.*

GRAEME CARROLL

I knew this would be my last fling. If I stopped again it would be for good. If I stopped again it would probably mean that they needed to defrost me. I hadn't been swimming long, though, when everybody suddenly started shouting wildly at me. I tried to make out what they were saying.

'Shelley, Shelley! Look, there's *dolphins!*'

'Where are they, where are they?' I shouted back.

Then I saw them. There was a pod of about twenty, swimming around and under me. I could see them blowing bubbles into the cage and eyeing Grub and Ian Gordon when they dived in to take a closer look. I thought back to the movie *Iron Will*. These creatures were like an answer from God. They were messengers, sent to remind me that I was part of a greater scheme. I no longer felt so alone. My pain dimmed.

Meanwhile, everyone else was going ga-ga! I felt like joining them shortly afterwards when the sun finally pierced the clouds and we broke free of the icy current. With the water temperature rising, I began to loosen up. My rhythm returned and the mood of my entourage lifted accordingly. They found their voices again and began to exhort me to greater effort. With the dolphins in our team, we were unstoppable.

After 90 minutes my dolphin escort veered away to sea again. They had done their job. I was stroking easily by now and Wollongong was within striking distance. As the kilometres fell away we attracted a new escort in the form of paddlers, kayakers and boaties. With Wollongong Harbour approaching everyone began counting off the distance to the landing. Our navigator's calculations showed we had travelled 79 kilometres since leaving Watson's Bay.

Five hundred metres from the beach, Grub said I could leave the cage. I had a fleeting thought that it'd be just my luck to run into a shark this close to the end, but I shrugged off my wetsuit anyway and started swimming to shore. As I got closer I could see the water getting shallower and clearer. Finally, I felt the sand between my fingers. I couldn't believe I'd made it. What a feeling! And what an amazing team effort from a group of people who'd hardly known each other a few months earlier. I tried to stand up but my legs were shot. I'd already warned Grub and Tammy that I'd need some help and they appeared at my side to lead me towards the welcoming party. The stopwatch halted at 6.19 p.m.

I had smashed Des's record by more than fifteen hours in posting a time of 12:24:07. More importantly, I had shown to myself and the Australian public that the 'new' Shelley Taylor-Smith could still do it.

Not that everybody was prepared to believe it. Of all people, Dick Campion chose to come out in the press and label the whole swim a farce. His argument was that the cage offered unfair assistance and that the swim had not conformed to FINA standards or rules. No one ever said it was conforming to anybody's rules. I had merely set out to swim from Sydney to Wollongong, using a cage designed according to the advice of the record holder. In fact, just about everything we had done was in response to Des's advice.

It was, at best, an ill-advised outburst from Dick. At worst, it was a churlish comment from someone who was meant to be promoting the sport, not deriding it. Others clearly took the same view when Dick subsequently lost his position as head coach of the Australian long-distance swimming squad.

By far the majority of reactions were positive. They were probably best summed up by leading sports journalist Mike Hurst, writing in the *Daily Telegraph Mirror* two days after the swim.

> Taken at face value, Taylor-Smith's swim appears superhuman. Perhaps it was, but her time could not be ratified as any kind of FINA 'world record' because conditions vary for marathon courses. Just as Steve Moneghetti can at best run a marathon 'world best' because road courses vary by elevation, surface and route, so do marathon swimming courses vary. Suffice to say Taylor-Smith holds the best time for swimming from Sydney to Wollongong thanks to a generous current, the skill of her navigator in locating it, and the courage and conditioning of the woman who refused to quit when the sea turned cruel . . .
>
> To the rest of us it was all about the challenge, the attempt, making the distance, defying the odds, pushing the limits of human endurance and mental resources. Taylor-Smith dared to confront all these boundaries and she succeeded in a way which was inspirational and a tribute to all those who facilitated her performance . . .
>
> By her effort this week Taylor-Smith proved again the capacity of great sportsmen and women to inspire their fellow Australians to find more in themselves.

To find more in themselves. Yes. I like that.

A • FISH • CALLED • SHELLEY

JUST WHO IS Shelley Taylor-Smith? Olympic gold medal winning swim coach Laurie Lawrence gave his assessment at a fund-raising dinner in early 1995. His poem was simply titled 'Shelley'. As you can imagine, his delivery was anything but simple.

Oh! Shelley Shelley! I saw you on the telly!
Heard a Dick from the south! Run off at the mouth.
Said that your shark cage pulled you along
when you swam 90k to Wollongong!

For seven years you've won the marathon crown
Guess it's time some bastard pulled you down
They won't mention your ability to endure pain
To swim through storms and driving rain
Or your induction into the Hall of Fame.

No! They won't mention
Nine dreadful hours in that stinking polluted Argentine river!
Losing control of your bowel, affecting your liver!
Nor the blood-sucking leeches! The five days in bed . . . then
    race 88k!
Are you right in the head?

Oh! Shelley Shelley! I saw you on telly!
They say you're addicted! Obsessed! Mad crazy!
But I haven't heard anyone say that you're lazy!

And I know you're not the kind to boast
But in New York you're the toast
of the town!
You wear the crown!
Manhattan Island! A four times winner!
The record too.
Shelley, is there anything that you can't do?

Oh! Shelley Shelley! I saw you on telly!
The night pitch black, the water grey
A bobbing lantern to show the way.
A nine hour ordeal in the freezing cold
How could anyone be so bold?

And so
You swam from England to France
If it had been me, I would have pooed me pants!
But now
Now you want to swim both ways
If you miss the tide it'll take three days
For most people one way's enough!

Shelley, you don't have to prove you're tough.
You've conquered infested, stinking water
In Europe they call you Neptune's daughter.
You've beaten oceans, rivers, cold water, lakes
You've got the kind of guts it takes.

Strength, courage, indomitable will
Polluted waters? You've drunk your fill.
You've been sucked by leeches, battered by storms!
Now you're chasing some simple reforms
You want to keep our harbours clean
Not polluted and stinking like places you've been.

Oh! Shelley Shelley! I saw you on telly!
Saw you beaten by Cunningham—I saw Grub cry
Saw him hang his head and question why?
Champagne to the winner—you raised your glass
Ever the lady, you showed real class!
No excuses! No wonder you're planting the seeds of inspiration.
Inspiration to the next generation of Aussie kids with goals and
    dreams
To make Australian sporting teams!

Oh! Shelley Shelley, you're so cool!
Meet ya at the swimming pool!

Thanks, Laurie. But how do I see myself? What are the
characteristics of a world champion?

They aren't easy questions. Like most people, I suppose I'm
still trying to understand myself. A little bit more gets unearthed
as time passes and trials mount. Some aspects of my personality
I've only come to appreciate in recent years. Others undoubtedly
still lie unrevealed beneath the surface.

This much I can tell you. Like my father, I have a great lust
for life. Even more so since I first felt the lump in my breast.
Benign or not, it was just the sort of thing to remind me of

my mortality. To remind me that there is so much to do and so little time.

And yet I also came to realise that it's not just about squeezing a million things into each day. It's the old quality versus quantity argument. I've always been one to race from one task to another. I 'do' something and then I turn my attention instantly to the next challenge. I'd never really slowed down long enough to savour the moment. And relaxation, well that was a completely foreign notion to me. Now I can see that many things of value can be missed if you're locked into the idea of relentless progress. My marriage breakdown, in particular, was partly attributable to my habit of juggling a thousand commitments and wearing a hundred hats. I simply didn't devote enough time to the relationship.

Finding the right balance is the trick. I was able to climb to the top of the world in my chosen field largely because of my constant striving to improve and go forward (practise makes progress, not perfect). But I have to question the price I paid elsewhere in my life, the areas that were necessarily neglected to make way for my swimming. It's every high achiever's dilemma. Perhaps, in the end, we need to be vigilant about where success and happiness collide.

There have been plenty of collisions for me over the years (and I'm not just talking about my car accidents). I know it's a cliché, but it can be very lonely at the top. Apart from the years with Peter, which started in 1987 and really ended in 1991, I've been single for most of my life. In recent years I've taken to calling Ben, my toy poodle, 'the man in my life' (apologies to any current suitors). He's my number one man and my number one fan.

It amuses me to think that some people have looked at my career and thought that I had it all. Hey, she's No.1 in the world. What could possibly be wrong with her life? I'm not saying that my swimming success hasn't brought me a great deal of joy and satisfaction. Of course it has. But it's one of the curses of individual sport that in the midst of your greatest triumphs you can feel your loneliest. Especially if you don't have a partner to share it with. It's a long journey to undertake on your own. And when you reach the top, the view may be spectacular, but you can't help thinking that it would be nice to have someone beside you to enjoy it with.

There are pitfalls even then. By definition, there are very few people who understand what it's like to be at the summit of individual sports. It's impossible for most people to grasp. I tried to talk to my husband and my friends about it, but it was no good. Even my sister couldn't always relate. The first difficulty they face is appreciating what they interpret as the sacrifices you make along the way. I didn't see them as sacrifices, as long as I was *choosing* to do them. They, on the other hand, would ask why I never drank or partied with them. My in-laws and my family probably thought that I was stubborn and anti-social. The perception was that I was never available for them. I had time for training, I had time for charity work, I had time for teaching, but I never had time for them. In my defence, I believed there was no other way. I was doing what was required to make it to and stay at the top. I was left feeling as though I could never fully satisfy anybody.

It didn't get any better once I reached the top. Very few people had any way of relating to the feelings I was experiencing. The pleasure I took in being rewarded for all my hard work. My desire to carve out a bit of history while I was there. Most of us don't get a shot at some kind of immortality and I was determined to etch my name in stone while I had the chance. And that meant more so-called sacrifices, more training and even greater support from those around me. It was a tough ask, but I'd always been very demanding of those around me in terms of support or recognition. It was a behavioural pattern I could trace back to the way my parents supported and rewarded me as a child. A very *destructive* pattern. One of a number I needed to change.

The lights began to flicker in my head after getting the bronze medal at Terracina. In the days immediately after the swim I suddenly realised that life would go on. I wasn't the world open water swimming champion any more, but the world hadn't ended either. It was brought starkly home to me as I watched Melissa struggling with the same things I'd struggled with before her. Because marathon swimming is not an Olympic sport, she simply wasn't getting the recognition she deserved. I vividly remember the look on her face at the press conference after the medal presentation in Rome as it dawned on her that the media really weren't all that interested in the long-distance event. Not when Kieren Perkins had just broken a world record.

It was like looking through a time tunnel. I could see my own hurt and bemusement in the period following my gold medal performance in Perth in 1991. While the media and sponsors were clamouring for a piece of fellow gold medallists Hayley Lewis and Linley Frame, I was getting 'Shelley who?'. I'd since come to understand how my sport would never command similar attention until it was included in the Olympics. I could see the sport in perspective. And I could also see that, regardless of whether it ever made it to the Olympics, there had to be more to life than the pursuit of medals and trophies.

The impression was reinforced when I returned from Italy and walked into my small Queenscliff home. It was crowded with trophies. The ones that couldn't fit onto shelves or fill corners of the living room burst out of boxes stacked in the storage room. Hundreds and hundreds of trophies. Looking at them all, it was abundantly clear that there *was* more to life. Who really gave a damn about them in the end?

In the end, whether I'm headed for heaven or hell, I'm not going to have to stand there with my trophies to prove myself. The undeniable truth was that the trophies had never been a ticket to anywhere in my life. They certainly hadn't been a ticket to happiness or personal well-being. Maybe, in pursuit of them, I'd learnt to deal with some of life's challenges. But, ultimately, I didn't want to be remembered for my swimming or my world records. I want to be remembered for *how* I went about my swimming. I wanted to be able to stand up and say that I was always committed to something. And I wanted my example to inspire others to make commitments to their dreams.

In pursuing that commitment, however, you need to remember that life is multi-faceted. When that commitment begins to exclude everything else, you have a problem. *I* had a problem. It's fair to say that my determination to succeed was sometimes all-consuming. I was seen as very driven. Very obsessed. And aggressive. It was almost the opposite to what I thought about myself. I saw my aggression as assertiveness, I saw my obsession as dedication, my drivenness as desire.

The Shelley before the cancer scare probably wouldn't have admitted this, but swimming was all that counted until 1994. I was totally consumed by my training and my next event. I never believed in short cuts. If you wanted to do anything, you had to do it right first time so you didn't have to do it again. I was very wrapped up in it all. I was only prepared to have fun at what I thought were appropriate times. I always believed things were done a certain way. I was so tunnel-visioned that I was often totally out of touch with what was happening around me. I was concentrating so hard on where I wanted to go that I was oblivious to everything else. I was totally unaware that my marriage was falling apart, for instance. If anyone tried to tell me it was, I wasn't listening. I knew best.

My drive was particularly apparent anywhere near a pool. I was focused as soon as I got into the water. Anyone who stood in my way had to watch out. Not that I'd walk over them, but I was there to work. I wasn't there to play. As a consequence, little things would upset me. They would appear to be mountains when they were only molehills. People always knew to stay away when I was in a mood. My attitude was that when the work needs to be done, do the work. Knowing when to stop was a problem. Especially for someone who likes to paste affirmations all over her walls. One of my favourites was:

I am a Rhinoceros—I have the
damn-the-torpedoes spirit, I am full
of energy and I can't wait to get up
in the morning and start charging.

I thought of myself as a rhino. And there was many a time when coaches tried to stop me charging. But until my body actually quit, I tended to ignore it. People would be asking what I was doing at the pool as I was coughing away, but I'd just keep saying that I was okay. For some reason, I always felt I had a point to prove to myself when I was sick. I believed that I could work through the sickness. That I could overcome *anything*. God knows why. But it reaches back all the way to my school days when I used to trot along, sick or not. My schoolmates thought I was the unhealthiest healthy person they'd ever seen.

It was no different in my adult life. I was absolutely smitten by the notion of overcoming all life's tests. I was mesmerised by such movies as *Chariots of Fire* and *Power of One* in which the characters defied all the odds to win out. I also drew inspiration from a line in the Ernest Hemingway novel *A Farewell To Arms*. In it he wrote that 'the world breaks everyone and, afterwards, some are stronger at the broken places'. I thought he was writing to *me*.

I shouldn't write in the past tense all the time. I still believe in many of those things. The difference is that I apply them more strategically now. I'm still a determined person, make no bones about that. But I try to treat my body and my self with more respect nowadays. I've opened my life to a little more fun. I don't get stressed so easily any more and I try to tread more lightly these days. You might say that the obsession is being treated, although I have no intention of throwing the baby out with the bath water.

The most obvious signs of my changing attitudes appeared after I came out of hospital following surgery on my breast. Friends noticed the change immediately. I was no longer living only for the next race. I was stopping to smell the flowers. In short, being the world champion was no longer my No.1 priority. It was no longer the be all and end all. I could see now that it had been my only yardstick for years, but I would have been defensive if you'd suggested it.

And the trophies? They now serve as doorstops in my new home.

What are my other qualities? I see myself as a leader. That's one of the reasons I'm a swimmers rep and it's also probably why I have my detractors. I've never been one to shrink from standing up for my beliefs, whether it be a funding issue or better conditions for swimmers. It has brought me into conflict with people from both the long-distance swimming community and the greater swimming hierarchy. But there's no regrets. Leaders must take a stand if they are to make a difference.

SHE WAS THE FIRST PERSON TO REALLY BELIEVE IN ME. SHE INVITED ME TO PERTH *to live and train with her in the lead-up to the World Championships trials and was there at the finish to congratulate me when I made the team. How many people in sport would go to their rivals and say come and train with me, come and see all my secrets? She didn't know what my motives were, or what I was capable of. For all she knew I could have been out there to use her up and then beat her.*

TAMMY VAN WISSE

Of those critics inside long-distance swimming itself, their main beef seems to be that I take too big a slice of the sport's small sponsorship and exposure pie. My counter to that is that they should stop worrying about what I'm doing and get out and boost their own profile. Ultimately, if we all do that, we will combine to lift the profile of the sport. And that's really what it's all about in the end.

It seems that I've also offended some in the wider swimming community by pushing for greater funding and recognition for both myself and the sport. The truth is, in a minor sport with loftier ambitions, if you don't push a bit you get left behind. I make no excuses for that.

You may have guessed my other traits. I'm very emotional. I'm a great believer in positive thinking and taking control of your life. As one of my favourite affirmations reads, 'If it is to be, it's up to me'. And while I believe we have the power to shape our lives, I also believe things happen for a reason. That's where my faith in God has been a real comfort.

You may also have divined that I'm an unashamed patriot. Having spent time in many countries, Australia is still the best place in the world as far as I'm concerned. Representing my country is the ultimate thrill, something that's obvious to any visitors to my home. The framed national anthem on my wall and the Australian and boxing kangaroo flags are a dead giveaway.

Oddly enough, it was an American who best summed up my feelings for Australia. As John F. Kennedy said in his immortal speech, 'Ask not what your country can do for you, ask what *you* can do for your country.'

OF • NEW • YORK • AND • • NEW • DIRECTIONS

HERE I WAS AFTER the Wollongong swim and Sydney was finally wide awake to my talents. A strange time to leave the city, you might think.

In reality, though, it was just a continuation of my new beginnings. Since the operation, everything in my life had been put under the microscope. I was 33, single, renting. Financially, Sydney seemed beyond my reach. And the training facilities just weren't there year-round. I decided I needed a fresh environment. That place was the Gold Coast.

But I'm getting ahead of myself.

After the incredible high of the Wollongong swim and the tide of media interest, I had to gird myself to return to the far-flung waters of Argentina in early February. As you already know, the Santa Fe and Parana swims hardly rate among my favourite destinations. Another Argentinian swim, at the coastal city of Mar del Plata, had also been added to the World Series itinerary this year. In all, I would have to complete three marathons between 5 February and 19 February. I was *not* looking forward to it.

There's no question I should have listened to my body this time. I was really in no shape to face Rio Coronda's murky waters less than three weeks after my taxing swim to Wollongong. Particularly since the race had been lengthened to 60 kilometres to honour the memory of Santa Fe's former world boxing champion, Carlos Monzon. I could really have done without the extra three kilometres, added so the race could start from the end of the street where he'd lived. And after the previous year's clash with a propeller, I had to wonder what else the swim might have in store for me.

I found out in the first fifteen minutes. After the standard chaotic start one of the other swimmers had to stop suddenly to avoid being run over by a boat. In the process he lashed his leg out and kicked me sharply in the shoulder. The kick did major damage. And there were more than nine hours to go! But I needed the World Series points, so I ploughed on in growing pain. It was a truly forgettable day as I finished fifth in the women's section. Rio Coronda, you'd done it again.

It didn't end there. The day after the swim I found out the real story behind Señor Monzon. It turns out that our boxer hero had not long been out of jail after murdering his wife by throwing her off a balcony. The word was that she'd made his coffee too weak. He didn't get to enjoy his freedom, though, as he died drunk at the wheel of his car soon after. I was disgusted. *This* was the man we'd honoured in the swim?

To cap it off, I was struck down once more by the Santa Fe specialty, diarrhoea and vomiting. This was an especially bad bout. When I emerged from my Parana hotel room after my usual drip-feeding, I felt like I'd been hollowed out. There were to be no miracles in the Rio Parana race on this occasion. With my shoulder still troubling me and my energy reserves non-existent, I had to withdraw from the swim after three hours. It was only the second DNF of my career, but I felt no dishonour in being fished out this time. There's only so much a body can take. The doctor who attended me later said I was so run down that I could only have got as far as I did on pure willpower.

I did drag my poor, depleted body along to Mar del Plata for the following week's swim, but only to act as a trainer for Kim Dyke. It was a winning combination, too, as I bellowed Kim on to victory. Then it was on the next plane home to try to recapture my health. I can't say I was sorry to be leaving the Argentinian waters behind.

If only they'd left *me* behind. Whatever bug I'd picked up this time took an enormous liking to its new host. The diarrhoea and the vomiting continued to plague me back in Sydney and to this was added a crippling lethargy. I felt completely wrung out, and no amount of vitamins or drips seemed to make a difference. I was certainly in no condition to contest the Australian national titles on 2 April. With that went any chance of selection for the Pan Pacs to be held in Atlanta in August.

I had other things on my mind, anyway. After three years in Sydney I was preparing to move base to the Gold Coast. There were several factors. For starters, I wanted my health back and I figured that the Queensland sun would help in that area. Then there was the cost of living in Sydney and the knowledge that I'd struggle to ever own a home there. The thought of a nice timber home in the Gold Coast hinterland really appealed. And there was also the attraction of the training facilities at Laurie Lawrence's swim school at Palm Beach-Currumbin High School, which offered more flexibility than the Warringah Aquatic Centre. The break with Grub wouldn't be easy, but his career was already taking off in another direction. I knew he would still be there for me when necessary.

The gradual retreat from Sydney began when I booked into a Gold Coast hotel. I wanted to get a feel for the place and get a taste of the atmosphere at Laurie's school, but my lingering illness meant I was generally confined to my room and long walks on the beach. Laurie must have wondered what sort of a crock he'd inherited. A couple of months slid by as I punctuated my stay with short trips back to Sydney. The World Series was set to resume with the Italian Riviera event in June, but it soon became obvious that I wouldn't be up to it. As it turned out, the event was ultimately cancelled amid more rumours of Mafia involvement.

My thoughts were a long way from Italy by then. At the top of my new set of priorities was a return to New York to take on the Guinness Book of World Records' solo mark for swimming around Manhattan. Now, to set the record straight (as it were), I thought I was attempting to better the 6:12:28 time I had set in 1985. I knew of American Kris Rutford's time of 5:53:57 set in 1992, but I didn't believe his mark had been ratified by the Guinness Book of Records. It was a distinction that was to lead to some confusion as my record attempt neared. As far as I was concerned, I would set a new women's mark either way if I bettered my 1985 time. Later I would find that the race organisers were promoting the swim as an assault on Rutford's time. It was no small difference of interpretation, but one I'd have to live with.

As I was saying. I'd decided to go for the record, reasoning that it had been sitting there quite long enough and that it would be a fabulous way to thank the Americans who'd had an impact on my life and my career. I guess you could say it was a nostalgic venture. Manhattan had played an enormous part in my early career and yet I hadn't swum there for six years. It would provide a fitting way to reunite the people who'd guided and encouraged me over the years. I would dedicate my new world record to them.

This would also be a great way to announce to New Yorkers that the Queen of Manhattan was still alive and kicking. After all, the Big Apple had been my second home for the past eight years as I spent up to ten weeks training there each summer. As a final consideration, I saw the attempt as a way to attract publicity to a swim that had always been underrated. I can see no earthly reason why the 'round Manhattan swim can't become swimming's equivalent of the world-famous New York Marathon and, ideally, part of the World Series circuit.

The plan first began to take shape after the worlds in Italy. I'd already made a tentative enquiry about tackling the record and had been told that, under the new committee of the Manhattan Island Marathon Swimming Foundation, there was now a specific day set aside each year for the solo record attempt. In 1994 it just happened to clash with the worlds. The next opportunity was scheduled for 14 July 1995, which coincided with a king tide.

The date had a nice ring to it. It was the seventh anniversary of my first world title, won at the 1988 World Cup in France. It was also Bastille Day. In addition, the timing meant it would serve as a perfect warm-up for the 1994/95 World Series final, to be held at Magog on 23 July. There *was* one concern. It happened to clash with the 1995 Pan Pacs on 9 August by way of Australian Swimming's ruling that swimmers not compete in the month prior to the championships. But, whether fortuitously or not, I ended up missing out on the Pan Pac team after withdrawing from the 1995 nationals. The coast was clear.

The swim had assumed greater significance by the time I sent off the paperwork and the entry money in April. It was now looming as my first opportunity to turn the year around after the mishaps in Argentina, the lingering illness and the frustration of missing out on the Pan Pacs. It would be my first major swim in more than five months and my only real test before the World Series final.

The call came back from the organisers to say that they had received my entry along with five others, all men. A few weeks later I got another call. All the guys had pulled out. You can read that any way you like. The most popular interpretation among my friends was that they didn't want to risk being overshadowed by a woman. No matter. I was still going ahead, so I began to assemble my support team. After countless late-night phone calls, Nancy had been confirmed as my trainer and Richard Kersh, my old assistant coach at Arkansas, agreed to paddle a kayak beside me. Karen Hartley, the original women's record holder for the swim, was coming too. I'd even managed to secure the services of my old boat driver. The only non-starters were Trisha Coulter, who was in my boat for my first Manhattan swim in 1984, and another former training buddy from Arkansas, Will Howe. Finally, there was Tammy, who I wanted to accompany me for moral and practical support.

As the day of the swim approached there were some intriguing twists. First, there was France's announcement that they were resuming nuclear testing at Mururoa Atoll. And here I was, set to swim on Bastille Day! As someone who takes a special interest in poisoned waters, I wasn't going to let the opportunity pass to make a small statement of my own. I would wear a black armband during the swim. It was sure to stir the curiosity of any media in attendance and I would soon have a platform to voice my disgust over the French tests. Unfortunately I made the mistake of showing my hand too early. When the organisers got wind of my intentions they threatened me with disqualification. No 'outside interests' were to be promoted during the swim, and that was to be the end of that.

Meanwhile, I had been put through a testing time myself in the months prior to the swim. I had relocated to the Gold Coast by now, but the new environment was yet to have any effect on my general health. Laurie began to wonder whether he'd got himself an athlete or a cot case. I was staggering from one flu-like condition to the next. At one stage I was coughing so hard that I tore the ligaments attached to my ribs. My voice came and went for the best part of two months and, no matter what I did, I couldn't seem to get well. I trained regardless, but it was hard to tell if I was making any progress. The most galling thing was that nobody could tell me what was wrong.

Until shortly before the departure date for New York. After a series of blood tests I was diagnosed as having recently suffered a bout of glandular fever. At least it was nice to know that there was a *reason* why I was picking up every virus going around. I wasn't a hypochondriac after all. With that question answered, I trained the house down in the last three weeks. Even so, by the time Tammy and I boarded the plane for New York it was questionable whether I'd done enough conditioning work to maintain the pace needed to break the world record. I'd already decided by now that I would skip the Lac St Jean swim after the World Series final because I didn't feel physically ready to face its freezing waters, particularly with my race weight considerably lower than normal. Instead, I planned to train some more in New York before going on to Atlantic City and the new World Series race at Long Island Sound.

Once in New York I had four days to fine-tune myself for the swim. Four sticky, enervating New York days. The best place to be in that weather was the pool. No wonder I was keen to get out to the Long Island Aquatic Club to do my laps under Dave Ferris's astute guidance. And I was flying! For the first time in ages I began to feel my old strength and rhythm returning. Maybe I *could* produce something special here. It helped that I felt so instantly comfortable in New York, staying at the Schnarr's familiar home in Flushing and finding my sponsored Ford car in the driveway.

I was slated to start the swim in the East River at 2.40 a.m. on Friday. We would be setting out from 96th Street before swimming into the narrow Harlem River and then into the expansive Hudson River. Travelling along the length of Manhattan Island we would then turn back up the East River and return to 96th Street. Forty-eight kilometres in all. And if I was to reclaim the outright record I would need to shave at least nineteen minutes off the time I had swum in 1985. Almost two minutes for every year since.

I felt up to the challenge by the time the team gathered in the ghostly light under a freeway flyover at 96th Street. Nancy and Tammy were to share the trainer's duties on my boat. After an organisational hitch, Richard would also be alongside them instead of in a kayak. The organisers had provided me with their own kayaker and it would be his job to stay abreast of the boat, forming a channel for me to swim through. Also on the boat were a navigator, two observers and a television crew from CNN. Karen was on the back-up boat with the MIMSF committee members.

After my greasing down I was led to the boat and transported to the middle of the river under the glow of a full moon. Watches were synchronised, a large time display was mounted on the cabin of the boat and, with the blazing camera lights upon me, I leapt into the East River and started swimming. Nancy and Tammy immediately struck up a chorus of cheers that bounced off the water surface and echoed deep into the still Manhattan night. Here we go!

My nerves were jangling through a combination of excitement and fear. It's very easy to get spooked swimming at night when your reliance on your support crew is absolute. Combine that with the adrenalin surge that comes with a record attempt and it's no surprise that my stroke rate started out at over 90 a minute. Overall, it was a promising beginning. The night was clear, the full moon improved visibility and the water was warm. The only disconcerting element was the realisation that the kayaker wasn't wearing any fluoro gear. I just couldn't pick him up in the khaki clothes he was wearing. The boat was no easier to see on occasion, either, as the CNN cameraman dazzled me with his spotlight. They were doing a tremendous job of promoting the sport, but they were doing a lousy job of helping my confidence. At times I couldn't see anything but light on one side and darkness on the other, an unnerving experience at water level.

At least my stroke was unaffected. I had moved smoothly down the East River and into the Harlem, where the river narrows beneath brooding tenements. As we passed beside Yankee Stadium and under a succession of footbridges, Nancy and Tammy filled the dark voids with a riot of hoots and whistles. They're not the sort of places where you want to feel alone.

We were making good headway on record pace when I started to notice a change in the water. I couldn't quite put my finger on it, but it tasted odd. I felt the nausea begin to claw at me and I had terrifying images of my first, abandoned Wollongong swim. Not *this* time, I thought. I just clenched my teeth and told myself to hang in there until we got through to the Hudson River, where there would be lots of fresh air and cleaner water. I wasn't told until later that I'd swum though an oil slick caused when a boatload of partying lawyers capsized earlier in the night.

Scarcely had I overcome the nausea when I let out a sudden scream. I had swum into a piece of broken pier and it had given me an awful fright. Worse still, it jarred my ribs and I began to feel my tender ligaments. After muttering at my team for not having warned me away from it (they hadn't seen it until too late) I continued on my way. Shortly afterwards I swam through the colourfully named Devil's Gate and into the Hudson River.

The Harlem River had been docile and sheltered. The Hudson was another matter altogether. The first sensation was of someone turning the lights out. In the narrow Harlem, buildings had cast their light over the water. On the broad Hudson, even under a full moon, I could barely make out the boat, let alone Nancy and Tammy. It's crucial for a swimmer to maintain eye contact with their trainer so that they can be reassured everything's okay. So when I lost track of the kayaker as well, I became really rattled.

On top of the rising anxiety I had to contend with a messy half-metre chop. I felt like a piece of clothing being tossed around in a washing machine. In quick order my rhythm, pace and technique deserted me. It was as though I'd never swum in rough water before. The problem was that there was all this water rushing down the Hudson with the tide while the forces underneath the surface were turning me inside out. I couldn't pull my arm under my body properly as the forces dragged it to the side. It was exasperating. I felt like I was going nowhere.

It wasn't the case. My progress had slowed, all right, but I still managed to reach the George Washington Bridge (about a fifth of the way down the western side of Manhattan) well before I expected. The first of the dawn's rays decided to make an appearance at about this point, helping to raise my spirits. But there was no denying that it was a hard grind. Because of concerns about the outfall from a huge sewage plant we would pass, I was being led out into the rough water mid-river. Although I was encouraged to learn that I was on record-breaking time, via a chalkboard held over the side of the boat, I was becoming increasingly frustrated by being tossed about in the chop. My ribs were hurting and the strength was draining from my arms.

The doubts began to multiply. I began to wonder if I could keep it up. The thought formed in the back of my mind that I couldn't take much more of this. There was also the knowledge that I had to swim the World Series final in nine days, with two more marathons to follow shortly after that. I could feel the termite-thoughts chewing away on my resolve. I'd have to answer them. In the end I told myself that I'd be satisfied if I could just make it to the bottom end of Manhattan. That's where I would turn back up the East River for the final leg. I'd let the negative thoughts have their say again then. But for now they'd have to take a back seat while I tried to put the turbulent Hudson behind me.

It was unquestionably the grimmest part of the swim. I was irritable from fighting the pain and I couldn't seem to get my rhythm back for the life of me. I wasn't even able to get a lift from the message that Laurie had called to say he was sitting in his loungeroom in his Australian tracksuit, cheering me on. And if that image couldn't draw a smile, what could?

I battled down the Hudson, mentally ticking off the familiar landmarks as I went. Finally, I could make out the World Trade Center's twin towers and then, off in the distance, the Statue of Liberty. We were nearing the tip of Manhattan and, according to the chalkboards, I was still about three minutes ahead of record pace. At times it felt like I would never get to the Wall Street end. There were apartment blocks and parks I'd never seen before. They'd obviously reclaimed some land, making the swim even longer. Just what I needed!

Still, my internal trade-off had worked. I was nearing the terminal for the Staten Island ferry and just beyond that I would leave the Hudson behind to enter the East River's kinder waters.

'Stop, Shelley! Hold up!'

I pulled up. What was going on?

'It's the Staten Island ferry,' called Nancy. 'We're going to have to wait for it to pass.'

'Can't we make it?' I shouted back. 'Won't they stop? They stopped for me before.'

'No. They're not stopping, Shell. We're going to have to wait.'

I couldn't bear it. Here I was, two-thirds of the way through the swim and three minutes ahead of the record, and suddenly I had to tread water. And they weren't stopping the clock. For four excruciatingly long minutes I had to wait for the ferry to pass. To try to calm myself I ate a banana and breathed steadily through my nose. Any lingering good humour I had about the day vaporised. Now I just wanted to get on with the job of breaking the record. This wasn't what I'd intended the swim to be. It was meant to be a happy reunion. It was meant to be *fun*. But I wasn't enjoying it one bit. By the time I got the signal to go, my hard-won break on the record had disappeared. I was back to square one. Instead of letting it get to me, though, I decided to use the frustration to spur me on. If I was determined before, I was now *driven* to go for the record.

As I came around into the East River again I readied myself to get some assistance from the tide. This would be more like it. Wrong. We had come in while the tide was still on the turn and instead of swimming with the flow I hit a patch where I felt the tide was running *against* me. This I didn't need. Not after the Hudson. Not after watching helplessly as my buffer disappeared. The messages were coming thick and fast to really push it now. What did they *think* I was doing?

It was a strange time. The water was much calmer, but I still felt as though I was spinning my wheels. And the communications from the boat began to dry up. I couldn't seem to get a straight answer from them about how I was doing. I found out later that at the end of this section, because of the tides, I'd actually fallen six minutes behind record pace. No one on the boat wanted to pass *that* information on. Every time I stopped for a feed and asked how I was going, Nancy or Tammy said they'd let me know at the next bridge. Then they'd urge me on and try to lighten the mood by cracking jokes. I was in no mood for jokes. I just let it all wash over me and put my head down and butt up. This was no joyful outing any more. The record was the only thing that would make it worthwhile.

Somewhere in my single-mindedness I found the key. My ribs stopped hurting, my rhythm returned, and I felt like I was in a pool. Where I'd recently felt as though I had weights attached to my feet (not an uncommon feeling in New York rivers), I now felt like I was flying across the surface. I just kept getting stronger and stronger. Sure, the tide had finally turned and was flowing in behind me. But I knew I was swimming fast as well. My stroke rate was climbing and the buildings were flashing by. I could see people running along the Manhattan shore and I was *overtaking* them.

Then I got the word. I was ahead of the record pace by about six minutes. From that point on I knew it was going to happen. I had the record! The last few kilometres buzzed by as the celebrations started on the boats. When I passed the finishing point the cheering reached a crescendo. My time of 5:45:25 had bettered Kris Rutford's record by more than eight minutes and hacked nearly half an hour off my 1985 mark. And yet my overwhelming emotion was of relief rather than elation. As I floated in the water I rolled over onto my back and burst into tears.

Back at 96th Street I accepted a plaque from the MIMSF commemorating my new record. I couldn't help but notice that they'd already inscribed a time of five hours and left a blank space for the minutes and seconds. I suppose I should have been flattered to know they had such faith in me.

After the initial flurry of media interviews and back-slapping, I returned to Nancy's home to freshen up. I was well satisfied with the result and pleased to be reminded that my mental strength was still intact. But there was no hiding from the fact that I had used up everything in the tanks to get over the line this time. Ordinarily I'd be ready to party after a big swim, but on this occasion all I wanted to do was go to bed. If I'd been reminded of my ability to push through pain, I was also reminded that there was a price to pay. While my body could endure a lot of punishment, it was also a fragile system.

Just how fragile I was to find out over the ensuing days when I didn't bounce back as I normally did after a swim. Even my celebratory night on the town fizzled out early when I hit the wall after a few drinks. It seemed the swim had taken everything out of me. It was time to listen to my body and take a break.

On the Monday night I was on the phone as usual, chatting to friends in Australia. I learnt that the house I'd bought on the Gold Coast just before leaving was going to be vacant on 23 July. That set my mind racing. If I went home now I could start moving in *and* capitalise on the incredible interest the swim had generated. If I stayed, on the other hand, I'd only punish my body more and further delay my full recovery. It seemed pretty cut and dried.

Only one thing. I felt an enormous obligation to the World Series organisers. I was a big drawcard in Magog, where I'd won for six years straight. And it *was* the super final. There was another consideration. Old habits die hard. I still had to be convinced that it wouldn't be a weakness to pull out of a race.

After much agonising I came to the conclusion that the decision was in fact a show of strength. That didn't stop my voice trembling a little as I told the organisers that I'd be pulling out of the final and the marathons in Atlantic City and Long Island Sound to return home to recuperate. It was ultimately one of the toughest *and* one of the best decisions I ever made. Tough, because I'm not a quitter and I was forfeiting the chance to defend my world title. But a good decision in that I had put into practice my new philosophy that there was more to life than swimming. I knew there were other challenges and responsibilities in life. One of those responsibilities was to my physical well-being. I could always attempt to reclaim my No.1 world ranking another year if it became a priority again.

It was a *smart* decision, too. Because, on reflection, it was clear that it was going to be best if I returned to Australia to exploit the media interest rather than go on to Quebec. World Series final or not, Magog would not carry anywhere near the punch of the Manhattan swim. As I'd realised since the Wollongong swim, with the exception of swims like Manhattan or the Channel I just couldn't expect decent media coverage outside Australia. And when the media focus *was* on me, I had to make it count. If that meant making the trip back to Australia prematurely, then so be it.

Back in the security of my new home, the pieces all fell into place. The key point to emerge was that I had to swim more often in my home country, where people could see me, if I really wanted to improve the profile of the sport in Australia. Not only would the sport benefit that way, but I would build my own profile as a consequence. The advantages were obvious. More sponsorship, more opportunities and, hopefully, a better platform to reach Australia's youth. The fact is, once my career is over, people in Australia won't be saying that Shelley Taylor-Smith won seven world titles in a row. When my name comes up they will talk about how they saw me on the news swimming from Sydney to Wollongong, or winning Sydney Harbour, or taking out the world championship gold medal in Perth. Perhaps they will remember me swimming around Manhattan.

I guess you could say that it's been a belated recognition of what really strikes a chord with the Australian public and sponsors. World titles are one thing. But unless they can occasionally see an Australian athlete performing in Australia, it's hard to make a genuine connection. Understandably, we like to be able to see our world-class athletes in the flesh, whether it be a Greg Norman or a Michael Doohan or a Cathy Freeman. So, while my world titles had been necessary to establish my credibility, they weren't ever going to count for much in

Australia while I continued to ply my trade where no one could see me. It was like operating in a vacuum.

Just as important was the realisation that when the cameras *are* on the long distance swimmers at the worlds or Pan Pacs, the medals don't carry much clout. When you look at the reaction to medals in the 25-kilometre event, you see that they quickly get overtaken by what's happening in the pool. That was even the case when I won a world championship gold medal in my home town. The fact remains that until long-distance swimming wins a berth at the Olympics it will continue to suffer in comparison to pool swimming. The frustration is that there is no inherent reason why that should be. You have the marathon in athletics. Why shouldn't the 25-kilometre event in swimming carry the same prestige?

Until such time as the sport receives an Olympic call-up, then marathon swimmers must use their imagination. And that's what I intend to do from now on. I'll be far pickier about the swims I do, whether they be selected World Series swims or record attempts. I'm determined to get some World Series races up and running in Australasia. By 1998, when the worlds are to be staged in Perth again (the swimmers liked it so much in 1991 they couldn't wait to get back), I'd like to see World Series races staged in Sydney, Queensland, Melbourne and possibly New Zealand.

When I do swim I'll be mindful of the lessons I learnt from the Wollongong swim. It's the scale that's important. For that reason I've got a Channel double crossing and a Newcastle to Sydney swim on my list. I'll be heeding other recent lessons as well. I'll be taking very good care of my body, particularly after the fright I got when I collapsed in my home a few months after the Manhattan swim. And I'll be saying no a lot more, because that's always been one of my weaknesses. It's dawned on me that I can't be everything to everybody.

Oh, and I'll be keeping my fingers crossed that the 25-kilometre event gets a place in the 2000 Olympics. You haven't seen the last of Shelley Taylor-Smith just yet.

RIVER • DEEP • MOUNTAIN • HIGH
• CONCLUSION •

IT'S BEEN A HECK of a journey so far, this life of mine. And I'm banking on there being a few more chapters to add before my story ends.

Would I have done anything differently? Regrets, sure, I've had a few (where have I heard that before?). But I believe I've definitely made more right moves than mistakes. I'll go further than that. I don't think I've *ever* made a wrong move. I'm not suggesting I'm perfect. But, as I've said before, in my philosophy of life there aren't any mistakes. Just new learning experiences.

It's all about taking risks and climbing the mountains that confront all of us in our lives. I figure I've climbed my share of mountains, emotional and physical. And, I'm glad to report, I've found something precious at each summit. An insight into my character. Or a new direction. Opportunity.

I hate to think how much rich experience I'd have missed out on if, for instance, I'd taken the easy option after losing my scholarship in Arkansas. By tackling marathon swimming instead, I opened up a whole new world. Similar rewards await everybody prepared to climb their personal mountains.

With one proviso. It can't be done alone. I may have been the one standing on the winner's dais, but it took countless people to put me there. Coaches, family, friends, handlers, sponsors, right through to the people who wrote supportive letters when I was preparing to swim the English Channel. I couldn't have done it without them. And I wouldn't have wanted to. **Life is a team sport!**

I just hope I've given something in return. Most importantly, I hope that my life has proved an inspiration for all those people who dare to dream and a heartening example of our ability to overcome the hurdles that inevitably confront us along the way.

And remember: If you do not quit, you will make it!

7 Taylor-Made Solutions for Creating Your Champion Mindset®

1. The Power of Success – Winning is achieving your goals and no one else's. It is not what you win, but how you go about your winning – your winning attitude!

2. The Power of Focus – Focus on what you want and you will create it – Focus on what you don't want and you will create it – we always get what we focus on!

3. The Power of Passion – The single most important ingredient to success is passion, the desire to follow your dreams no matter what!

4. The Power of Goals & Outcomes – The small steps taken each day are the short-term goals that help you know and feel what winning is. Enjoy the journey!

5. The Power of Choice & Action – Say "stuff it" and "flush it" to any doubts. Just keep telling yourself, "I'm doing the best I can do" and then the doubts will go away.

6. The Power of Persistence – There are no disappointments in life, just new learning experiences. If it is a mistake and you learn something, then it's been a learning experience, and it's no longer a mistake.

7. The Power of Now – Now is all you have, to live your life to the full, moment by moment, being yourself 100%. You are "present" in the now when you experience yourself being 100% in everything you create and achieve.

For more information on motivation, goal setting, personal development, open water swimming, swim coaching and Shelley Taylor-Smith

Visit: www.championmindset.com.au

CAREER • HIGHLIGHTS

• AT A GLANCE •

1988-94	International Marathon Swimming Federation's No.1 woman's ranking
1991	IMSF's No.1 overall ranking (men and women combined)
1987-98	Australian National Marathon Swimming Champion (except 1991 & 1995)
1983-98	Set 15 World Race Records in Open Water/ Long Distance/Marathon Swimming
1984-98	51 International Marathon Swims. First-placed woman 45 times, second-placed four times, third-placed twice, fifth-placed twice and Did Not Finish (DNF) twice.
1984-98	Won 9 races outright.

• AWARDS AND HONOURS •

Dean's List, University of Arkansas, 1984, 1985, 1986

Who's Who of American Colleges and Universities 1985/86

Inducted Amateur Sport Hall of Fame, Johnstown, Pennsylvania, USA 1986

Induction International Marathon Swimming Hall of Fame, 1990

Australian of the Year finalist 1990, 1991

Australian Female Athlete of the Year, 1991

Long Distance Swimmer of the Year, *Swimming World* magazine 1989, 1990, 1991, 1992, 1993

Long Distance Swimmer of the Year, US Swimming Federation 1985/86

Australian Swimming Inc. Long Distance Swimmer of the Year 1991, 1992, 1993

Rotary International Award for Contribution to Sport, 1994

Perth, Western Australia 'MV Shelley Taylor-Smith' Ferry, 1997

Chairman, FINA Athletes Commission, 1998

Honorary Secretary, FINA Technical Open Water Swimming
Committee, 2000-2009

Australian Centenary Sports Medal, 2000

Swimming Australia Hall of Fame, 2000

Rotary International Paul Harris Fellow Medal, 2002

Induction into International Swimming Hall of Fame, 2008

1st International Women's OWS Chief Referee, FINA World Open
Water Swimming Championships, 2010

Patron, Esther Foundation, 2010-present

Named one of '50 Iconic Australian Women', 2011

Induction Inaugural West Australian Womens' Hall of Fame, 2011

• YEAR BY YEAR •

1998	• 1ST OUTRIGHT	48km 'Round Manhattan Island Race (USA)
1997	• GOLD MEDAL	25km Pan Pacific Swimming Championships, Fukuoka (Japan)
	• GOLD MEDAL	25km Team Event, Pan Pacific Swimming Championships, Fukuoka (Japan)
1995	• RECORD	48km 'Round Manhattan Island solo (USA)
	• DNF	88km Hernandaria–Parana World Series (Argentina)
	• 5TH WOMAN	57km Santa Fe Worl Series (Argentina)
	• RECORD	79km Sydney to Wollongong solo
1994	• BRONZE MEDAL	25km World Swimming Championships, Terracina (Italy)
	• 1ST WOMAN	42kn Lac Magog World Series (Canada)
	• 1ST WOMAN	36km Italian Riviera World Series final
	• 2ND WOMAN	Hernandarias–Parana World Series
	• 2ND WOMAN	Santa Fe World Series

1993	• GOLD MEDAL	25km Pan Pacific Swimming Championships, Terracina (Italy)
	• 1ST WOMAN	Long Island Sound Charity swim (USA)
	• 1ST WOMAN	35km Atlantic City World Series (USA)
	• 1ST WOMAN	40km Lac St Jean World Series (USA)
	• 1ST WOMAN	Lac Magog World Series
	• 1ST WOMAN	66km Six-Day Italian Riviera World Series
	• 3RD WOMAN	Hernandarias–Parana World Series
	• 1ST WOMAN	Sante Fe World Series
1992	• 1ST WOMAN	30km Sylvan Lake World Series (Canada)
	• 1ST OUTRIGHT	Atlantic City World Series (USA)
	• 1ST WOMAN	Long Island Sound charity swim (USA)
	• 1ST WOMAN	Lac Magog World Series (Canada)
	• DNF	25km World Cup, Lac St Jean (Canada)
	• 1ST WOMAN	Six-Day Italian Riviera World Series
	• 1ST WOMAN	Santa Fe World Series (Argentina)
1991	• 1ST OUTRIGHT	Sydney Harbour International Marathon
	• GOLD MEDAL	Pan Pacific Swimming Championships, Sylvan Lake (Canada)
	• 1ST OUTRIGHT	Atlantic City (USA)
	• 1ST WOMAN	Lac St Jean (Canada)
	• 1ST WOMAN	Lac Magog (Canada)
	• 1ST WOMAN	32km Capri to Naples
	• 1ST WOMAN	Santa Fe (Argentina)
	• 1ST WOMAN	29km All Saints Bay (Brazil)
	• GOLD MEDAL	25km World Swimming Championship Perth
1990	• SOLO CROSSING	English Channel
	• 1ST WOMAN	Lac St Jean (Canada)
	• 1ST WOMAN	Lac Magog (Canada)
	• 1ST WOMAN	Capri to Naples
	• 2ND WOMAN	25km International Challenge, Perth
1989	• 1ST OUTRIGHT	'Round Manhattan Island race (USA)
	• 1ST WOMAN	Lac Magog (Canada)
1988	• 1ST OUTRIGHT	'Round Manhattan Island race (USA)
	• GOLD MEDAL	World Cup, Lac Leman (France)
1987	• 1ST OUTRIGHT	'Round Manhattan Island race (USA)
1985	• RECORD	'Round Manhattan Island solo (USA)
	• 1ST OUTRIGHT	'Round Manhattan Island race (USA)
	• 2ND WOMAN	Lac Magog (Canada)
	• 5TH WOMAN	Atlantic City (USA)

1984	• 1ST WOMAN	'Round Manhattan Island race (USA)
	• 1ST OUTRIGHT	25km Seal Beach Rough Water Swim (USA)
1983	• RECORD	American women's four-mile (6.4km), Beaver Lake (USA)

the spirit to win and the will to excel are always measured one stroke at a time

• ABOUT SHELLEY TAYLOR-SMITH •

Champion Mindset® Consulting Founder and Director **Shelley Taylor-Smith,** is best known as the Motivational Expert with keynote motivational speaking presentations, workshops and coaching programs.

Using her thirty plus years of experience as athlete, coach, writer and consultant Shelley helps individuals in the sporting world from beginner level onwards as well as business people on performance and lifestyle issues to discover the mental toughness to stay on top of your game despite the daily obstacles you face in your business and career with her everyday life motto: "Get Up, Get Over It & Get On With It."

The true grit of this Aussie woman is shown in her commitment and passion to her twenty three year old dream becoming reality and as Honorary Secretary for the FINA Technical Open Water Swimming Committee (2000-2009). Shelley trained the officials and coordinated the Inaugural 10km Marathon Swim at the 2008 Beijing Olympic Games.

Known more today for her patriotism and passion than her world titles (and beating the blokes), Shelley Taylor-Smith is passionately committed to one and only mission: to help you achieve your birthright.... and be the Champion you were born to be!

Just as dedicated out of the water as she was in it, Shelley is Patron of the Esther Foundation, dedicated to helping young women in the leadership and community program based in Perth, Western Australia. http://www.estherfoundation.org.au (15% of profits of sales of 'Dangerous When Wet' is donated to the Esther Foundation).

Shelley resides in her hometown of Perth, Western Australia.

Champion Mindset Consulting Contact Details:
Perth Office: +618 6102 4568 — Sydney Office: +612 8005 8033
Mobile: +61 414 594 245 — Fax: +618 6210 1414
Skype: shelley.taylor.smith
Email: champion@championmindset.com.au
Web: www.championmindset.com.au.

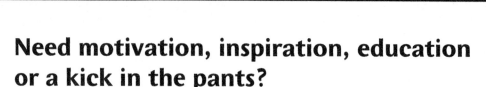

READY. SET. ACTION.

Gain control of your life, business and career and create your own Champion Mindset!

Need motivation, inspiration, education or a kick in the pants?

Kick your day off right... from the start!

Champion Motivational thoughts personally written by Shelley Taylor-Smith are guaranteed to be quick to read, quick to motivate and quick to inspire you to leap into your day!

Receive the complimentary fortnightly "Champion Motivations" newsletter. Register today at www.championmindset.com.au/inspire.htm

Subscriber benefits include....
#1 Start Achieving More Success!
#2 Become More Confident!
#3 Attract Everything You Deserve in Your Life!
#4 Receive "8 Taylor-Made Steps to Accelerate Your Success" Report
#5 8 Ways to Think Like Champion Michael Phelps! (MP3)
#6 Obtain Valuable **FREE** Products, Articles and Interviews!
#7 Be the First to Discover Great Breakthroughs!

And remember...

"If you don't quit, you will make it!"

Shelley Taylor-Smith
B.Sci.Ed
Success Coach & Motivational Expert

CHAMPION MINDSET

Perth Office: **+618 6102 4568**   Sydney Office: **+612 8005 8033**
Mobile: **+61 414 594 245**   Fax: **+618 6210 1414**
Email: champion@championmindset.com.au
Skype: shelley.taylor.smith
Facebook: www.facebook.com/shelley.taylor.smith

www.championmindset.com.au

CHAMPION MINDSET® CONSULTING PO Box 2178 Claremont North WA 6010 Australia

**Patron, Shelley Taylor-Smith
proudly supports the Esther Foundation.**

**15% of all profits of sales of "Dangerous When Wet –
The Shelley Taylor-Smith Story" goes to the Esther Foundation.**

The Esther
Foundation

restoring lives in need

"To encourage and empower individuals in need to attain their full potential"

The Esther Foundation facilitates an extensive and multi-award winning young women's residential health, development and leadership programme, the largest of it kind in Australia. Programme participants include children, young women and mothers with children, all between the ages of 13-33 years.

The extensive recovery programme that the organisation provides offers a safe and structured residential environment to support young women dealing with issues stemming from substance abuse, depression, self harm, eating disorders, sexual abuse, domestic violence, teenage pregnancy, family breakdown, bullying, mental health concerns and offers early intervention assistance for parents unable to cope with teenage behavioural concerns.

The positive profile that this organisation holds within the community has been highlighted simply through its work with young women in crisis and the remarkable success stories and outcomes that have resulted from this work. The program has been commended by many government and non-government agencies and is supported by many business and governmental leaders within our community.

The organisation is a non-profit and non- Government organisation that has always been funded through corporate donations and fundraising initiatives.

For more information go to:
http://www.estherfoundation.org.au

CHAMPION MINDSET® PROUDLY PRESENTS

MASTER OPEN WATER SWIMMING CLINICS

Who Better to Learn from than the Best!
Attention: All Coaches, Athletes, Officials & Swimmers

... INCLUDES GET WET WITH THE CHAMP.

THIS IS YOUR OPPORTUNITY TO ELIMINATE YOUR FEARS, IMPROVE YOUR SKILLS AND BUILD CONFIDENCE!

7-time World Marathon Swimming Champion, Shelley Taylor-Smith teaches you first hand her passion for Open Water Swimming... and turn your love-hate relationship around so you too will be the Master of your next Open Water swimming competition.

Training is a passion of mine and I've had the pleasure of sharing with businesses throughout Australia and internationally in New Zealand, Spain, Italy, Japan, USA, Dubai, Hong Kong, China, Singapore, Brazil and Argentina for the last 10 years.

My experience in providing clinics to referees and officials for open water swimming has extended to helping national federations and organising committees in the preparation, planning and co-ordination of 10 World Swimming Championships, over 50 World Cups and the Beijing Olympic Games 2008 10km Marathon Swim; in my role as FINA Honorary Secretary, FINA Technical Open Water Swimming Committee 2000-2009.

Since retiring from international competition in 1998, I have focused my energy on supporting individuals and teams to master open water swimming; sharing with people of all levels from international to masters and recreational.

In recent times I have worked alongside groups such as Australian Swimming Team, Brazil Swimming Federation including Brazil Swimming Coaches, Masters Swimmers, Referees and Officials, Western Australian Surf Lifesaving High Performance Team, Australian Surf Lifesaving Clubs and Western Australian Masters Swimming Clubs.

The Mastering Open Water Swimming Clinics include:

"DRY" THEORY PRACTICAL COMPONENT:

- Open water swimming – what works, what doesn't
- Race preparation
- What additional training will benefit you
- Goal setting
- The mindset – blocking out self doubt, fears and unwarranted thoughts
- Focus – getting what you want out of the race

"WET" PRACTICAL COMPONENT in open water:

- Starts – surf dashes and water starts
- Drafting – how to effectively draft, swim in waves and find the path of least resistance
- Sighting – how to sight, how to use landmarks, when to sight, when not to
- Buoy turns – roll technique, flags and buoys, how to turn in a group
- Finishes – body surfing, positioning and strategies

For all enquiries contact: Shelley Taylor-Smith
Founder & Director, Champion Mindset Consulting

Perth Office: **+618 6102 4568**   Sydney Office: **+612 8005 8033**
Mobile: **+61 414 594 245**   Fax: **+618 6210 1414**
Email: champion@championmindset.com.au
Skype: shelley.taylor.smith
Facebook: www.facebook.com/shelley.taylor.smith

CHAMPION MINDSET

www.championmindset.com.au

CHAMPION MINDSET® CONSULTING PO Box 2178 Claremont North WA 6010 Australia

Living ON Purpose Celebration Sale
CHAMPION MINDSET® PRODUCTS & SERVICES

www.championmindset.com.au

Please RUSH me the following orders: (all prices inc. GST)	RRP	My Order
1. **Create Your Own Champion Mindset 7CD set** 12 hrs being coached to achieve your goals by the World Champion herself, Shelley Taylor-Smith & 90 page ultimate step-by-step manual **PLUS BONUS** 8th Resource CD. Purchase today and receive personally autographed copy of "Dangerous When Wet - The Shelley Taylor-Smith Story" - **NOW ONLY $297** Total savings $268	$595	.... x copies
2. **Goal Setting and Time Management 4 CD 8hrs Package** With Shelley Taylor-Smith & Australia's No. 1 productivity coach, Lorraine Pirihi. A complete one day workshop covering the hot topics of motivation, goal setting, time management and productivity - and no more excuses! - **NOW ONLY $147**	$197	.... x copies
3. **The Champion Starter Kit** (includes all items 4,5,6,7,8 & 9) - **NOW ONLY $299**	$350	.... x copies
4. **Shelley's 69 Personal Best Champion Motivations - CD** - **NOW ONLY $20**	$29.95	.... x copies
5. **The Power of Success - 7 week Online Coaching Program** - **NOW ONLY $155**	$177	.... x sign up .... x copies
6. **My Champion Motivational Goal Planner - NOW ONLY $10**	$19.95	.... x copies
7. **Dangerous When Wet -** The Shelley Taylor-Smith Biography personally signed copy! Includes complimentary bookmark.- **NOW ONLY $20**	$29.95	.... x copies
8. **Inside the Champion Mindset - CD - NOW ONLY $20**	$39.95	.... x copies
9. **How to Become the Champion Of Your World - CD & Workbook** - **NOW ONLY $30**	$49.95	.... x copies
10. **Bookmarks - $2 each or 10 for $15**	$2 ea or 10 for $15	.... x copies
11. **Champion Motivation Cards - $4.50 each or 5 for $15**	$4.50 ea or 5 for $15	.... x copies
12. **Secrets of Great Public Speakers Exposed!** (Includes free bonus gifts worth $357) - **NOW ONLY $25**	$29.95	.... x copies
SUB-TOTAL		
Postage & Packaging Australian orders: $9.90 for first product, $15 for 2, $20 for Champion Starter Pack. Overseas Orders - $25		
My Champion Order Total		

Name: _____ Position: _____

Company: _____

Address: _____ Postcode: _____

Telephone: _____ Fax: _____ Mobile: _____

Email: _____

Please charge my: ☐ VISA   ☐ MASTERCARD   ☐ BANKCARD   ☐ CASH / CHEQUE

Credit Card Number: ☐☐☐☐ ☐☐☐☐ ☐☐☐☐ ☐☐☐☐   Expiry Date: _____ /

Name on Card: _____ Signature: _____

Cheques made payable to **Champion's Mindset® Consulting** www.championmindset.com.au

FAX YOUR ORDER TO: + 61 8 6210 1414 **OR EMAIL:** office@ChampionMindset.com.au

Perth Office: +61 1300 78 41 70   **Sydney Office:** +61 2 8005 8033   **Skype: shelley.taylor.smith**

CHAMPION MINDSET® CONSULTING PO Box 2178 Claremont North WA 6010 Australia

Shelley Taylor-Smith has rewritten the record books and set new standards in one of the roughest sports imaginable — marathon swimming. Seven consecutive world titles, a world championship gold medal and head-to-head victories over the best men in the sport have marked her as one of the supreme athletes of the 1980s and 1990s. On her triumphant march through a career spanning twelve years she has earned a place in the Guinness Book of Records for the fastest swim (male or female) around New York's Manhattan Island and captivated Australia with her record-shattering swim from Sydney to Wollongong. And she hasn't finished yet.

Shelley has shared her story with Ian Cockerill: from her memories of growing up in Perth to her drama-filled reclamation of the 'round Manhattan record. Like Shelley herself this book is spirited, uncompromising and right from the heart. Behind her rise to success life dealt Shelley some heavy blows which are captivated in this riveting story of an amazing woman's life. Above all, Dangerous When Wet is about belief in oneself, triumph over adversity and the power of positive thinking.

15% of profits of sales donated to THE ESTHER FOUNDATION

ISBN 1-86448-075-0

9 781864 480757

Front cover photograph: Harvie Allison
Back cover: Tom Rovis-Hermann
Cover design: April Briscoe

CPSIA information can be obtained at www.ICGtesting.com
Printed in the USA
BVOW06s0843080816

458297BV00012B/114/P